THE TASTE OF MY MORNINGS

THE TASTE OF MY MORNINGS

TONY ROBERTS

Shoestring Press

All rights reserved. No part of this work covered by the copyright herein may be reproduced or used in any means—graphic, electronic, or mechanical, including copying, recording, taping, or information storage and retrieval systems—without written permission of the publisher.

Printed by imprintdigital
Upton Pyne, Exeter
www.digital.imprint.co.uk

Typesetting and cover design by narrator
www.narrator.me.uk
info@narrator.me.uk
033 022 300 39

Published by Shoestring Press
19 Devonshire Avenue, Beeston, Nottingham, NG9 1BS
(0115) 925 1827
www.shoestringpress.co.uk

First published 2019
© Copyright: Tony Roberts
Cover photograph: Chris in Carnac

The moral right of the author has been asserted.

ISBN 978-1-912524-26-6

for Chris

'I do love nothing in the world so well as you'

&

in memory of Jim Todd

'Oh, Mama, can this really be the end…'

My whole point of view about literature was affected by Taine's methods of presentation and interpretation. He had created the creators themselves as characters in a larger drama of cultural and social history, and writing about literature, for me, has always meant narrative and drama as well as the discussion of comparative values.

    Edmund Wilson 'A Modest Self-Tribute' (1952)

Last night I was reading Lord Acton's introduction to a series of lectures on modern history. He offered as a truism that needed no underlining or amplification: 'Historians, learn by writing, rather than by reading.'

    Robert Lowell to Elizabeth Bishop (December, 1955)

CONTENTS

Preface   1

PART ONE: POETS OF AMERICA   3

With the Topnotch Tates at 'Benfolly', 1937   5
Archibald MacLeish: Collapsing Star   18
Malcolm Cowley among the Poets   29
Allen Tate in Paris   39
Robert Penn Warren at Oxford   48
Seeing Robert Lowell Plain   57
All's misalliance: Robert Lowell in England   64
Approaching James Dickey: A Cautionary Tale   74
Maxine Kumin's Territory   86
The Hard Losses of Louise Glück   98

PART TWO: POETS IN AMERICA   109

Czesław Miłosz in Exile   111
Time away: Louis MacNeice's America   123
Dylan Thomas roars across America   132
Charles Tomlinson & America   141
Michael Mott: delving into the shadow   151
Ted Hughes in Boundless Suburbia   163

PART THREE: CRITICS HERE & THERE   173

Alexander Herzen in London   175
The Shelf Life of Robert Browning (1812–2012)   183
Matthew Arnold Lecturing America   188
Ford Madox Ford: a fish in not quite the right water   200
Remembering Wilson & Trilling   208
Petted and fussed over: William Empson & America   218
Regarding William Styron   227
Al Alvarez at Risk   236
Jim Burns, Jonathan Ellis   247

Adam Kirsch and Michael Hofmann: Hobbyhorsing	252
Stefan Collini *Common Writing*	263
Richard Holmes *This Long Pursuit*	267
Robert Hass & Stephen Burt	271
The Lamentations of Arthur Krystal	276
James Wright: A Biography	282
Anthony Rudolf *European Hours*	286
The Lives of Robert Lowell	290

PREFACE

The Taste of My Mornings was written during my favourite working hours, about poets whose work has given me real pleasure. The title also makes a rather obvious reference to my first prose compilation, *The Taste in My Mind* (2015). As with its predecessor, this is a collection of essays written for literary magazines. It is again preoccupied with the American experience of twentieth century poets. I include a number of pieces on critics, too, for the simple reason that those chosen are among the writers I admire.

From childhood I retain—in a residual form at least—the vivid enthusiasm of a fan for people and ideas which interest me. These essays are essentially celebratory then, and—as a fan—I have generally been keen to push on from the poetry to the life of the poet. Hence the biographical slant in many pieces. The approach is predicated also on the disputable belief that if the writing is the important life to the reader, the lived life offers a high window on it. I do not go as far as Sainte-Beuve's *tel arbre, tel fruit* (the fruit is like the tree), though I do treat my subjects, in effect, as characters in their own work (as well as being figures resident in my imagination).

A word about the preoccupation with America: it reflects a lifelong interest in the country, its culture and history, an enthusiasm fuelled by the time I spent there in the early 1970s, as a student and teacher, and by many subsequent visits. In his journal Alfred Kazin expressed it perfectly: 'I love to think of America as an idea, to remember the adventure and the purity, the heroism and the *salt*.'

Always intriguing, C20th American poetry differs from British in its greater commitment to modernism and what evolved from it, as well as to the intensity, the life and death struggle, of some of its poets in producing their art. There is often a Whitmanesque, vernacular boldness, a sizeable scale and eccentricity in the American poetry of this period. It is as if the poet were aware that he or she had a continent to shout across. In a 1959 letter, an unimpressed Ted Hughes was to describe it in the following terms:

'American taste in poetry is basically, aside from sophistication & hep, like their taste in cars.'

The allure of America for British writers has generally been one of the following: money, prestige, academic resuscitation, love, a sometime vague glamour—or plain, old-fashioned curiosity. Many of the most successful British poets came to the States at one time or another. It might have been a formative, comforting or frustrating experience, but it was an experience. And American poets took to Europe as a rite of passage, an education, a breather or—as in the case of Robert Lowell—ostensibly to teach.

This book begins and ends with Lowell as his work has interested me the most. Fortunately, since he knew almost everyone, the ripple effect of reading him has drawn in almost all of the other writers I have written about. Another recurrent figure in my thinking has been Matthew Arnold. Today one may read him 'for his tone rather than as a guide' (as Clive James wrote of Sainte-Beuve, Arnold's mentor), but there is no denying his contribution to modern criticism. His example has been influential in the writing lives of some of the best of twentieth century critics: T. S. Eliot (who regarded him sniffily), Edmund Wilson (who Americanized him) and Lionel Trilling (his first modern biographer). More recent critics who have engaged with Arnold include Stefan Collini in England and Adam Kirsch in America.

On February 28th, 1884, at the Authors' Club in New York City, Arnold advised his audience of young authors to 'Put your heart into your business.' It remains a handy maxim.

Tony Roberts
Manchester, 2019

Part One: Poets of America

WITH THE TOPNOTCH TATES AT 'BENFOLLY', 1937

It is a potentially disastrous situation—one almost wills it to be: Allen Tate and his wife, Caroline Gordon, are furiously busy with their novels; their house guest, Ford Madox Ford, is dictating to his secretary (the engagingly named 'Wally' Tworkov) while her sister, his companion Janice Biala, sits painting. Out on the lawn of 'Benfolly' the young and callow Robert Lowell intones his own Miltonic sonnets in an olive-green tent. 'It's awful here', writes Biala. 'In every room in the house there's a typewriter and at every typewriter there sits a genius. Each genius is wilted and says that he or she can do no more but the typewritten sheets keep on mounting. I too am not idle. I sit in the parlor where I paint on three pictures at once in intervals of killing flies.'

The reason that this was not one of the great literary combustions, with five simmering egos in a hothouse summer and unreliable basic amenities, has a lot to do with their individual preoccupations—and mutual respect. Irritability seems to have been largely suppressed, intellectual wrangling muted. As Allen Tate wrote in a late 'New York Review of Books' piece, 'It was a situation perversely planned by fate to expose human weakness. There were no scenes.'

The nineteenth century 'Benfolly'—'one of the damnedest houses in the world to my notion', wrote Caroline Tate—sits on a hill above the Cumberland River three miles from Clarksville, Tennessee. It had been bought with the aid of a generous $10,000 'loan' from Tate's brother Ben, a coal executive who alone in the Tate family had made money. To the improvident Tates it was Ben's 'folly' and in an irony that could not be escaped—as Allen Tate told Malcolm Cowley—a man who had famously 'taken his stand' against industrialization had been one of its beneficiaries.

To her friend Sally Wood, Gordon described the house as being in 'the old neighborhood' near the Kentucky border where her ancestors the Meriwethers had settled when they came westward from Virginia. 'Benfolly' stood in eighty five acres, partly worked by what Lowell called a 'token tenant' farmer. The two-storey brick house stood somewhat weathered and given to a number of privations and failings, but with its two tall chimneys, its columns and porch it had stood a century. Until they filled it with guests, as they did habitually, the eight roomed mansion added an eccentric spaciousness to the living experience of the nomadic Tates.

Some suggestion of the oddity of the internal design of the house comes from a remark made by Gordon to Wood about Ida the cook, who 'often goes upstairs when she means to go downstairs—she says this house baffles her—as it has me these many years'. In fact the lowest floor was the basement at the hill end and the ground floor where the back of the house looked over the Cumberland ('deadwood-bordered' and 'the color of wet concrete' at the time of Lowell's visit). Aside from the kitchen and a small bedroom, the floor was one long dining room from front to back, boasting a long table and a central fireplace where the guests met to eat and talk under a Confederate flag. To Sally Wood and others the room resembled their memories of Parisian cafés. The other two floors had bedrooms and parlours, negotiated by narrow stairs.

Although the depressed economic climate meant that even the Tates could afford servants, they nevertheless found 'Benfolly' a demanding residence, being determinedly encouraging in their Southern hospitality. In September 1936, Gordon was declaring ruefully, 'We will probably never open Benfolly again till one of us writes a best seller.' Then the success of *None Shall Look Back*, Gordon's atmospheric novel of the War Between the States, would allow them to live there for a year, she decided.

The house suited Caroline Gordon. A country girl born in Todd County, Kentucky, in 1895, she grew up at Merry Mont, near Clarksville, at her family's plantation home known as 'Woodstock'. Although the family itself did not have to work the land, Gordon grew up with keen appreciation of the outdoors. Her romanticism was perhaps more immediately sensuous than her husband's. Gordon's South was both historical and vividly immediate, as we see in her letters ('The miasmal mist rose from the river in great clouds. It actually curled up over the back porch. It was almost like being on a boat in a storm').

Tate was equally fiercely Southern, but in other ways. This poet and polemicist's early life had been infused with his mother's mythology of the South. Apparently a native of Fairfax County, Virginia, Eleanor Custis Parke Varnell Tate had made much of her side of the family's connection with 'Chestnut Grove', an old farm house built on the land of 'Pleasant Hill', a mansion burned in the Civil War. Tate was to use this as the setting for his novel of the South's decline, *The Fathers*. For Tate, whose early life had been lived in a succession of homes, rural life had not the same attraction. Gordon wrote to Wood in 1926 that Tate 'has the strangest attitude toward the country—the same appreciation you'd have for a good set in the theatre. I think Allen feels toward Nature as I do toward mathematics—respectful indifference. He walks about the garden hailing each tomato and melon with amazement—and never sees any connection between planting seeds and eating fruit.'

Although Tate might have been more comfortable indoors, he was certainly not without practical skills. Gordon wrote of 'a most elegant desk, a combination book case and desk which he has built'. When Lowell visited, Tate explained to him that a poem is a work of craftsmanship, exhibiting some of his carpentry, 'a tar-black cabinet with huge earlobe-like handles.'

In May, 1937, the Tates were back at 'Benfolly' after two years away, with their twelve year old daughter, Nancy, moving furniture and settling their work spaces. Gordon had the servant's room, since their cook lived out. Tate held fast to that desk ('his masterpiece') pushed into the dank corner of the dining room. They were each at a critical juncture with their work, Gordon trying to finish her latest novel, *The Garden of Adonis*. She had been particularly hard-pressed with the autumn deadline ('I think it's absurd for me to get out another novel so soon but Scribner's insist that the iron is hot and must be struck quickly'). *None Shall Look Back*, recently published, had sold about 10,000 copies ('Of course Margaret Mitchell has taken all the trade,' she wrote. 'I think I might have made some money but for her').

Tate had eventually been making headway with his novel, though he was not a novelist by instinct, according to Gordon. Also, the 'Benfolly' atmosphere had hardly been conducive to his writing ('Allen has never been able to work there'). The bulk of the one hundred and forty pages of *The Fathers* that Cleanth Brooks was to be impressed with later in the summer of 1937 had been written at 'Monteagle', while visiting with Andrew Lytle, his fellow Agrarian.

At this point in his career, Tate was still involved, at least in the literary public's mind, with Southern Agrarianism and his Fugitive past. As a student at Vanderbilt University in Nashville, Tennessee, the young Tate had established a reputation as a hard-headed, highly talented student with an emerging understanding of European Modernism that had some impact upon his teacher, the poet John Crowe Ransom. Taken along to meetings of an off-campus group that called themselves the Fugitives, who met to discuss philosophy and then poetry, Tate had shone. When the group produced a magazine their influence began to spread. In 1930 a number of the Fugitives published together a collection of essays, *I'll Take My Stand: The South and the Agrarian Tradition*. This conservative, anti-industrial 'manifesto' (which often makes uncomfortable reading today) held together for a while some disparate talents. Benefiting from the skills of Ransom, Tate and the young Robert Penn Warren in particular, the movement made its mark nationally and contributed to the notion of a Southern Renaissance in literature, contextualizing the work of other notable writers like William Faulkner, Ellen Glasgow and James Branch Cabell.

However, fame can be a lean provider. The Tates were itinerant of necessity. Their fierce commitment to their art was highly impressive but never particularly rewarding financially (unlike the prose and poetry of their close friend, Warren). Tate had achieved critical success with his *Reactionary Essays on Poetry and Ideas* in 1936, a collection of his essays and reviews that adopted a position indebted to Eliot ('Modern poets are having trouble with form, and must use "ideas" in a new fashion that seems wilfully obscure to all readers but the most devoted', it began). Among impressive reviews, the caution of Tate's friend Malcolm Cowley was shrewd: 'it almost seems that his essays are being written by three persons,' he wrote in 'New Republic', 'not in collaboration but in rivalry'. He explained that 'Tate is a Catholic by intellectual conviction (though not by communion), he is a Southern Agrarian by social background, he is a man of letters trained in the Late Romantic or Symbolist tradition—and these are three positions that cannot be reconciled anywhere short of Nirvana.' The consequence, according to Cowley, was that he responded to 'the civil war inside his mind by the process of reducing everything to abstractions'.

Tate was to be less successful with *The Fathers* and with his poetry collection, *The Mediterranean and Other Poems* (1936), which had been privately printed but not distributed. However, with a high profile as essayist/reviewer and as the author of books on Jefferson Davis and Stonewall Jackson, Tate had finally arranged with Scribner's Maxwell Perkins for the 1937 publication of his *Selected Poems*, which would assure his status as a leading poet (and contain almost all of his best work). To augment his precarious income from reviewing, he had also recently turned to teaching (at Southwestern University in Memphis) and embarked on a lecturing tour, returning to 'Benfolly' in late spring, having invited the Ford Madox Fords to join them there.

Ford, the English modernist, editor of 'The English Review' and 'The Transatlantic Review', had mentored Gordon in New York, for which she was permanently grateful. She had met him at the age of twenty-seven and acted briefly as his secretary (though a little disconcerted at the heavy Ford dictating in his underwear and sweating in the summer heat). When he found out that she had a novel in poor shape, she recounted how 'He heaved another sigh and said, "You had better let me see it."' An effort to encourage her led to Ford 'taking my dictation for three weeks'. The resulting novel, *Penhally*, was the beginning of Gordon's long career as a novelist.

Always eager to support new talent, Ford had also promoted Tate's work, as well as lending the two of them his Paris apartment. As Tate later remembered, 'This homme de lettres, who had been a great editor and was now the greatest living British novelist, lived in Spartan frugality. His flat consisted of a petit salon furnished with a divan.' Ford had helped Tate secure a Guggenheim Fellowship for 1928, while attempting to find his poems a British publisher. Always a generous critic of those whose work he liked, Ford liked Tate's poems, especially the one he had helped inspire on a day-long Cassis picnic, where he had mentioned to Tate how some of Troy's refugees may once have paused there:

> Where we went in the boat was a long bay
> A slingshot wide, walled in by towering stone—
> Peaked margin of antiquity's delay,
> And we went there out of time's monotone
> – 'The Mediterranean'

From Toulon Ford wrote to Tate in September, 1936:

> I have just got your MEDITERRANEAN—and it's lovely. I suppose I may be pardoned for liking the first poem best since it brings back the occasion... which was a happy one... And after that AENEAS AT WASHINGTON and then PASTORAL and SHADOW AND SHADE; and then TO THE LACEDEMONIANS and THE MEANING OF DEATH in, I think, that order. But they are all astonishingly level in quality. You have got hold by now of a sort of lapidary sureness and hardness that puts you, I should think, alone among the poets

Like the Tates, Ford Madox Ford knew hard times, despite an exceptionally prolific writing life. By the mid-1930s his reputation guaranteed only a hand-to-mouth existence, punctuated by necessary travel ('It would be impossible to find any three English people connected with books who would not automatically put a spoke in any wheel of mine that passed them by,' he wrote to Hugh Walpole in December, 1930).

In October 1935 he and the Polish-American Biala took a short trip to Geneva, where Ford worked on his latest book, *Portraits from Life*, before returning home to Villa Paul in Cap Brun, Toulon. Here their ground floor rooms overlooked the sea, its beautiful views and their garden compensations for the basic amenities. There he wrote his autobiographical paean *Provence* ('where I have lived for nearly all my spiritual as for a great part of my physical life'). Although *Provence* had been published in March 1935 to 'the most enthusiastic notices Ford ever received' in America and his *Collected Poems* appeared in October, the Fords were penurious again by Christmas, which led to a return to Paris and, after the failure of Ford's thriller, *Vivre le Roy*, some much required journalism.

By November of 1936 they found it necessary to return to America, where Ford could find work more easily, though neither he nor Biala really wished to stay there. In January the American edition of his *Great Trade Route,* a sort of travel book and autobiography, appeared to some acclaim. In February Biala's second art exhibition took place at the Gallery Passedoit in New York, while Ford busied himself with a radio broadcast and public speaking engagements. The two travelled to Boston for the March publication of the entertaining *Portraits From Life* and then, at the end of April, they took up the invitation from the Tates to stay with them at 'Benfolly', where they were to live and work until they all decamped for Olivet College and the 1937 Writers' Conference in July, after which Ford was to remain there teaching until December.

At 'Benfolly' Ford completed dictating *The March of Literature*, his idiosyncratic survey of its history 'From Confucius' Day to Our Own'. He described the book to publisher Stanley Unwin as 'covering, comparatively, the whole of Literature from the Chinese to, say, Mr. Hemingway in a not too, but yet sufficiently, erudite manner'. While Ford worked on his book, Biala focused on her 'cryptic, lusciously painted' canvases 'that hovered between abstraction and representation' (according to Roberta Smith in a 'New York Times' obituary).

Ford loved the Tates but, according to Tate's biographer Radcliffe Squires, 'He found "consorting" with them "an exhausting intellectual undertaking"' and consequently reacted negatively at times to his surroundings. 'This is one of the noisiest spots in the world,' he wrote to George Bye, 'what with children and chickens and birds and cows and steamboats and Tennessean voices and doors slamming in the wind.' Not only was his exhaustion a consequence of his extremely poor health and the effort of completing the book. He was also involved by Tate in the academic politics of Vanderbilt University. Tate's teacher John Crowe Ransom, aggrieved at being undervalued, had been considering a move to Kenyon College, Ohio. 'Consorting with the Tates', Ford wrote in a letter of June 11, 'is like living with intellectual desperados in the Sargoza [sic] Sea.' Yet, always the professional, Ford could boast of having completed his thousand words a day.

The Fords exerted their own pressures on 'Benfolly' life that summer. Their arrival had been preceded by the arrival of 'eighty pounds of Janice's pictures'. Then Ford turned out to be suffering from 'insomnia, indigestion and gout'. Then there were the bathetic moments. With Fordian flourish, on one occasion he attempted to solve the problem of the house cistern running dry by sinking a washtub containing twigs (a Sussex dew pond) into the ground. It proved a dismal failure.

Besides, the tireless, diminutive Gordon had a combative streak easily raised in anticipation of any potential confrontations. She had written to Sally Wood (in November, 1927) of Robert Penn Warren's first wife, 'I would have thrown her out of the window the first week but for my deep affection for Red.' Now she stood ready for the painter, a 'hellion' on their previous visit. Part of the problem had no doubt been the clash of temperaments, but part was the matter of food. Ford's health was not good and his preference for French cooking could not be accommodated. 'Ida, with the occasional assistance of her mother Electra, the washerwoman, could not even cook Tennessee, much less French', wrote Tate. Fortunately on this visit things went better from the start, according to Gordon:

> —but not without strife. I took Janice by the horns last night before she'd had time to get really obnoxious and

explained to her that while I seemed very feckless I had in my way a system and that it didn't include French cooking by a Tennessee negro or by me either................ It's dreadful to feel that way about a guest but I knew she would run me nuts and ruin my book if I didn't smack her paws off the bat.... I just made up my mind I wouldn't take any of her damn nonsense... She takes a spanking well, is extremely amiable this morning and resolved to be good.

It was into this company that Robert Lowell stumbled in late April, having driven through 'plains of treeless farmland, and an unnatural, unseasonable heat' from Nashville to Benfolly, his bumper 'mashing the Tate's frail agrarian mailbox post', as he described it in a short essay, 'Visiting the Tates'. 'Wearing last summer's mothballish, already soiled white linens, and moccasins, knotted so that they never had to be tied or untied', the young man climbed out and turned his back on the 'peeling, pillared house', to disguise the damage.

To Caroline Gordon, who thought it 'the strangest visitation we ever had', the event had its own weird comedy. With characteristic zeal she recounted how she and Tate had been out enjoying the lemon lilies when the young man arrived and proceeded to urinate with his back to the house:

> We stood there eyeing him sternly and were on the point of shouting "defense d'uriner" when he came up to Allen, regarded him fixedly and muttered something about Ford. Something made us treat him more gently and ask him into the house. He is a young man named Lowell from Massachusetts who heard Ford lecture in Boston and as he wasn't getting on well at Harvard decided to come south to learn how to write. We kept him overnight and sent him on to Nashville to learn further about writing. I think Ford really rescued him from a bad situation. His family decided he was crazy because he wants to be a poet and had him in a

psychopathic sanitarium. He does have a queer eye on him but he is very well behaved and affable, but imagine a Lowell (yes, the poor boy's mother is a Cabot)— imagine one coming all the way from Boston to sit at Southern feet.

Just as Lowell didn't remember the urinating, Gordon did not choose to comment on the post box. Then again she had plenty to occupy her mind beside the genial young man and her house guests, with the deadline pending.

Robert Traill Spence Lowell 1V had made hard weather of his life to date. The single and unhappy child of a union between the Winslows and Lowells of Boston, 'Cal', as he was known from boarding school days, enrolled at Harvard in 1935 but dropped out in spring 1937. He found the environment did not sufficiently engage his interest, plus there were family difficulties consequent on a premature engagement to Anne Dick, a distant cousin of one of Lowell's friends. At twenty four Dick was a little older than Lowell and his infatuation with her was to his mother, Mrs. Charlotte Winslow Lowell's mind, a symptom of his difficult relationship with herself.

The situation exploded at Christmas 1946 when a note from Lowell's father about Dick's visiting Lowell in his Harvard room without a chaperone caused Lowell to strike his father. His irate mother contacted the psychiatrist Merrill Moore, a family friend, with a view to having her son treated. Moore had a more profitable idea. Since he was also a Tennessee poet and a Fugitive, Moore instead gained approval for engineering a social meeting for Lowell with Ford Madox Ford and a leave of absence from Harvard. The twenty year old could journey south to meet Ford and Moore's friends, the Tates, and possibly study with John Crowe Ransom at Vanderbilt, thereby maintaining his commitment to poetry while simultaneously removing him from Boston and his fiancé.

It turned out that Ford was not speaking to the young man who arrived with his tenuous invitation, but by then Tates had invited him in. To Lowell he had, as he recounted, 'crashed the civilization of the South', and he was to stay much longer than one night. As he remembered that first visit to 'Benfolly', the conversation with Tate had been highly stimulating to him:

> After an easy hour or two of regional anecdotes, Greenwich Village reminiscences, polemics on personalities, I began to discover what I had never known. I, too, was part of a legend. I was Northern, disembodied, a Platonist, a puritan, an abolitionist....He quoted a stanza from Holmes's 'Chambered Nautilus'— 'rather beyond the flight of your renowned Uncle.' I realized that the old deadweight of poor J.R. Lowell was now an asset. Here, like the battered Confederacy, he still lived and was history.

The way Tate could rip through the canon 'coolly blasting, rehabilitating, now and then reciting key lines in an austere, vibrant voice', proved beyond doubt what Lowell had thought on his journey down: that Tate was the kind of literary model he needed. 'Reading over the "Fugitive" poets on the train', he remembered, 'I decided Allen Tate is very topnotch, a painstaking technician and an ardent advocate of Ezra Pound.'

Tate was more circumspect. To Andrew Lytle, on May 19th, 1937, he wrote, 'The Lowell boy turned up twice, and we like him but feel that he is potentially a nuisance.' Undaunted by his reception, Lowell took literally their comment that an extra guest would have to pitch a tent on the lawn: 'A few days later, I returned from Nashville with an olive Sears, Roebuck umbrella tent. I stayed three months.' To his mother he wrote, 'I feel convinced that I have never worked so hard or reaped such favourable results before.' He managed to secure $8 a week from her in order to live adequately through the summer there.

Though the Tates both privately admitted to first thinking Lowell was 'mad' (sadly prophetic), gradually they grew to be fond of him, urging the young man to neatness and bathing. Gordon was the first to be mollified by the uninvited guest. By July 10th she was writing:

Ford saw him in Boston and told him to go south young man and learn how to write. He promptly came. Ford was so enraged at being taken literally that he doesn't speak to him at the table. He's such a nice boy. Drives me out to Merry Mont to haul in buttermilk etc., flits the dining room—the handiest boy I ever knew, in fact. When he isn't doing errands he retires to his tent whence a low bumble emerges—Robert reading Andrew Marvell aloud to get the scansion. I've given Ford hell about not speaking to him, and he now addresses him as 'Young man.'

Ford's sensitivity to being studied in ill health was more the cause of his early rejection of the young poet. His concern turned out to be prescient:

I hear you huffing at your old Brevoort,
Timon and Falstaff, while you heap the board
for publishers. Fiction! I'm selling short
your lies that made the great your equals. Ford,
you were a kind man, and you died in want.
 – 'Ford Madox Ford, (1873–1939)'

Conversation was perfunctory in the mornings since Gordon, the dedicated professional, hurried her writers off to work to avoid the delay rich exchanges might bring. At lunch it was a different matter. Wally Tworkov confessed herself astounded at the lunch time conversations. 'I was to discover, after a week of lunches, when visitors were most frequent, that the animated talk around the table was not about the Spanish Civil War which was then taking place and which was preoccupying most of my friends in New York, but about the Civil War between the States.'

It is not surprising in this conservative Southern stronghold where Lowell remembered seeing an engraving of Stonewall Jackson, as well as the Confederate flag over the fireplace. To the Tates, the War Between the States had become a literary as well as a military affair. Tworkov on the other hand was politically engaged, 'a rabid Communist' in Gordon's view: 'she asked me shyly the other day, "How wise would it be to have the Daily Worker sent to me here? I can't live without it?" I think she thought she might be ridden off of Benfolly on a rail if caught with a copy of the Worker.'

We have Ford's perspective on the hosts' Confederate sympathies in a much earlier letter, quoted in Max Saunders biography, *Ford Madox Ford: A Dual Life:*

> all the Tates' friends are from Kentucky or Tennessee or Virginia. It is rather queer: because of the Civil War you see American history quite reversed. Lincoln is the villainous bastard ... who ruined the world & Stonewall Jackson the only hero. It is queer & rather ghostly & pathetic, being buried amongst the relics of a lost cause... & hearing that if only Lee had not lost Gettysburg the world today wd be ...Elysium ... No industrial system: no Middle West: only kindly & courteous people of pure English blood! ... of course it is rather like the French royalists—but really queerer and more passionate.

Passions were held in check that summer. There was the sortie out to Vanderbilt on behalf of Ransom (who decided anyway to move on to Kenyon College). Then in mid-July, together with Ford and Biala and with Robert Lowell in tow, the Tates set off for Olivet College. On July 10 1937, Caroline Gordon wrote her friend, 'we have lived through the summer and the Fords, too, are still breathing though a little wan. We've really got through beautifully but you can imagine how it's been.'

ARCHIBALD MACLEISH: COLLAPSING STAR

Few C20th American poets could boast of being as popular or successful as Archibald MacLeish (1892–1982) and few have had their readership collapse so quickly. Yet, particularly in his early lyric poems, he could be outstanding.

When he came to choose representative work to make up *The Human Season: Selected Poems 1926–1972,* the poet showed himself to be fully aware of the fragility of reputations (if not specifically of his own). In a foreword to the selection he reacts to the habit of anthologizing only a handful of a poet's work, by asserting that 'a poet like a novelist or a critic or anyone else hopes to be read, not tasted'. His selection for *The Human Season* is intended, therefore, to give access to his lifetime's concerns, to act as he puts it as 'not a choice *from* but a representation *of*. He is keen to venture wider through his oeuvre to find poems that 'represent attempts to come to terms with the tragic sense of time and change which afflicted the generation of the two Great Wars'. For an outward-looking poet like MacLeish this makes perfect sense.

He arranged his selected poems under headings, rather than chronologically, in order to give some sense of their breadth of preoccupation: 'Autobiography and Omens'; 'Actors and Scenes'; 'Love and Not'; 'Strange Thing ... To Be an American'; 'Illustrations'; 'The Art'; 'News from Elsewhere'. Even so, *The Human Season* can only also be a 'taste' of a very industrious writer. While some us would not doubt have preferred a chronological arrangement, rather like a shadowy biography, MacLeish's works well. It did, however, encourage at least one reviewer to claim that the best poems—the often anthologized ones—were all written before 1930. I must agree that many of his best poems *are* early ones—'Ars Poetica'; 'You, Andrew Marvell'; 'The End of the World'; 'L'An Trentiesme de Mon Eage', for example—but there are fine later ones, too, and significantly more of them than are generally chosen. The best of these bear comparison with some of the finest poems of his time and, taken with the book-length

Conquistador (1932), are reason enough to deplore the relative eclipse of Archibald MacLeish's work.

However it must be said that even in his own day MacLeish was something of a controversial poet. Partly this was connected with the man himself. Reading Scott Donaldson's excellent *Archibald MacLeish: An American Life* (1992) it is easy to be enamoured of his subject's achievements. He was a man of staggeringly varied and enviable talent, with a lifelong commitment to public service. Poet, athlete, lawyer, journalist, Librarian of Congress, government director and speechwriter, Harvard professor, he was also highly competitive, ambitious and, to those his charisma failed to touch, arrogant and distant. 'Archie', as he liked to be known, also opened himself to criticism because of his tendency to take a public platform, to lecture other writers on their commitment, particularly during the Depression and in wartime ('We cannot escape our duty as political animals').

Archibald MacLeish was born to well-to-do parents in a not-quite fashionable Chicago suburb, his father a businessman of Scottish origin, his mother a college principal eighteen years younger. Although the three children had great advantages, their father was somewhat remote. Nevertheless, MacLeish was encouraged by his mother who devoted herself to public service. His success began at prep school and never ended. At Yale he excelled on the football field and in the lecture room, becoming a member of Phi Beta Kappa and winning awards which stirred his literary ambitions. He also met Ada Hitchcock, later a celebrated singer, who would remain married to the poet for 65 years (despite his infatuations).

After Yale MacLeish chose law, possibly to avoid the business career his father favoured for him. Typically he excelled there, too. What it did not do was assuage his literary ambitions. After his first year of law he married and, when America entered the war in 1917, he went to France, eventually to join the field artillery as a second lieutenant. In December of that year Yale University Press published MacLeish's first collection of poems, *Tower of Ivory*—to mixed reviews. After some months in France, MacLeish was recalled to America as an instructor and so ended his war.

Tragically his younger brother, Kenneth, a navy pilot, died on active service ('And down those burning skies / Fell like a shattered star').

After law school, MacLeish turned to teaching while also practising law. He juggled his responsibilities with a little journalism and, when about to be offered a position with the firm, decamped with his family to Paris in September 1923 to pursue his literary dream, financially supported for the first year at least by his father. The poetry continued to appear in France and America (*The Pot of Earth*, 1924). Eliot published him in the 'Criterion'; he appeared in Marguerite Caetani's 'Commerce' and in the 'Nouvelle Review Francaise'. The poet also made close friendships in Paris with other Americans, notably Hemingway and Gerald and Sara Murphy, endured some privation and continued to gain recognition at home, where he and the family returned five years later. Meanwhile, ever-blessed with connections—on this occasion Dean Acheson—MacLeish had made a three month trip to Persia (Iran) for The League of Nations.

Back home MacLeish was persuaded by Henry Luce to work for his magazine, 'Fortune'. It was employment that enabled the MacLeish family to weather the Depression and the poet to travel extensively in America and to China. This also deepened his commitment to social causes and focused his poetry on his economically suffering countrymen. At 'Fortune' he was able to write on a variety of subjects: housing, Roosevelt, the Senate, Montana wheat farming, Japan.

MacLeish later reckoned *The Hamlet of A. MacLeish* (1928) began his reputation, though there were some intemperate responses to it (particularly by Edmund Wilson, who parodied the style in 'The Omelet of A. MacLeish'). He triumphed again, however, with *Conquistador*, which earned him the first of three Pulitzer prizes. He also wrote 'The Fall of the City' (1937), the first verse play performed on radio, with Orson Welles as the announcer. And then in 1939, at President Roosevelt's urging, MacLeish became Librarian of Congress. His success in the role led to his employment as Assistant Secretary for Public Affairs, then to involvement in the establishment of UNESCO.

In 1949 he became the popular Boylston Professor of Rhetoric and Oratory at Harvard, a position from which he finally retired in 1962. In 1958 he had been instrumental in obtaining the release of Ezra Pound from St. Elizabeths Hospital in Washington, a psychiatric hospital in which Pound had been incarcerated since 1946 for treason. This in spite of the fact that Pound often spurned him ('he was a very silly man who had some remarkable gifts', Archie believed). MacLeish had also won a Pulitzer Prize for Drama in 1959 with his play about Job, 'J.B.'. In retirement he never stopped writing, his last poems more personal, exploratory, restless. When he died in 1982, it was acknowledged that Archibald MacLeish had lived a full life of highly laudable public service.

From this distance in time MacLeish ideas about poetry are always interesting to read. Clearly he gave a great deal of thought to it. When he taught at Harvard he was given no direction as to what to teach, and later remembered, 'I came to the conclusion that what I really wanted to do was put together everything I'd ever wondered, or guessed, or hoped, or imagined about the art of poetry, and try it on young minds and see what I could learn.' In an interview for 'The Paris Review' in 1974, he spoke of what he learned: 'I tried to find out for myself what poetry is, what it *really* is. I began to understand that it is a part of a process which extends beyond poetry but which is most apparent *in* poetry, of trying to *see* human experience, trying to see "the world". "The world" being what a man feels *about* the world. Now if you realize this—what the purpose of your art is—you come to see that you are laboring at your art not only to make works of art but to make sense of your life... If you have succeeded at all you have become part—however small a part—of the consciousness of your time.'

The second aspect of the controversy that surrounded Archibald MacLeish was to do with his modernist poetry itself. Few failed to accept his success at writing clear and accessible verse. 'As one gets deeper and deeper into the essential, which is the human situation in the world, one is practically compelled to use simpler and simpler language', he explained. Still, there were those who criticised him for a facility they felt superficial, even unoriginal. It was also felt by some that his excellent control of technique masked insufficient ambition as a poet. That certainly does not square with his own view of his ambition as expressed in his *Reflections* (1986): 'a poem is a means of comprehending humanity, a means of comprehending human life and to a very considerable extent, the only means we have—the only means in which you use the emotions as well as the intellect at the same time—to live understandingly, to live in a considered way the life we live'.

MacLeish's poetry at least tries to do justice to these beliefs. His single most anthologized poem is in homage to the symbiosis of emotion and intellect. 'Ars Poetica' is a poem built from metaphor which concludes with the paradox: 'A poem should not mean / But be.' This perfectly modernist position might be expected to have pleased Eliot (a great early influence on MacLeish) and his idea of the objective correlative (as with the lines, 'A poem should be equal to: / Not true.') though in one of his letters Robert Lowell quotes Eliot calling MacLeish 'a better librarian than poet', which gives a hint of the carping MacLeish met with some of his fellow poets.

'You, Andrew Marvell', probably his other most anthologized poem, addresses Marvell's *carpe diem*, 'To His Coy Mistress' (with its reference to our inability to 'make our sun / Stand still'):

> And here face down beneath the sun
> And here upon earth's noonward height
> To feel the always coming on
> The always rising of the night

The exotic locations in the poem may be explained by the fact that MacLeish had just returned from Persia at the time of its composition. He was always captivated by notions of the place of man in the vastness of the universe, the stars and notions of eternity. His biographer, Scott Donaldson, pointed to 'the most prevalent image in MacLeish's writing: insignificant man adrift in space on the spinning earth. The idea is captured in 'Le seul malheur est que je ne sais pas lire', where the speaker is prompted by an old sailor in a fez looking up the stars, to recognise that he cannot read into them.

Two memorable poems capture the France of the 1920s. 'Years of the Dog' looked backward twenty years to the wonderful Paris when fame was to be had 'flushed like quail / in the / Cool dawn'. The poem remembers Joyce who lived on scraps and Hemingway ('with the supple look like a sleepy panther'), who 'Whittled a style for his time from a walnut stick / In a carpenter's loft in a street of that April city.' While MacLeish celebrated his close friends he was also quick to point out in later life that 'what was going on in Paris was infinitely more important than the few Americans who were there'. There were the young who 'flooded' into Europe and all the artists, not only Joyce but Picasso and Stravinsky and others.

Among the most famous of the Americans in Paris and the South of France in the 1920s was the charismatic and ultimately tragic couple, Gerald and Sara Murphy. In 'Sketch for a Portrait of MME G—M—' MacLeish skilfully explores the issue of identity, privacy and influence:

> The room, made probable, made real, became
> As strangely visible as if it were
> The shape of something she was thinking of.
>
> And there were afternoons when the snow fell
> Softly across the wind and in the mirrors
> The snow fell softly, flake on flake, the vague
> Reflected falling in the long dim mirrors,
> Faint snow across the image of the wind,—
> And there were afternoons when the room remembered,
> When her life passed in the mirrors of the room.

This poem, with its fascinating perspective, might be said to look back to the Augustans (or at least to T.S. Eliot) and forward to Leonard Cohen. Another poem clearly indebted to Eliot is the excellent 'L'An Trentiesme de Mon Eage'. 'In his thirtieth year (the title from Ezra Pound's 'Hugh Selwyn Mauberley:' Unaffected by "the march of events", / He passed from men's memory in l'an trentiesme/ De son eage') the poem begins, 'And I have come upon this place / By lost ways' and concludes:

> By words, by voices, a lost way—
> And here above the chimney stack
> The unknown constellations sway—
> And by what way shall I go back?

Like the painfully self-conscious Prufrock, the speaker in this poem wonders too about turning back and descending the stair, except here the ways are anyway lost (and man is again mocked by the sway of 'unknown constellations').

Man's aloneness is most remarkably witnessed in 'The End of the World'. In the summer of 1924, after a year in Paris, the MacLeish family took a trip to the coastal town of Granville in Normandy, where they watched a travelling circus, the sea unquiet, and the flaming torches potentially dangerous, as the poet remembered. In MacLeish's surreal poem the octet gives us the crazy, comical hyperactivity of the circus while the sestet literally takes the roof off and

> There in the starless dark the poise, the hover,
> There with vast wings across the cancelled skies,
> There in the sudden blackness the black pall
> Of nothing, nothing, nothing—nothing at all.

The final line of this powerful poem gives us the equivalent of the stunned eye-witness testimony we are used to after today's outrages, set against the realisation of life's meaninglessness. Perhaps the poem is a critique of World War 1 and of post-war European madness.

The suffering and the loss of his brother in what MacLeish saw as that unnecessary, 'commercial' war preoccupied him for some years. In 1924 he visited Kenneth's grave for a ceremony commemorating the American dead. It resulted in the poem 'Memorial Rain', which expressed his antipathy, contrasting the hyperbole and hypocrisy of the official position with the silent dead and the purifying rain. 'The Silent Slain' also memorialises MacLeish's brother's sacrifice, this time evoking the eleventh century French epic poem, 'The Song of Roland'. In his poem the speakers turn at the sound of battle to the Roncevaux Pass battlefield where they come upon the heroic dead. He also wrote 'Lines for an Internment', feeling bitter because fifteen years after the event the mood at home had changed: 'Nobody would talk about the war, and it was just more than I could bear to see the whole thing just wiped out with a wet sponge. The American Legion started parades, the whole thing became very hard to take.'

'The Young Dead Soldiers' was his one anti-war poem written during his time in Washington. In *Reflections* he recalled, 'I wrote that in seven minutes at my desk at about five minutes of eight one morning when I was called up to the Treasury and asked for something that they could use.' It was wanted for propaganda but he kept it, seeing it as a poem. It is a strongly rhetorical piece, dependent on the repetition of the soldiers' words, their essential message being: 'They say: Our deaths are not ours; they are yours; they / will mean what you make them.' The war continued to be a part of MacLeish's imagination for many years. In 'Speech to Those Who Say Comrade', for example, he returns to it:

> A French loaf and the girls with their eyelids painted
> Bring back to aging and lonely men
> Their twentieth year and the metal odor of danger.

Perhaps not unconnected with the war poems, another that has stirred many readers is 'Immortal Autumn'. The poem looks at the human condition with 'grave and level voice' (and gives rise to title of the selected poems). Fall is the 'human season' to the poet, in its clarity, its solitude, it spaciousness. Freed of the clutter of the year and before winter buries us, in autumn man can communicate with past and future:

> It is the human season. On this sterile air
> Do words outcarry breath: the sound goes on and on.
> I hear a dead man's cry from autumn long since gone.
>
> I cry to you beyond upon this bitter air.

In his 1948 collection, *Actfive*, the poem 'Winter is another country' has a similar plangency. Despite his attractive limpidity of diction and the innocence of his use of rhyme, MacLeish manages in these lyric poems to retain what Hamlet refers to as 'the heart of my mystery', so that we are tantalised by glimpses, by half-knowledge more influential for not being spelled out: 'The image seen but never seen with sight. I could endure this all / If autumn ended and the cold light came.'

There are other fine poems in the *The Human Season*, urgent public and political calls to arms, such as 'Brave New World', which dwells on 'our failure to seize the moment of triumph, to reassert our commitment to the things we really believe in, to the American Revolution'):

> Your countrymen who could have hurled
> Their freedom like a brand
> Have cupped it to a candle spark
> In a frightened hand

Then there are those more personal poems, almost confessional, which have worn better, poems such as 'Broken Promises', the 'Hotel Breakfast' ('suddenly / across the table, / you.') and the fearful 'Unfinished History':

> I wrote this poem that day when I thought
> Since we have loved we two so long together
> Shall we have done together—all love gone?

'Broken Promise' came out of a combination of images of a lover standing in a doorway with a star visible under the lintel. For MacLeish, Ophelia 'is very naturally associated with the emotions with which that poem deals' and the stars are there again:

> I think, O, my not now Ophelia,
> There are not always (like a moon)
> Rememberings afterward:

> I think there are
> Sometimes a few strange stars upon the sky.

There is also in the *The Human Season* a brief extract from *Conquistador*, just long enough to send an interested reader to that book-length poem to consider, as it were, whether MacLeish could challenge his talent. Although this poem deals with Spain's' conquest of Mexico (with Cortez and Montezuma in Bernal Diaz' account) by dealing with the end of Western expansion it becomes, in the poet's own words, 'a metaphor of the American situation'. It is gritty and very modern, so that one wonders, as MacLeish did, why 'the poem has slipped so completely out of sight':

> What are the dead to us in our better fortune?
> They have left us the roads made and the walls standing:
> They have left us the chairs in the rooms:
>   what is there more of them—
>
> Either their words in the stone or their graves in the land
> Or the rusted tang in the turf-root where they fought—

Technically MacLeish makes Dante's *terza rima* work over the length of his epic by skilfully substituting assonance for rhyme:

> And the stain of the foam on the long flank of the swells:
> And they gave us the signals for night with the swung lanterns
> And the chains came in: foul with the tatters of kelp

Conquistador boasts evocative, sensuous lines throughout ('his desire was in their limbs as an / Odor of plums in the night air'; 'the 'Broken melon smelled of a girl's robe'; 'we slept / eyelids covering many stars'). In exploring the great national question of America's mission and its cost, I think he was right to believe in the poem's relevance.

In death MacLeish has profited even less than he might have feared in his foreword. *The Oxford Book of American Poetry* (2006), for instance, selects just three of MacLeish's poems, while Rita

Dove's *The Penguin Anthology of Twentieth Century American Poetry* (2013) has only one, the ubiquitous 'Ars Poetica'. At the end of Scott Donaldson's biography the author quotes a friend speaking of 'how forward-looking MacLeish was at eighty-seven'... He 'was not content to be known as the author of such anthology pieces as 'Ars Poetica,' or 'You, Andrew Marvell... His eye was ever on what lay beyond the next horizon'. At his best, as in *The Human Season* and in *Conquistador*, Archibald MacLeish deserves to shine in the constellation of American poets of the last century.

MALCOLM COWLEY AMONG THE POETS

> Trust me to be here, not complaining,
> not making excuses, not letting my envy speak,
> not ever slipping a knife in the back.
> In other things don't trust me too far.
> – 'Prayer on All Saints' Day'

The chronicler of the Lost Generation, Malcolm Cowley (1898–1989), was a literary critic, editor and poet. Though always drawn to poetry, his work in other fields marginalized that talent. One consequence was that he was able to neatly organize his life's verse, which focused largely on the intellectual and emotional development of a literary expatriate and 30s radical. His collection, *Blue Juniata*, appeared first in 1929, reappearing—each time augmented—as *Blue Juniata: Collected Poems* (1968) and *Blue Juniata: A Life* (1985). In a selection of his letters, *The Long Voyage* (edited by Hans Bak in 2014) Cowley offers interesting perspectives on his fellow poets and on his own verse.

A Pennsylvania farm boy, Cowley was educated at Harvard, which he left on two occasions: firstly for the American Field Service in France and then with the American army. Graduating in 1920, he moved to Greenwich Village, married and became a free-lance writer, initially book reviewing at the going rate of one or two cents a word. Pressing needs required him to sell on the review copies (as he explained in *Exile's Return: A Literary Odyssey of the 1920s*) and also take a job writing advertising copy. This doubtless prompted his generosity during the Depression. In his essay 'The New Republic: 1934' Alfred Kazin remembered Cowley as editor: 'not knowing what else to do for the hungry faces waiting to see him, [he] would sell the books there was no space to review and dole out the proceeds among the more desperate cases haunting him for review assignments'.

With a fellowship from the Field Service Cowley studied at the University of Montpellier (1921–3). He spent time in Paris with French modernists and expatriate American writers, including

Hemingway and Fitzgerald. In *Exile's Return* he recalled, 'Almost everywhere, after the war, one heard the intellectual life of America unfavourably compared with that of Europe.' Cowley flirted with Dada ('a literary movement that would outdo the politicians in lunacy') and fervently embraced modernism. In the 1930s the economic nightmare made him an active Communist fellow traveller. Unfortunately, his support for Stalin finally compromised him, professionally and personally. He was later to acknowledge guilt for his 'sins of silence, self-protectiveness, inadequacy, and something close to moral cowardice'.

Cowley became literary editor of 'The New Republic' in 1930, when Edmund Wilson left to work on *The American Jitters*. He was to lose that position ten years later as a result of ideological restructuring, though he continued with a weekly book page. In 1942 he worked very briefly in the Federal Office of Facts and Figures before being pressured to resign over his political activities of the 30s, a blow to Cowley both as citizen and family man. The following years were comparatively more secure. He received a Mellon Fellowship to work on American writers, famously reviving Faulkner's career with *The Portable Faulkner* (1946). In 1948 he became literary consultant to Viking Press, where he encouraged Kerouac and Cheever among others. Subsequently he was elected to the National Institute of Arts and Letters and later became its president (1956–9 and 1962–5). He also turned to lecturing, at Washington, Stanford, Michigan and the University of Warwick, continuing to publish prose, particularly on the 1920s and 30s because he believed, as he said in 1974, those writers 'were much more ambitious to produce a masterpiece than writers today'.

Ambitious himself, Cowley was always a controversial figure, given his personality, politics and pre-eminence in the literary world. Looking back on his thirty-two year old self he wrote, in *The Dream of the Golden Mountains* (1980): 'he was awkward, credulous, either rash or exuberant at moments, and usually persistent… He never forgot that he came of people without pretensions, not quite members of the respectable middle class. He was slow of speech and had a farmer's silences, though he was not slow-witted; people were fooled sometimes.' Alfred Kazin saw something of the actor there: 'Whenever you crossed Malcolm directly, he would sidle into his familiar role of the slow-moving and slow-talking country boy from western Pennsylvania, clear-minded and deliberate'.

Mary McCarthy had only a negative view of reviewing for the taciturn editor at 'The New Republic' in her *Intellectual Memoirs*, while her one-time husband, Edmund Wilson, wrote of Cowley's 'characteristic tactlessness'. His friends could be enemies, too, like John Dos Passos or Ernest Hemingway. Cowley features in the latter's story 'The Snows of Kilimanjaro': 'And there in the café as he passed was that American poet with a pile of saucers in front of him and a stupid look on his potato face talking about the Dada movement with a Roumanian who said his name was Tristan Tzara, who always wore a monocle and had a headache'.

* * *

The letters of the young Cowley to his closest friend, Kenneth Burke, speak frequently of his commitment to poetry. They show him to be highly conscious of form (a lifelong preoccupation), while keen to be unorthodox. Perhaps in the long term he did not work hard enough at the craft. In a 1982 'Paris Review' interview he acknowledged, 'I wanted to go on writing poetry, but I always had the feeling that I couldn't write any poem that didn't come to me.' He certainly had some success in the early days, with Wilson at 'Vanity Fair' and Harriet Monroe at 'Poetry'.

Prompted by Hart Crane's efforts, *Blue Juniata* appeared in 1929, bringing Cowley an advance of $125. For this 'book of his days', as he called it in a late poem, he wanted unity above all; hence he arranged the collection in sections with prefatory notes. 'I think,' he wrote to Allen Tate at the time, 'that the book as a whole is better than any single poem in it. At any rate, it's not a scrapbook, a collection of unrelated poems by the same author.' (He was to 'arch his back and purr' at Tate's 'flattering judgment' in print.)

The autobiographical nature of Cowley's oeuvre is signalled by its title. Blue Juniata is both a Pennsylvania river and a sentimental ballad still remembered in Cowley's boyhood. The poems of the first section are narratives of general decline. They deal with woods and farmhouses, barns and mines, railroad hands, village wives and war veterans. What the community has in common is its poverty. The poems have an eye to detail and the telling phrase: 'night insects creak like rocking chairs'; 'the bottom land / was ribbed and gaunt as the horses'; cold hills lie 'staring down at our cornfields hungrily'. 'The Blown Door' captures the collective narrative of failed lives:

> a broken pane upstairs in the east bedroom
>   that let the northeast rain
> beat down all night on the red Turkey carpet;
> nobody puttied in another pane.

The prefatory 'Note' to part II explains that these poems are largely set in New York during the post-war years of poverty, where the poet and his friends 'made a kind of religion out of the sordid', reflecting their lost illusions. The prevailing mood, cynical and detached, features fragments of pathetic conversation, song lines, images reminiscent of Eliot's early poetry. The titles watch the clock: 'Mortality', 'So Perish Time' and 'Winter Tenement':

> When everything but love was spent
> we climbed five flights above the street
> and wintered in a tenement.
> It had no bathroom and no heat
> except a coal fire in the grate
> that we kept burning night and day
> until the fire went out in May.

The 'Valuta' section relives the exploitation of post-war Europe by 'the profiteers of the exchange' and 'the pilgrims of art' who are 'following the dollar' across Europe, enriched by the collapse of currencies. It may be the Dada influence but the poems have a deadening gaiety. Cowley rises to the decadence of the 'Carnaval in the Midi' and to the 'Château de Soupir: 1917', where the odalisque Yvette entertains her Senator lover by running nymphlike through the woods, he in pursuit while ominously

> The mist creeps riverward. A fox
> barks underneath a blasted tree.
> An enemy machine gun mocks
> this ante-bellum coquetry
> and then falls silent, while a bronze
> Silenus, patron of these lawns,
> lies riddled like a pepper box.

Like Pound, in 'Ezra Pound at the Hôtel Jacob', the speaker rejects but cannot shake his own country, though there is 'nothing grand' about it he reckons in one poem and announces, in another, that he will not return home. It is a posture in a crowd of posturings.

'The City of Anger', part IV, returns the exiles to New York. Beneath the indignation is 'a longing for utter ruin, a feeling of timeless melancholy, dry, reckless, defeated, and perverse'. Often jaunty, these poems are frequently dedicated to friends presumably on the same wavelength (Crane, Tate, Burke, Loeb). Part V, 'The Dry Season', speaks of 1930 as a time on the unsettled brink of middle age, when Cowley and his peers were bound by professional and domestic commitments. The mood is expressed pithily in the opening of 'The Mother' ('It was a noon of freedom, / an afternoon in chains') and viscerally in the title poem ('Take out your heart and wring it between your hands'). This section also features Cowley's most anthologised, patriotic poem, 'The Long Voyage', an odyssey begun on his return from Spain in 1937:

> Now the dark waters at the bow
> fold back, like earth against the plow;
> foam brightens like the dogwood now
>   at home, in my own country.

In an October 1941 letter Cowley described several of these poems as being connected, 'the product of 'my mood at the moment... the break-up of a world that deserved to be broken up, but not by the people who are doing the breaking'. 'The Lost People' revisits the Lost Generation ('the habit /of little treacheries, the friends unliked, / the joyless orgy').

'The Unsaved World', part VI, deals with Cowley's fellow-travelling politics. Each poem is dated—in both senses of the word. There are propaganda pieces about injustices and sacrifice ('dying for tomorrow'), about the marching dead who have given all and the future for which they paid ('O children born from, nourished with our blood.'). 'The Last International' and 'Tomorrow Morning' were used—lamely—by 'Time' magazine as ammunition against Cowley during his short stint on the government payroll.

There are well-realized poems, like 'Leander', 'Natural History' and the nostalgic 'The Flower and the Leaf' in section VII, the poet wondering on the fortunes that befell his literary companions. Always, as he tells us in 'The Urn', these young exiles possessed 'an urn of native soil':

> —a parcel of the soil not wide enough
> or firm enough to build a dwelling on
> or deep enough to dig a grave, but cool
> and sweet enough to sink the nostrils in
> and find the smell of home, or in the ears
> rumors of home like oceans in a shell.

In the elegiac last section 'The Red Wagon' follows the little boy rolling downhill on his toy, passing through his life until 'Sweat clouded his heavy spectacles. / His white hair streamed in the wind.' To live is to witness in 'Log in the Current', while in 'From Where the Forest Stood' time and progress have levelled the landscape of a life. At the poem's end the poet muses: 'There must be giants among them, / but distance makes them all look smaller than the men / and women we knew.' 'Prayer on All Saint's Day' considers poignantly what the poet's late mother would make of his achievements and the 'absences' that displease him (a request turned down, a friend unsupported).

There are some first rate poems in *Blue Juniata: A Life* while, as Cowley suspected, they work better collectively. And yet the reader ultimately feels that the autobiographical coherence is a constraint. The 'Notes' direct us overly; themes are circumscribed. Cowley's constant references to names, the snatches of dialogue and the songs carry, cumulatively, a weight of disappointment, as if the poet's success had been failure. Their dominant mood is loss; any joy is hysterical. What Cowley wrote of the lives of his fellow exiles, is also true of his own poetry: it is a search for an identity that fits—and it has its borrowings from others.

* * *

The letters in *The Long Voyage* show Cowley establishing his niche as poet-critic. Conrad Aiken and Allen Tate were his chief correspondents, though Hart Crane was also a friend. As an aspiring poet Cowley had approached H. D., Harriet Monroe and Amy Lowell. As the editor of 'The New Republic' he published Cummings, Moore, Stevens, Williams and younger poets including Berryman, Bogan, Roethke, Rukeyser and Richard Wright among many others. Cowley's dealings with Robert Lowell had a public dimension not tied to poetry and he jousted with Randall Jarrell in print. In *Exile's Return*, he wrote at length of Eliot, Pound and Cummings.

Cowley was forthright and partisan in his estimates of other poets (at least in his letters). Robert Frost's reputation, for example, irritated him. Writing in 1944 he complained, 'I don't like Frost—or to be more exact, I don't like the sort of veneration that surrounds this honest but rather minor poet.' Of Edna St. Vincent Millay he wrote, 'We thought her classical sonnets were insufferably mannered.' E. E. Cummings he found repetitive but inventive. He admired Louise Bogan, a friend of his first wife's ('In her work she was truly one of the incorruptibles').

Cowley seems to have had a vexed relationship to the poetry of T. S. Eliot. In *Exile's Return* he reckoned that by 1922 Eliot was 'most fervently worshipped by young poets' for his technique, his constant new departures and defence of the intellect against the emotions. 'In those early poems... he was endowing our daily life with distinction', whereas in 'The Waste Land', 'He not only abused the present, but robbed it of vitality. It was as if he were saying, this time, that our age was prematurely senile... that it was forever condemned to borrow and patch together the songs of dead poets.'

Much later Cowley partly blamed 'The Waste Land' on Ezra Pound's severe editing technique with its indifference to sequence. Pound, he felt, was a seminal influence on poetry and 'deserved the credit for discoveries which other poets were using, yet it seemed to me that some of the others—notably Eliot and Cummings—had a great deal more to say'. He felt that 'the central and always obvious meaning [of the Cantos] is nothing that throws light on any real dilemmas, past or present'. Nonetheless, Cowley would always publicly support Pound's right to recognition.

Cowley's relationship with Archibald MacLeish and his work was complicated. Although he shared Allen Tate's admiration for MacLeish's Pulitzer Prizewinning *Conquistador* (1933), according to Hans Bak, 'Cowley critically reviewed MacLeish's work through the 1930s'. Writing to Wilson in June 1940 Cowley defended the writers of the 1920s against MacLeish's published argument that they failed democracy in their defeatism, 'I have always felt that MacLeish was all right emotionally but a very sloppy thinker, with the result that he lets his emotions carry him into a succession of weak positions.' He also was to describe MacLeish's style as 'inflated'. On the other hand he was beholden to MacLeish for the government job that had unfortunately ended badly.

In Bak's view, 'Making the acquaintance of Aiken in Boston was a catalyst: it propelled [Cowley] away from Boston's literary conservatism and toward a distinctly modern poetry.' Conrad Aiken's commitment to strong rhythms, to poetic consciousness as a religion and to the thematic pursuit of identity seemed to Cowley, in 1918, 'a successful development of most of my present tendencies'. Bak noted that 'Despite their different temperaments—Cowley thriving on literary contacts, Aiken prickly and wilfully reticent, resistant to public exposure or self-promotion—the two men got along well.' On Aiken's death, Cowley confessed that he regarded his friend as a 'father figure'.

Aiken had not been an easy 'father' to have. As their first meetings Cowley wrote, he 'is now criticizing poetry for *The Dial*. He is getting so unpopular that he can't get anything published in a magazine'. Cowley would clash with Randall Jarrell over Aiken in 1941, after Jarrell had criticised his 'pet lamb' for his negativity about other poets. In turn Cowley lamented Jarrell's 'dandysme' as a writer of reviews ('Poetry enters them only as a target'). Jarrell had the defter touch in a letter to 'The New Review' where he wrote, 'That my reviews seem to Mr. Cowley disproportionately severe indicates a divergence of our tastes which can hardly fail to be a source of gratification to us both.'

Cowley's friendship with Allen Tate began in 1924 when Tate came to Greenwich Village at Hart Crane's urging. He first considered Cowley a snob who 'looked like a truck driver' but that scathing view did not last, plus Cowley was an excellent publishing contact for the southerner to make in the north. Their long friendship survived political disagreements. Tate's reactionary regionalism and Agrarianism might seem at odds with Cowley's Communist sympathies, but they at least shared criticism of 'our business civilisation'. Besides, as Cowley remembered in *The Flower and the Leaf* (1985), 'both of us put literature above politics and in literary matters we were likely to agree'. A little over a year before Tate died, Cowley wrote to him, 'The years since 1924 have made us brothers.'

One mutual friend he kept close as long as possible was Hart Crane, to whom he had written: 'you are one of two or three people who can write a twentieth century blank verse, about other subjects than love, death and nightingales and in other patterns than ti tum ti tum ti tum ti tum ti tum'. When in September 1929 Crane arrived at the Cowleys to work 'in peace' on 'The Bridge', Cowley wrote to Tate, 'I can hardly use the word in connection with him. Like certain mountains, he has his own storms, his local weather. The phonograph is playing, the alcohol bottle uncorked.' It remained uncorked until Crane committed suicide in April, 1932. A decade later Cowley wrote to Burke: 'Hart had the impulse of a prophet, spoke in the voice of a prophet… But at heart he didn't believe in anything.'

Malcolm Cowley's prose reminiscences are part of the American century. He once said: 'Writers often speak of "saving their energy," as if each man were given a nickel's worth of it, which he is at liberty to spend. To me, the mind of a poet resembles Fortunatus's purse: the more spent, the more it supplies.' I cannot claim that Cowley's poetry purse was large or that it never emptied, but he knew that himself. To Robert Penn Warren he wrote in July 1967: 'The spirit hasn't stirred in me … to write many new [poems], but I have a curious mania for revising old ones, as if I felt that each of the poems written long ago was begging me to chisel away at the rough stone and give it a final form.' He was, he said, 'senilizing my juvenalia'.

ALLEN TATE IN PARIS

> The thirtieth, not yet the thirtieth year
> Of wonders, revelations, whispers, signs
> – 'Fragment of a Meditation'

In his *Memoirs and Opinions 1926–1974* Allen Tate has a colourful essay, 'Miss Toklas' American Cake', recounting his first experience of London and Paris in 1928 and 1929. At that time, the poet, editor and formidable polemicist was already influential, being known as both a Modernist and a leading contributor to the revival of the Literature of the American South, dubbed 'The Southern Renaissance'. Tate had just published *Stonewall Jackson: The Good Soldier* (1928) and *Mr. Pope and Other Poems* (1928) which, along with the support of prominent friends, had earned him a Guggenheim Fellowship to study abroad. At this time Tate stood on the cusp between his precocious beginning and a lauded career in which he was to influence generations (including galvanising poets as different as Robert Lowell and Geoffrey Hill).

Despite the heavy commitment of time required for his current project, a biography of Confederate President Jefferson Davis, the trip enabled Tate to explore his regional identity at a distance geographical as well as historical. Tate's Southernness was a complicated affair, partly real—he was Kentucky born and also cherished a Virginia legacy his mother persuaded him of—partly symbolic and partly in defiance of the North's ignorance of the region. He also wrote essays while in Europe, at least one of crucial personal importance, 'The Fallacy of Humanism', which pointed the way toward his eventual Catholicism. Tate further revised his celebrated Emily Dickinson essay there, wrote French-influenced Modernist poems ('Mother and Son', 'Message from Abroad') and worked on others, including a fated long poem and a revision of his greatest, 'Ode to the Confederate Dead'. Equally important for this most 'networked' of writers, Paris and London offered a significant extension of friendships and contacts: T. S. Eliot and Herbert Read among others in London, Ford Madox Ford, John

Peale Bishop and the more celebrated American expatriates in Paris (Hemingway, Fitzgerald and Stein).

The twenty nine year old Tate had lived in New York since late 1924, working on his poetry, reviewing and writing freelance for 'The Nation' and other periodicals, while supporting himself as a janitor. He had married the aspiring novelist Caroline Gordon that year, a fellow Kentuckian, who would shortly give birth to their baby, Nancy. The Tates had developed friendships with Hart Crane, Mark Van Doren, Malcolm Cowley, Ford Madox Ford and others while in New York. All were left behind on September 29th, 1928, when they sailed for Europe on board the S.S. America. Recounting the hazards of their first overseas trip, Tate wrote to his long-time friend, the author Andrew Lytle, of the unnerving swells and gales that had hounded them. Caroline Gordon, in a letter to her friend Sally Wood, described enduring 'a fearful voyage. A storm, two points below a hurricane'.

They arrived unscathed, but hard-pressed financially. Generally 'The Guggenheim stipend was enough for sustenance but not enough for the luxury of the grand tour', Tate remembered. Yet after a few days in London, he had to petition the Guggenheim Foundation for permission to write two review articles before January 1st to tide them over until the next foundation payment, since travel and settling in had been so costly. His intention had been to remain in England until January, in order to work in the Oxford libraries before moving on to Paris. Gordon was disappointed at this, being desperate to work herself. While a French nurse was affordable, she judged, an English nurse was not. 'Six weeks, with no interruption,' she wrote ruefully, 'would enable me to finish the novel I've been working on now for three years'. *Penhally* told the story of the decline of a landed Kentucky family over four generations.

By the end of October Tate had also begun complaining: 'What a God-smitten climate fair Albion is!' They had visited Robert Penn Warren, currently in Oxford on a Rhodes scholarship and working on his biography of John Brown. Tate wrote of being weakened by 'the miasmal airs' of Oxford. 'How inferior the English are', he continued in the same ill-tempered vein. Warren found them lodgings in Oxford notwithstanding and it turned out to be 'a grand place to work' after all, according to Gordon. While there Tate wrote an article, 'American Poetry since 1920', plus a revised draft of his Emily Dickinson essay, though he made little progress on the long poem.

One significant attraction of London for Tate was an opportunity to meet T.S. Eliot (and, as it turned out, to form a friendship with Herbert Read). As Read remembered, they met at one of the editorial gatherings for 'The Criterion', 'perhaps introduced by Uncle Tom'. According to his first, tactful biographer, Radcliffe Squires, Tate 'was taken by F. V. Morley to a Criterion luncheon' where he met the two. Be that as it may, Tate established a firm relationship with Read from the first, while with Eliot only a productive one. In Tate's words 'the twelve years between Mr Eliot and myself were like the Grand Canyon that only after some years seemed to silt up'. His reported initial impression was of Eliot as a man with an affected British accent who gave very little of his background: a 'Sphinx'. And in a 1932 letter Tate would write with irritation: 'I think Eliot is pretty hopeless about contemporary poetry, at least so far as my part is concerned; he took five poems of mine in 1929, but not one of them ever appeared.' Over the years their acquaintance 'almost imperceptibly became friendship'. In Tate's opinion this happened because, 'I never tried to imitate him or become a disciple'. For Tate, the Southern man of manners, Eliot's 'literary reticence' became 'the highest form of civility'.

While he was eager to meet Eliot, Tate turned down the opportunity of an introduction to Yeats on the grounds of shyness (John Berryman acted more boldly a decade later). He did however attend a party at Harold Monro's flat, Monro being 'a gloomy spirit' according to Robert Frost whom Tate met there. Monro, the famed owner of the Poetry Bookshop in Bloomsbury, published the *Georgian Poetry* anthologies. Frost attempted to involve Tate in the party conversation by using him to illustrate the difference in regional accents. Tate reported later to Donald Davidson he 'disliked him instinctively', though after Frost's death he concluded that, though he was no reader of the poet either as a young or old man, 'I am convinced that he wrote some of the finest poems of our time, or of any time.'

No doubt the British inability to distinguish Southerner from Northerner did little to endear them to Tate. According to his best biographer, Thomas A. Underwood (*Allen Tate: Orphan of the South* (2000), the Southernness of the Tates made him feel self-conscious among the British Modernists. Allied with a bad cough and the fog and cold, it led him to uproot Gordon, baby Nancy and their friend the poet Léonie Adams whom they had met in Oxford. In late November the little group took the boat from Newhaven to Dieppe, the cheapest crossing. Arriving in Paris, they rented two rooms at the Hotel de Fleurus. At the end of January 1929 they were to move into Ford Madox Ford's cramped apartment at 32 rue de Vaugirard, where the toilet was a drain without a seat. The compensations would be a view of Saint-Sulpice and the opportunity to live rent-free for six months when the fifty-five year old novelist, Gordon's mentor, sailed for America.

Tate recounted his Paris time with some irony in the 1971 Toklas essay: 'I was about to plunge into the French experience which young literary Americans in the twenties thought they must have or remain sorry provincials.' The truth was that Paris would hardly broaden his mind since conversations with French writers rarely happened and 'the work I did every morning in Ford's flat might have been better done in New York, or Richmond, or Nashville'. And yet while the trip may have been unnecessary, France helped focus Tate intellectually, being filtered through his Southern perspective. There were feelings of cultural consanguinity, for example. As he would remark in a 1935 essay entitled 'The Profession of Letters in the South': 'In religious and social feeling I should stake everything on the greater resemblance [of The South] to France.'

Initially Paris pleased the Tates in other ways, especially given the exchange rate and the availability of good, cheap alcohol after Prohibition America. Gordon's snap judgment had been that café society was somewhat overrated: 'The Dome and Rotonde are really quite terrible… A sort of super-Greenwich village. They actually appall. Allen says the Select is better. I haven't been there yet.' What soon floored them was the flu. The winter of 1928 brought recurrent bouts. A time of rum and aspirin, Gordon reported to Wood the following July: 'we have been having steadily one hell of a time. First we had grippe, then grippe again, and then more grippe: three main bouts, with slight attacks sprinkled in between.'

Soon their limited French and the departure of Ford, on whose company they had tended to depend, exacerbated their illness. They had socialised frequently, playing sonnet-writing games at Ford's apartment, and Tate had regularly accompanied him to the Café Les Deux Magots to play cards ('Russian Banque') and drink brandy. 'He is really one of the best men I have ever known' wrote Tate to Lytle. Gordon was to echo the sentiment, praising Ford's generosity and encouragement in her own work (and Adams's). The loan of the apartment had been a gift in appreciation of her assistance in retyping a bulky manuscript of his.

The Tates eventually developed friendships with other writers in Paris. These tended to be Southerners like John Peale Bishop—a friend of Fitzgerald and Edmund Wilson—who currently lived with his wife in a chateau twenty kilometres from Paris, and Julien Green, an author who at least wrote in French. Then there were visits from 'Red' Warren and Hart Crane, travelling courtesy of a legacy from his grandmother.

The key essay Tate produced abroad was 'The Fallacy of Humanism', which Eliot gladly took for the 'Criterion', it being '*admirable* for our purposes' as he assured Tate in February 1929 (although privately, to mollify Paul Elmer More who had been criticised in the essay, he declared that Tate 'is still in growing pains, and his style is heavy and uncouth'). Eliot did not, however, take Gordon's story 'Funeral in Town', because he doubted that the magazine's readers would 'make much of it'. Instead he encouraged her to send more.

The importance of Tate's essay is now perhaps biographical: an attack on the New-Humanism, an American literary critical movement initiated by Irving Babbitt, which had its source in Matthew Arnold's view of Literature's moral heart. To Tate, 'The humanists quarrel with literature because it cannot give them a philosophy and a church; but they keep turning to literature because they cannot find these things elsewhere.' He believed literature could not carry the weight of expectation. 'The religious unity of intellect and emotion, of reason and instinct, is the sole technique for the realization of values', he concluded. In the essay he does not go so far as to subscribe to religion himself but clearly, intellectually at least, this is his direction. He wrote to Herbert Read at the time, 'I am not "in the arms" of any church; though I am convinced there is only one church capable of meeting us with a really warm embrace.' Looking back in 1975, the Catholic Tate would see this essay from one perspective as 'an attack on myself'.

He reported to Mark Van Doren in January 1929 that he had written five hundred lines of the long poem, 'But the trouble is I can't understand the lines I wrote two weeks ago. I oughtn't to be writing a long poem. It is unfortunate, of course, that I didn't see that before I was given a salary to write it.' In the end Tate dropped it, no doubt partly because of the onerous weight of the Jefferson Davis biography. Since he was strapped for sources, this work relied greatly on the many volumes of *The Official Records of the Union and Confederate Armies* in the American Library. The War Between the States fascinated him, he reckoned, because 'a military subject ... permits me to indulge my preadolescent hero-worship of the great generals'.

The seasonal seesawing of the weather continued to frustrate the Tates. In March he was writing of going every afternoon at four to sit at a table outside Les Deux Magots. Yet come summer they were still being challenged by its uncertainty: 'I cannot get used to its being so cold in July: Allen is positively bitter about it. He makes patriotic speeches about the climate', wrote Gordon. When pressure came from his publisher about competition for the Davis biography, Tate 'leaped out of his sick bed and began typing madly' so as not lose money. They were both typing madly according to Gordon, day and night until the book was dispatched to the publisher on July 4th .Tate later confessed that, although deep in her novel, his wife broke off to write three chapters of the biography for him, based on his notes and outline.

When Ford returned to the Paris apartment, the Tates left for Brittany, where they learnt on July 19th that his mother had died at Monteagle, Tennessee. Theirs had been a fraught relationship. The family returned to Paris in September to be greeted with celebrity introductions, which began at Sylvia Beach's 'Shakespeare and Company' bookshop. There Tate was introduced to Hemingway. On the first meeting the two strolled from the bookshop to the terrace of the Café Voltaire where they discussed, over vermouth cassis, two of Tate's positive reviews of Hemingway's work and Ford's impotence, a subject of interest only to Hemingway who was characteristically lethal about his former editorial employer. The famously charming Tate had met Hemingway at a time—as his biographer Scott Donaldson observed—when he 'made people want to please him'. If privately Hemingway believed, as he said, that Tate's 'Ode to the Confederate Dead' held 'the lifeless-est lines to Dead Soldiers ever read', he still knew a good critic and potential acolyte when he saw one.

The two became good enough friends to attend the bicycle races at the Vélodrome d'Hiver most Sundays for three months, where Tate was to be 'a somewhat sardonic high priest of the cult' according to another Hemingway biographer, Carlos Baker. The novelist continued to hold Tate's critical opinions in regard over the years. He had earned the Hemingway stamp of approval, being recognised as possessing 'moral guts'. 'So I was adjusted to the Hemingway myth', wrote Tate. It did not hurt that as a favour, the latter had patiently read an early copy of *A Farewell to Arms* overnight and pronounced it 'a masterpiece'. Many years later the admiration turned sour, after Tate had read Hemingway's memoir *A Moveable Feast* (1964): 'I couldn't have known then that he was the complete son of a bitch who would later write about certain friends, all of them defenselessly dead'.

Tate felt F. Scott Fitzgerald to be a better writer than Hemingway and though they met no more than a dozen times, he also liked him better, 'even though he was not as good company'. The Tates met the Fitzgeralds at a dinner party with their mutual friends, the Bishops. He enjoyed meeting Zelda ('not a beautiful woman but immensely attractive, with the Southern woman's gift for conversation that made people feel that she had known them for years'). In contrast he found Scott's opening question insulting: 'Do you enjoy sleeping with your wife?' Bishop dismissed the question as being a favourite Fitzgeraldian tactic to find out how one dealt with a disconcerting situation. Privately, to Carlos Baker, Tate called Fitzgerald a 'fatuous' drunk.

Another incident occurred in December, when he and Warren were café crawling with Fitzgerald in Montmartre. At some point—according to Tate's version—'Red' Warren said he admired *The Great Gatsby*. Fitzgerald dared him to repeat the remark and threatened to hit him if he did. When he repeated it, Fitzgerald jumped up apparently, grabbed Warren's overcoat, put it on and disappeared. Presumably he had been suffering from the stress of trying to reproduce work of such quality. If Tate publicly admired Fitzgerald as an author, in a letter to Fitzgerald's biographer Arthur Mizener fifteen years later he was to write provocatively, 'It was his very romanticism which kept him from ever learning more about the American rich [who were his subject] than a little boy knows about cowboys and Indians.'

It is little surprise that Tate was wary of the expatriates, then, and his reservations were confirmed when he got to know Gertrude Stein, friendly, imperious and 'mad as the March Hare'. On one occasion he bumped into her walking around the Musée de Luxembourg with her poodle, 'Basket'. She spoke to him of 'Presidential timber' and concluded, 'No Southerner can afford to know any history.' Tate, the imaginative biographer, was appalled. On another occasion he attended Stein's lecture in American literature, urged by Hemingway who had been summoned back into favour. In her salon she lectured to the men in her audience on American literature, while the women, segregated, were entertained by Stein's companion, Toklas. She took her audience up through literature before arriving at the summit, which had been reached in her own work, leaving Tate again appalled.

By the end of their time in Paris the writing had been going better for Tate. In a letter of early November he told Andrew Lytle: 'I'm working hard on my book of essays and at my Poem and poems.' The 'essays' refer to the collection *Reactionary Essays on Poetry and Ideas* (1936); the 'Poem' to 'Ode to the Confederate Dead'. (This was the ode the sixteen year old Geoffrey Hill would read in 1948. It 'struck me like a bolt from heaven', he remembered; 'overnight I became a modernist.') The fellowship ended, the Tates sailed for New York on January 1st, 1930. Near the end of another 'ghastly trip', Gordon declared her hatred of leaving the French capital: 'I didn't do much to amuse myself there—just sat around in cafes, but it was all so nice & easy. I gained 15 pounds, in spite of working like a dog!' Husband and wife were to return to Paris in June 1932 for seven months, another trip financed by a Guggenheim fellowship, this time for Caroline Gordon.

So the Tates had weathered their first European adventure. At the time of their return to America, Gordon's success with *Penhally* was a year away. As for Tate, *Jefferson Davis: His Rise and Fall* (1929) had been published to good reviews, further extending his reputation. The next step would be his contribution to the conservative Agrarian manifesto, *I'll Take My Stand* (1930), which he and his friends had been contemplating for some time. He had become a professional Southerner.

ROBERT PENN WARREN AT OXFORD

Describing his friend Allen Tate's memory of the incident as 'a bit garbled', Robert Penn Warren wrote of an evening's café-crawling with F. Scott Fitzgerald in Paris in December 1928. It ended abruptly after Warren praised *The Great Gatsby* and its author took threatening exception. In his version, the twenty-three year old seized his coat and, with a few choice words to Fitzgerald, stalked out. Behind this contretemps lay Fitzgerald's feeling that his best writing days were behind him. Robert Penn Warren, on the other hand, stood at the beginning of an uninterrupted, prolific and highly acclaimed career as a poet, novelist, and critic.

The Kentucky born Warren had arrived in Oxford two months earlier as a Rhodes Scholar. An alumnus of Vanderbilt University, Tennessee, where he met poets Allen Tate, John Crowe Ransom and other Southern conservatives who were to become at first literary 'Fugitives' and then anti-industrial 'Agrarians', he completed graduate work at the University of California (M.A. 1927) and Yale. As with Tate, his two years abroad were to reassure him in his Southernness while releasing him from its confines ('as soon as I *left* that world of Tennessee... I began to rethink the meaning ... of the world I had been living in without considering it').

Before he left Oxford, 'Red' Warren would complete his biography of the abolitionist zealot in *John Brown: The Making of a Martyr* (1929), largely finish a poetry collection (finally appearing in 1936 as *Thirty-six Poems*) and write 'The Briar Patch,' his essay contribution to the manifesto *I'll Take My Stand: The South and the Agrarian Tradition* (1930). He would also turn to fiction with a long story called 'Prime Leaf', which appeared in the yearbook 'American Caravan' in 1931. That would lead eventually to his novel on the Black Patch Tobacco Wars, *Night Rider* (1939). In the course of time Warren would promote the work of New Criticism as a teacher and co-author of the seminal *Understanding Poetry* (1938) with Cleanth Brooks, whom he met at Oxford, win Pulitzer Prizes in both fiction (*All the King's Men*, 1946) and poetry

(*Promises: Poems 1954–1956*; and *Now and Then, 1978*). He would earn the Presidential Medal of Freedom in 1980 and become the first Poet Laureate Consultant in Poetry in 1986.

Warren was first and last a poet, ruminating on the human condition and on the past. In a 1966 interview he explained, 'The South is a special case. It lost the war and suffered hardship. That kind of defeat gives the past great importance.' As a poet, he began under the influence of Hardy, Eliot, and the Metaphysical poets. Many years later he would describe his affinity with Hardy: 'I would single out the notion of fate; a fatalism was deeply ingrained in the Southern mind... A sense of entrapment. I think you can probably make a case that Hardy touched this nerve. Another thing was Hardy's use of folk materials, his portraits of little ironies of folk-life.' Warren had discovered *The Waste Land* as a sophomore and spoke of being 'completely overwhelmed' by it ('It was certainly a watershed in my life and the lives of many of my friends'). The Elizabethans and Jacobeans greatly appealed to him also, but 'the metaphysical strain, I began to feel, was not for me at a technical level'.

Fortunately for Warren he had an early conduit for his verse experiments in his old roommate Tate, always eager to promote his work in the modernist and vernacular styles. 'You have placed everything I have ever published,' Warren wrote in thanks; 'you might as well start an agency.' Tate also recommended his friend to an agent who gained him a contract for writing the John Brown biography.

Warren's dramatic imagination had been influenced by old family stories and tales of the Civil War, and now refreshed by his correspondence. Other Southern friends were 'ferociously restudying American history'. Allen Tate had gone from Stonewall Jackson to Jefferson Davis as biographical studies; Andrew Lytle worked on Nathan Bedford Forrest; Donald Davidson's poems, *The Tall Men*, inhabited the old South. As Malcolm Cowley, who knew Warren wrote, 'most of his world is reduced to stories'. And those stories, as Alfred Kazin observed, dealt with guilt and the Fall of Man: 'In a sense all of Warren's work could be called *The Legacy of the Civil War*' (the title of his 1961 essay). If as a Southerner he felt 'trapped in history', that gelled at the time with 'the other half of my life, in which my sole passion was John Donne, John Ford, Webster's plays, Baudelaire'.

He found the Oxford of 1928 much tamer than all this: dull in fact. In September he had been researching his Brown book in Harpers Ferry and elsewhere, in Virginia. Now at New College, facing an October 11th term commencement, he found the climate 'hellish', his digs an 'ice house' with the privations of the period (baths and toilets hardly to hand) but with a scout to light the fire, open curtains, etc. He lived with five others, dined in gown in the Hall, with occasional invitations to the High Table and to join the dons for coffee.

The Tates, busy Americanizing Paris, swooped in for a visit but were immediately driven away by Tate's flu, though they returned at the month's end to try working there briefly. Warren aside, Caroline Gordon had not been much impressed by the Rhodes Scholars who had been their travelling companions across the Atlantic, as she noted in one of her wonderfully tart letters: 'There were forty Rhodes scholars on our boat—really quite terrible creatures, most of them. The honour of Tennessee is in the hands of a young man named Dogberry, who had the effrontery to refer to me as "the wife."' Warren himself subscribed to her view.

His early impressions of the English were in part even less favourable, but delivered to Andrew Lytle on October 18th with youthful hyperbole: 'I like the English… the English men, that is. Did you ever see anything in your life as generally ugly and uninviting as the British female?' Australians, he went on are 'sons-of-bitches' and, though he liked the South Africans at Oxford, 'The Americans, I grieve to relate, are not a thing to make one proud.' In the same letter he went on to criticise 'The New College literary gents' for holding that Rupert Brooke was the first and last great modern poet'. On the other hand, 'There is some good company, tobacco (pretty bad),' he writes, 'drink, books, and dulness. Great dulness. Rain. There is something like a narcotic about the whole dump, which is rather pleasant in its total effect.' He had an official 'moral tutor', who warned him against debt, time wasting, women and so on.

A veteran student by now, Warren understandably took some of the academic trappings airily, though it would cost him later. He also had some independence as a graduate and a Rhodes Scholar, one of a small number of American students there. He intended to read for the B. Litt. degree; learnt archival and textual skills for the reading of Chaucerian and Shakespearean texts; and 'soaked' himself in sixteenth and seventeenth century poetry. There was the possibility of a D.Phil if his scholarship could be further extended. His supervisor, Percy Simpson (author of a monograph on Shakespeare's punctuation) had been described by another as a 'patient soul'. He was not really sympathetic to Warren as an American though, having established his student *was* an American and not an Australian ('no American has ever distinguished himself with us').

That Christmas Warren left for the Tates who had taken rooms at the Hôtel de Fleurus, pending the loan of Ford Madox Ford's tiny Paris apartment. It was at this time that the eventful meeting with Fitzgerald took place. Warren soon took off for the Côte d'Azur in the company of the college friend who had driven him from Oxford. He had decided on teaching, as Tate told their friend Andrew Lytle: 'Red is, in short, about to toss the sponge high in the air and become a professor.' Early the next year, however, Warren was writing to Tate of 'suffering a mental, moral, and spiritual collapse' though being physically in good health.

Taking Dr Johnson's prescription of society as a cure for loneliness, he subsequently wrote, 'I have been to five cocktail parties, two theatre parties, four dinners, one shooting party, five poker games, and to church since my return to Oxford' [since the Christmas vacation]. He turned the poker at least to his advantage (£5) and not for the last time. He showed a writer's concern for the John Brown work: 'as the sheets pile up, I become more and more humble and distressed on the subject of biography. I reread and revise and the more I do those things the flatter the thing seems to become. God help me'. And yet the book was a necessary part of his education as a writer and, 'in a way a question of homesickness'.

Warren was also committed to staying in Oxford between terms to use the library in peace, but also for the company of a British girl he had met ('an exception which to some extent supports our favorite dogma about the daughters of Britain', he wrote to Tate). It was not long before he was disciplined for breaking college rules over the girl's presence in his room. Surviving the scrape, by late March he reported 'a second wind and a completely new enthusiasm' for his work. Tate sounded relieved, writing to Lytle that the reader is 'simply amazed at the subtlety of the presentation'.

Preoccupied as he was by John Brown, Warren returned also to the subject of his poetry, wondering whether he should try his collection on Harper's in the hope that publication would encourage him to write better poems. Although only 'Oxford City Wall' was known for certain to come from these days, Warren worked also on 'Tryst on Vinegar Hill'. He was not sure that the poem did not have 'some rather grave flaws in it', he wrote to Allen Tate in April 1929, intending to return to it when he had time for reflection. It appeared in 'This Quarter' in the January-March issue of the following year.

The gravest flaw in the poem is in its conception, in the racism that disqualifies it. It follows a pair of African-American lovers to a graveyard, where their lovemaking allows the dead 'to spread / Their fingers to the little spark / Of warmth the living bodies own'. Since his own death in 1989 Warren's reputation has wavered, partly as a result of these early poems. In 2007, for instance, a controversy erupted regarding the Poetry Society of America. Warren was cited as evidence for its supposed racism, from lines in 'Pondy Woods', a poem which inhabits a similar perspective to 'Tryst on Vinegar Hill'. It should be pointed out that Warren's attitude was to evolve with the times, and also that racism (and anti-Semitism) was endemic within the writing community in both the south *and* north in those days—as it was in the movies and everywhere else.

Less contentiously, 'Empire' appeared in that summer's issue of 'This Quarter'. The poem sails through empires misread, found and lost. Part confrontation with Whitmanesque optimism and equally atmospheric, it addresses the new America, 'bastard to memory', a 'new lamb' in jeopardy being without a sense of the past:

> Always at night
> the land-wind lifts. Follow, there is a path
> down through the dunes, I recall, which brings
> us to the beach. The wind, east, will swerve
> only at dawn. Behind us in the duneland
> the cicada, cold in the salt grass, sings
> no more. I think that we can understand
> each other, talking here, while we observe
> the foam in calyx on the patient sand.

At this period Warren handled history and landscape better. He had the rhetoric and the subject matter. Perhaps the most successful poem of the period, 'Kentucky Mountain Farm', was written and published in parts between 1927 and 1932. 'History among the Rocks', part of the sequence, appeared in 'New Republic' in December, 1928. A symbolic poem that focuses on the eternality of stone in the historical landscape of fallen and transient lives, it takes Warren back to a Kentucky he imagines as much as remembers. The power of the poem may be glimpsed in the opening section where Man is addressed in 'Rebuke of the Rocks':

> Then quit yourselves as stone and cease
> To break the weary stubble-field for seed;
> Let not the naked cattle bear increase,
> Let barley wither and the bright milkweed.
> Instruct the heart, lean men, of a rocky place
> That even the little flesh and fevered bone
> May keep the sweet sterility of stone.

If the other poems he was working on while at Oxford were 'not so hot' at least his publisher was pleased with the John Brown book, which was set to appear in the autumn. Unfortunately Warren's eyes gave him trouble, an ongoing problem since an adolescent accident had left him almost blind in one. His rigorous routine would not have helped: 'I work until four every day, then paddle a canoe up the river, have some tea at an inn, and return in time for dinner. I amuse myself in the early hours of darkness and return to college at ten-thirty, and work for two more hours. I am getting an incredible amount of work done under this regime.'

During the summer Warren returned to America. There he unsuccessfully attempted to persuade his publisher, Payson and Clarke, to take his poems to fulfil their book option—or to free him from it. Nor could he interest Viking, though both publishers were willing to have him undertake a biography of the ardently Southern antebellum politician, John C. Calhoun, an idea he prompted as a vehicle for one of 'the family'. Moving on to San Francisco, he joined his girlfriend, Cinina Brescia, who was teaching Spanish and Italian. They married in Sacramento, but kept the news quiet so as not to lose his scholarship. This was a judicious act on more than one front, for Cinina was poison to some of Warren's friends. After a visit from Warren and his fiancé to the Tates, in November 1927 Caroline Gordon had reported: '[she] felt that she must live up to her descent from the Borgias and raised as much hell as she possibly could all the time'.

Warren had the opportunity over the summer to visit with his Nashville friends ('they are on fire with crusading zeal and the determination to lynch carpet-baggers'), to have dinner in New York with Edmund Wilson, an early champion of his poetry, and to meet Wilson's friend the editor of 'The American Caravan', Paul Rosenfield, who had published parts of 'Kentucky Mountain Farm' and was also interested in Warren's fiction ideas. Returning to Oxford in autumn 1929 and buoyed by winning a little at poker (£11) after having lost his wallet, he became more cheerful about the place. He determined to work on the satires of the dramatist John Marston and to commit himself to the degree, though his letters to the Tates and Andrew Lytle suggest that their Agrarian project was also on his mind. He was also reviewing for Wilson at the 'New Republic' (on Merrill Moore and Thomas Jefferson).

Warren was drawn to Paris again that Christmas, telling 'John Marston to go to hell for a time'. His Brown biography had been published to *some* impressive reviews ('a capital piece of work' wrote H. L. Mencken). He seemed satisfied, given that the subject always created partisan feelings. The biography succeeded most crucially in recognizing the complexity of his subject (Brown's 'elaborate psychological mechanism for justification') and in its dramatic narrative drive:

> The sheriff's hatchet flashed in its downward stroke to release the trap. The rope spun through, jerked heavily with the weight below, and vibrated for a moment. Over the entire field—the cluster of officials, the officers sitting their horses, the steady ranks of militia—there was no sound.

The Tates returned to America in the first week of 1930, completing plans for *I'll Take My Stand* and involving Warren as one of the essayists. At length he chose, warily, to write on the 'negro' for his essay, 'The Briar Patch'. As the editor of his letters, William Bedford Clark, has written, 'Warren's misgivings were well-founded. His essay, which accepts the "fact" of segregation as a given but argues for a fuller recognition of the dignity of the Black American "as a man," was and would remain controversial.' According to his biographer Joseph Blotner (author also of a Faulkner biography and an entertaining autobiography, *An Unexpected Life*):

> One of the sources of the Southern Literary Renaissance was the impact upon a whole generation of their return home after exposure not just to Europe but also to the whole milieu of the literary avant garde. Friends such as Tate would remain receptive to the experimental, but this openness did not always extend to areas of thought and feeling.

The attitude of some of Warren's friends, less enlightened than his, reflected their belief in the status quo. Warren, in contrast, was to move on. In a 1970 interview he spoke of how he saw the process of writing as 'modifying, testing, and exfoliating older values'.

Back at Oxford he worked at the Marston thesis, learning that his Brown book was not selling well but soon absorbed in writing

'Pale Leaf'. He was delighted to hear that the Tates had been helped to purchase an antebellum farmhouse outside Clarksville, Tennessee, which they named 'Benfolly' for his brother Ben's largesse. In a congratulatory letter Warren also informed them of the courses he would teach at Southwestern College in Memphis (now Rhodes College), since he had decided not to return to Yale to complete his fellowship and had also declined a post at the University of Southern California.

Robert Penn Warren was granted his B. Litt. in Elizabethan Literature from Oxford in 1930 and went home to the Agrarian fray. At heart he remained the poet, one whose work gathered major critical attention with the passing decades. 'If I had to choose between my novels and my *Selected Poems*,' he said later in life, 'I would keep the *Selected Poems* as representing me more fully, my vision and my self. I think poems are more *you*.' He also remained a Southern writer wherever he lived ('I can't be anything else. You are what you are'), producing work in several genres, which resonated beyond the regional.

SEEING ROBERT LOWELL PLAIN

In the centenary of his birth the major American poet Robert Lowell is back in focus, if not quite in fashion. This year he is the subject of an excellent biography, *Robert Lowell: Setting the River on Fire*, by Kay Redfield Jamison, and his *New Selected Poems* has also appeared. After proofreading his first *Selected Poems* in 1976, the year before his death, Lowell acknowledged, 'Autobiography predominates, almost forty years of it.' Another, more comprehensive route to his life, however, is through the letters. Here we may, in Robert Browning's words, see the poet 'plain'.

A charismatic figure emerges from the pages of Saskia Hamilton's *The Letters of Robert Lowell* (2005) and from *Words in Air: The Complete Correspondence between Elizabeth Bishop and Robert Lowell* (ed. Thomas Travisano and Saskia Hamilton, 2008). While the poet's early, strident voice matured into compassion and finally weariness, the man we meet in the correspondence is amusing, admiring and optimistic as well. This is the poet who wrote in an 'Afterthought' to *Notebook 1967–68*, 'In truth I seem to have felt mostly the joys of living; in remembering, in recording, thanks to the gift of the Muse, it is the pain.'

Lowell was born into an old New England family. After a rebellious childhood complicated by a dominating mother with whom he always 'competed' and an ineffectual naval father, he dropped out of Harvard to study with the influential Southern poets, Allen Tate and John Crowe Ransom. He also formed a friendship with the poet and critic Randall Jarrell, married the first of three writer wives, Jean Stafford, and published the Pulitzer Prize winning collection, *Lord Weary's Castle* (1946).

Lowell suffered bipolar disorder throughout his life, being institutionalised sixteen times or more. One early manifestation was religious zealotry. Infidelity became a wearying later symptom, weighing on Lowell's second and steadiest marriage, to Elizabeth Hardwick, with whom he had a daughter. After a highly successful career in poetry—especially with the ground-breaking *Life Studies* (1959)—and a time dabbling in celebrity and politics, America soured for him. In 1970 he turned to England, found a new wife, Lady Caroline Blackwood, and produced his last works during a period of increasing turmoil. He died returning to Hardwick at the age of sixty.

The Letters of Robert Lowell offer an eloquent self-portrait. Central to the collection are the fascinating glimpses of the evolution of the poet and finally the poignant letters at the time of the Hardwick divorce. We begin with the fierce commitment of the neophyte. In the opening letter the nineteen year old petitions Ezra Pound to accept him as an apprentice, offering to bring the necessary 'steel and fire' to one who he feels has 're-created what I have imagined to be the blood of Homer'. The young Lowell expects to make his way by his writings, he tells his parents, 'not because I was a Lowell at Harvard'. Arriving unannounced in Tennessee, he soon learns from Tate to 'know better what I need to do to advance, and [be] less inflated with my doings and writings.' There is maturity in his recognition in a letter to his early teacher, the poet Richard Eberhart, 'I'm in no hurry for recognition. I have no doubt in my ability to produce in the end.'

Although new to the poetry scene his potential was recognised by his mentors. He had impressed Eberhart and reached out to Pound, Eliot and to Frost who had seen his work as an undergraduate. To him he writes in July 1947: 'Thanks for what you said in your letter. We are really old friends now.' Lowell's friendships were sincere, but also valuable. He made further connections through his time as Consultant in Poetry to the Library of Congress (1947–8). A gregarious man who lived for poetry, Lowell constantly networked via notes, invitations, letters and reviews.

As well as promoting the work of friends, he also supported them. Breakdowns and depression were not uncommon among the poets of his generation. To Theodore Roethke he writes of 'some flaw in the motor' in the fact 'that to write we seem to have to go at it with such single-minded intensity that we are always on the point of drowning'. Lowell goes on to hope, 'There must be a kind of glory to it all that people coming later will wonder at.' He begins a letter to John Berryman: 'I have been thinking much about you all summer, and how we have gone through the same troubles, visiting the bottom of the world.' At Jarrell's breakdown he writes 'Your courage, brilliance and generosity should have saved you from this, but of course all good qualities are unavailing.'

Being habitually generous in tributes to others Lowell defends Ezra Pound, whose fascist comments are not to be condoned, 'Yet as a poet he is a hero, full of courage, and humor and compassion.' He comforts T.S Eliot's widow, Valerie: 'there was no one else who could both write and tell us how to write, no one who spoke with such authority and so little played the role of a great man'. In another mood his wit could be barbed. He begins a letter to Allen Ginsberg, 'I think letters ought to be written the way you think poetry ought to be. So let this be breezy, brief, incomplete, but spontaneous and not dishonestly holding back.' He could be acid, too. Of Spender he writes, 'You know he bites the boot he licks.'

We learn a lot about Lowell's attitude to his own poetry from these letters, particularly his reluctance to declare finished versions: 'Revision on revision, then worst of all tinkering, sometimes just for a change', as he tells Eliot of 'Thanksgiving's Over' in 1949. Throughout his career he worried about 'spoiling by polishing'. Metre had always been a preoccupation but he was gradually lured towards a breakthrough to a conversational style. Not long before *Life Studies* appeared he explained to William Carlos Williams that he has been 'experimenting with mixing loose and free meters with strict in order to get the accuracy, naturalness, and multiplicity of prose, yet, I also want the state and surge of the old verse, the carpentry of definite meter that tells me when to stop rambling.' Above all he was desperate not to repeat himself as a poet. As early as 1952, in the largely fallow period between books, he writes to Allen Tate 'I think I'm going into new country, and will not be repeating my old tricks'.

One could get 'boxed up' by the machinery of metre, but not only by that. Lowell began to see that his characteristic rhetorical impulse—the explosive diction and symbolism—needed to change also. With *Life Studies*, as he put it to Randall Jarrell: 'I've been loosening up the meter, as you'll see and horsing out all the old theology and symbolism and *verbal* violence.' It was a change that paid dividends for both poet and audience, as Lowell learned in reading on the West Coast: 'I found reading aloud that I wanted more humor, more immediate clarity, fewer symbols, more of the good prose writer's realistic direct glance.' He needed to tap into his own experience directly, and was to do that from then on.

'Writing's hell, isn't it?' The rollercoaster emotions of creativity—the exhilaration and depressions—fuelled Lowell's bipolar condition. Letters that make reference to it are affecting, whether written at the height of mania ('This has been like purging the Augean stables, but I'm in mysteriously wonderful and rugged shape') or during the depression that followed. After his first breakdown he explains to an ex-lover: 'By the time I reached the hospital I was completely out of my head... I was a prophet and everything was a symbol; then in the hospital: shouting, singing, tearing things up—religion and antics. Then depression (extreme) aching, self-enclosed, fearful of everyone and everything anyone could do, feeling I was nothing and could do nothing.' A decade later he described this as the 'Messianic bestial glow' followed by 'dark months of indecision, emptiness etc.' Always the poet (and in an effort to be uplifting), he admits to Roethke, 'We even bring back certain treasure from our visits to the bottom.'

Lowell learned to accept his attacks as part of his character, before a change to lithium treatment stabilised his condition, making him more hopeful. He could at times even write of it dispassionately, as in a 1965 letter: 'Every year or two, I have a breakdown and am in a sanitarium for about a month, never much more. Often there are girls or a girl, and it's all messy and hard as hell on Lizzie.' His first marriage foundered on his sudden, intense Catholicism and incipient mania. Lowell's liaisons with young women began later, not confined to his bipolar episodes.

Lowell met Elizabeth Hardwick at Yaddo, a writers' colony, where he described her to his friend Peter Taylor as 'slip-shod, good humored, malicious (harmless) and humorous' and to another as 'a Southern girl (a New York character now) full of gossip'. They met and married in 1949, the year after his divorce from Stafford. In the wake of his first breakdown he reported to his mother that Hardwick had been 'marvelously brave, ingenious and sympathetic'. So she was to remain, despite his manic episodes, infidelities and ultimately their divorce.

The *Letters* include many of Lowell's to Elizabeth Bishop, his 'favorite poet and favorite friend'. *Words in Air* offers more: both sides of their correspondence in its entirety. These are generous, loyal and loving exchanges over thirty years. In January 1962 Bishop wrote, 'When I think of how the world and my life would look to me if you weren't in either of them at all—they'd look very empty, I think.' On March 10, 1962, Lowell replied, 'how indispensable you are to me, and how ideally we've really kept things, better than life allows, really'. In the exchange of letters with Bishop, who lived a significant part of her adult life in Brazil, we have more insights into Lowell's thoughts on his work and often the best of him as a person.

The relationship began in 1947 when Bishop was thirty-six and Lowell thirty. She had published *North & South* the previous year and he *Lord Weary's Castle*. Both were in an uncertain romantic position in their own lives, which led Lowell to long-cherish an idealised notion of their compatibility. In August 1957, in a manic state he would make advances to Bishop during a visit by her and her partner, Lota de Macedo Soares. Forgiven, he explained that he had always assumed that they might marry, that 'asking you is *the* might have been for me'.

The letters are not love letters in the romantic sense as much as the eager correspondence of friends who enjoy each other's work and offer to critique it ('I am dying to see the ballad and the other new poems'). As early as December 1947 Lowell declares himself flattered by the fact Bishop gave some of his poems 'such a thorough going reading'. These are of course letters about their day-to-day lives as well: family, houses, jobs, plans, vacations—and gossip on the literary life. In writing to Bishop, Lowell loves to recount the conversations that corner him at meetings and parties. When Auden tells him Southerners [the New Critics] should keep off criticism because they are not good at it, he cheerfully reports the comment adding that Auden should perhaps do the same, 'but the remark did my wicked New England heart good'. There are many amused references to their mutual friend Jarrell's antics, to Pound's, to Marianne Moore, Mary McCarthy, Roethke and Berryman who is 'utterly spooky, teaching brilliant classes, spending week-ends in the sanitarium, drinking, seedy'. Spender is almost rehabilitated: 'to my surprise [he] turned out to be very pleasant—no poet, though'. Self-deprecation or a dash of realism saves them from vanity with respect to their own merits and successes. Lowell reports 'front page glowing reviews in the *Times* and *Tribune*, one in *Newsweek*, interviews in all three. I can't say I don't find it very occupying and exciting, but what use?'

Their exchanges also provided opportunities to try out anecdotes, ideas and images and, in Lowell's case, to promote his friend's career: 'I was on the Bollingen and National Book Award committees and tried to get the prizes given to you and/or Randall.' On another occasion he writes, 'Whenever I meet a publisher I give him your address.' Both poets shared some similar problems, with alcohol dependency and depression, for example. They exhibit great sympathy and tact for each other's reverses, notably in their love lives.

A great contrast in the letters is between Lowell's relentless ambition for his verse and Bishop's quiet perfectionism. As Lowell's friend and colleague Grey Gowrie wrote, reviewing the second major biography of Lowell, *Lost Puritan* (in the 'The Daily Telegraph', February 1995): 'Like readers today, he loved Elizabeth Bishop's geographical, noticing poems. But he never doubted that speaking for and to America at a peculiar moment of history counted more.' If the comment hardly reflects current verdicts on Bishop's fine poetry, it does make a valid point about Lowell's perception of his task. Yet he was endlessly admiring of her work, fearing in contrast that he tended to 'beat the big drum too much'. As he admitted on April 24th, 1952, 'You always make me feel that I have a rather obvious breezy impersonal liking for the great and the obvious—in contrast with your adult personal feeling for the odd and the genuine.' Bishop, in turn, was flattered by such comments as, 'I think I read you with more interest than anyone now writing. I know I do', and not a little humbled given her great admiration for his work. In July 1960 she pleaded, 'Please never stop writing me letters—they always manage to make me feel like my higher self... for several days.'

Lowell's absorption in writing shows throughout their exchanges. In July 1948 he confesses, 'Sometimes nothing is so solid to me as writing. I suppose that's what vocation means—at times a torment, a bad conscience, but all in all, purpose and direction.' Towards the end of his love affair with metre, Lowell turned increasingly to the example of Williams and Bishop herself. In December 1957 he wrote with a generous nod, 'But really I've just broken through to where you've always been and gotten rid of my medieval armor's undermining.'

The crowning pleasure of this correspondence is their use of language, the observations made, the wit that both poets exhibit. Lowell, for instance, writes of Roethke 'mammoth yet elfinlike, hairless, red-faced'; of opera rehearsals as 'A world of hurry, craftsmanship and controlled calculated tantrums'; of a colleague's son as 'a quiet, slow boy, wavering between being awfully nice and turning to vegetation'. Attempting autobiographical prose he writes, 'It starts naked, ends as fake velvet' and on his wife's evasiveness on details of musical terminology, 'Her replies are more airy than clear.' He misses Bishop, 'Oh what a gap and blank and sorrow that you are so far away.' Of the depression following a manic attack he writes 'talking about the past is like a cat's trying to explain climbing down a ladder'. Bishop is equally memorable in their exchanges and excellent with anecdotes, at one point comically capturing her pet toucan in the rain with the image of Brancusi's 'Bird in Flight'.

Letters too are birds in flight and perhaps it is, after all, impossible to see someone 'plain', except in the literal sense of Browning's poem. And yet there are enough glimpses of the inner man in these wonderful letters to fashion an impressively life-like Lowell portrait. And to have them *and* the poetry is the greatest gain.

ALL'S MISALLIANCE: ROBERT LOWELL IN ENGLAND

> Ours was never a book, though sparks of it
> spotted the page with superficial burns:
> the fiction I colored with first-hand evidence,
> letters and talk I marketed as fiction—
> but what is true or false tomorrow when surgeons
> let out the pus, and crowd the circus to see us
> disembowelled for our afterlife?
> – 'Marriage'

'Yet why not say what happened?' Robert Lowell asked in 'Epilogue' and saying what happened had, by the end of his glittering career, become synonymous with the premier American poet. In fact the idea had dogged him since his autobiographical work in *Life Studies* (1959), his great, game-changing collection. Lowell (1917–77) remained ambivalent about this. After castigating the fallen world in his early, richly rhetorical poetry he had turned to public address and to autobiography as a lens for history. Yet he was always aware of the complexity of the idea of truth and keen to point out the craft behind autobiography. Without craft, poetry would be merely baffled self-expression. As he explained in a 'Paris Review' interview of 1961, 'Your actual experience is a complete flux. I've invented facts and changed things.., so there's a lot of artistry, I hope, in the poems ... the reader was to believe he was getting the *real* Robert Lowell.'

In England, in Lowell's last years, the poetry became more personal, closer even than in *Life Studies* to 'the *real* Robert Lowell', though at times the art suffered. Initially energised by a new love, a new country, Lowell became entangled in the events of his life and confounded by vacillation, ill health and the bipolar condition that had undermined him since his thirties. That he produced so much good work in revised versions of *Notebook* (1970) (*For Lizzie and Harriet* and *History*), in *The Dolphin* (1973) and *Day By Day* (1977) is a tribute to his tenacity, honesty and, of course, artistry.

After a number of years in the public eye in America, through Democratic politics and anti-war protest, Lowell needed a retreat. As he confessed to his lifelong friend Blair Clark in May 1970, England presented an opportunity: 'Things seem rasped and low in America, and here I sigh gladly into the somewhat different air. I'm thankful to get away for a stretch.' Lowell had been offered a (non-teaching) Fellowship at All Soul's College, Oxford, for April 1970 and subsequently a two year teaching post as Professor of English at Essex University at a salary of £4,000, which approximated his Harvard income. For a man steeped in European history and literature, as well as a privileged New England tradition, the chance of spending time in England provided a further incentive.

Within a week of his arrival at All Souls Lowell's life turned upside down. Faber held a party in his honour. Among the guests was the aspiring author and member of the Guinness family, the 38 year old Lady Caroline Blackwood, whom Lowell had met three years earlier in New York. This time they gelled. Lowell had had numerous affairs in his twenty-one year marriage with the writer Elizabeth Hardwick, though these had generally been associated with his manic periods. (To Hardwick he had earlier written, in 'Obit', the fine, chilling lines 'After loving you so much, can I forget / you for eternity, and have no other choice?') This new relationship proved the exception. In a poem to Blackwood he 'wondered who would see and date you next, / and grapple for the danger of your hand' ('Mermaid'). He also captured something of the renewed optimism she brought him in the opening poem to *The Dolphin*, 'Fishnet': 'Yet my heart rises, I know I've gladdened a lifetime / knotting, undoing a fishnet of tarred rope'.

After the Faber party the couple returned to her home in Redcliffe Square, Kensington, where Lowell effectively took up residence. In the following weeks they took trips to Ireland and the Lake District, while Hardwick waited anxiously for news of the accommodation Lowell was supposed to be finding so that she and their daughter, Harriet, could join him. What she heard from Lowell was, according to 'On the End of the Phone', only 'My sidestepping and obliquities'.

At the end of June Hardwick learned of the affair, being understandably furious, particularly since she had given up her teaching post at Barnard College and Harriet had been removed from school. ('My utter contempt for both of you for the misery you have brought to two people who had never hurt you knows no bounds.'). Perhaps under the pressure of events Lowell's behaviour became erratic; another manic attack was on the way. After an incident at All Souls and an escapade involving locking Blackwood in her Redcliffe Square home away from her girls, she decamped to Ireland while Lowell was hospitalized at Greenways Nursing Home, London. He described his early symptoms in 'Redcliffe Square' as an 'old infection': 'lowered good humor, then an ominous / rise of irritable enthusiasm'.

Hardwick flew to visit him, assuming that this would be another of those manic Lowell infatuations which often expressed a desire for a new start, a symptom of his mental state. She worried over the rumours of his neglect at the hospital, tidied him up, determined finally that he was in safe, then returned to New York, offering to be there for him *if* he needed her. Lowell wrote appreciatively to her of their time together, 'You couldn't have [been] more loyal and witty. I can't give you anything of equal value.' Clearly the three were tangled in their relationships. Blackwood returned but was unwilling to house Lowell until he was perfectly well. As he put it in 'Runaway', 'At the sick times, our slashing, / drastic decisions made us runaways.' The episode served as a warning to Lowell about Blackwood's limited ability to handle him in illness (especially given her commitment to her girls), something that Hardwick had done loyally, valiantly and repeatedly for many years.

In October Lowell began teaching at the University of Essex. He had been looking forward to it, he told Hardwick, because 'teaching is so much easier and more dependable than writing, tho so much less'. He had been working on the sonnets that became *The Dolphin,* which documented his problematic relationships while controversially using Hardwick's letters. Despite the order the book imposed, the real order of events became disastrously confused, as can be seen by the letters exchanged at the time. In

October 1970 Lowell wrote to Hardwick, 'Even if I returned for good, if that has meaning, almost all would be unsolved.' Although he credits their marriage as being 'both rib and spine for us these many years', he also writes of his 'useless, depressed will' and of his love for Caroline. Lowell's vacillation was chronic. He wrote to Adrienne Rich on the same day, the 21st, telling her it was 'Hard to tell what is right or even possible.' Much as Lowell loved and respected his wife, he felt the marriage had foundered. He continued, 'I imagine I'll get divorced, and all may be well, but the loss will never go.'

At the beginning of November Lowell wrote to his friends Peter Taylor and Mary McCarthy that he anticipated returning to Hardwick. Five days later he mooted the possibility of a return ('Maybe you could take me back, though I have done great harm.'). Even this early in his relationship with Blackwood (still married to the father of her daughters, Israel Citkowitz), Lowell sensed the impossibility of his relationship with his new, younger partner: 'To go on seriously toward marriage with Caroline against the grain, the circumstances, our characters etc. is more than can be got away with. We don't think we can, and are in accord.' He further said (then retracted), 'I do find though that even for such a careless person as me one is cemented in habits beyond belief. I had to come to England and live with practically a new wife to learn my whole being is repetition of things once done.'

Essex did not turn out to be the dream he had first imagined, either. He found the university architecturally dull, second rate, the students less motivated than his Harvard students, but his opinion fluctuated. To Hardwick he reported in November, 'My classes are small and quiet, the Poetry Writing rather retarded after Harvard, a good one in Shakespeare'. Later, teaching 'King Lear', he reckoned his students 'mutely thumb through their texts. I got so weary, I hardly read the brief assignments I gave. I am hoping to live off my royalties and "papers".'

Crucial to everyone's well-being was the 'baffling vacillation'. It was to feature in his poem 'Doubt': 'From the dismay of my old world to the blank / new—water-torture of vacillation!' He had warned Hardwick in October that he did not think that he could return to her. He loved Caroline, 'but allow me this short space before I arrive in New York to wobble in my mind. I will be turning from the longest realest and most loved fragment of my life.' He visited at Christmas, staying with Blair Clark, to whom he admitted, 'I don't know yet what will happen, but I increasingly fear the blood I'll have to pay for what I have done, for being me.' The visit proved calmer than he anticipated, his daughter a pleasure to be with. Yet it held nothing for Hardwick, except the knowledge she was losing him. His new life, he confided to John Berryman, 'fills me with uncertainties that mount up terror'.

In terms of his poetry the one significant gain may have been the presence of Frank Bidart, a former student of Lowell's, who had helped him revise and expand his collection *Notebook 1967–68* into *Notebook* (1970). While in New York that Christmas Lowell had Bidart meet him to look over the ninety-odd sonnets he had so far produced for *The Dolphin*. Although dolphins were not part of the book's narrative at that time, they became associated with Blackwood in Lowell's mind (beautiful, 'bigger-brained than man and much more peaceful and humorous', he explained to his daughter). They also were to feature in a manic episode when he bought several antique versions for Blackwood's country house, 'Milgate' (Maidstone) where they were to move in the summer and Lowell would imagine himself among the squirearchy.

In the New Year he returned to London, moving in with Blackwood at 8 Redcliffe Square. Then in February his marital vacillation became irrelevant after the disclosure of Blackwood's pregnancy. It took some weeks for Lowell to inform Elizabeth Hardwick. He worried about losing his daughter, had to put off his plans for a New York visit, though feeling himself reborn at the news. Poetry took him to Scandinavia and Holland for readings. Other distractions presented themselves, firstly Jonathan Miller's production of his translation of 'Prometheus Bound', then a genealogical Orkneys adventure with Jonathan Raban, who would edit Lowell's *Selected Poems* in 1975. Robert Sheridan Lowell was born on September 27th.

The weekly trips to Essex became a drag on Lowell's spirits, while *The Dolphin* began to take shape as a narrative of the end of one marriage and the beginning of another. Word reached Hardwick that what Lowell referred to as his 'rather grinding autobiography' might not augur well. In December Lowell wrote to Bidart again requesting his help, this time in reworking *Notebook* into what would become two books, one public, one personal (*History* and *For Lizzie and Harriet*). 'This all began,' Lowell wrote ominously, 'by trying to get around the mounting pressure on me not to publish *The Dolphin*. (For moral reasons.) And indeed, it must wait.' But it could not, because he was as compulsive about his desire to publish as he was to write.

He ignored warnings by friends like Stanley Kunitz ('There are details which seem to me monstrously heartless') and Elizabeth Bishop about the use of Hardwick's letters in the forthcoming book. She famously warned him, in a letter of March 1972: 'One can use one's life as material—one does, anyway—but these letters—aren't you violating a trust? IF you were given permission—IF you hadn't changed them…etc. But *art just isn't worth that much*.' The advice was unheeded because, as Lowell had admitted to her years before, 'I may have gotten into a rather mechanical appetite for publishing.'

Lowell might have given 'Lizzie' the best of the lines in these poems as he claimed; she is still the supplicant:

> You left two houses and two thousand books,
> a workbarn by the ocean, and two slaves
> to kneel and wait upon you hand and foot—
> tell us why in the name of Jesus.
>   – 'Hospital 11'

The irony is made clear in 'Records' where Hardwick sees him as 'doomed to know what I have known with you, / lying with someone fighting unreality'. What could he say? Lowell was now settled in England with a new love. While America continued a lure of sorts—he wished to return 'temporarily'—there were binding commitments here. In January 1972, Blackwood's six year old daughter was badly scalded. Then they shared the little daily dramas of living and the attempt to civilise their baby son.

In October the Lowells flew to New York to finalise divorce proceedings before going on to Santo Domingo, where he and Hardwick divorced (as did Blackwood and Citkowitz), then Lowell and Blackwood married. The settlement with Hardwick soon began to seem punitive, 'a barracuda settlement', since he gave up most of his trust fund, their apartment in New York and his cousin's home in Castine, Maine.

1973 promised more travel (the Rotterdam Poetry Festival), more leisure (fishing in Westmorland), Harriet's visit—and publication of the three collections. *History* and *For Lizzie and Harriet* did little to mask the arrival of *The Dolphin*. The critical response ran from the favourable English to the insulting American. Most famously Adrienne Rich wrote in the 'American Poetry Review', 'this is bullshit eloquence, a poor excuse for a cruel and shallow book' describing it as 'one of the most vindictive and mean-spirited acts in the history of poetry'.

Rich stood on Hardwick's side at least. Marjorie Perloff's *New Republic* review in early July suggested that Harriet and her mother deserved their treatment. The controversial use of private letters seemed neither vindictive nor mean-spirited in intention. Lowell's latest biographer, Kay Redfield Jamison, denies a moral case was involved in his writing the book, 'only a human and artistic one' for which overwhelming precedent existed. It could be seen as an unfortunate consequence of being intimate with an autobiographical poet.

The fury and the heartbreak passed and, though Hardwick interrupted their relationship, she did not end it. Lowell continued teaching at Essex in the spring but moved to Massachusetts in the autumn to teach again at Harvard before returning to 'Milgate' at the end of term. Some sort of balm, if not vindication, came in 1974 with the award of the Pulitzer Prize for *The Dolphin*. Lowell gave a reading tour of the American South in the spring, before again returning to 'Milgate', but in truth his relationship with Blackwood was being undermined by their health and life style. Even in *The Dolphin* we have a strong sense of the turmoil of love and its blindness:

> I watch a feverish huddle of shivering cows;
> you sit making a fishspine from a chestnut leaf.
> We are at our crossroads, we are astigmatic
> and stop uncomfortable, we are humanly low.
> – 'Fall Weekend at Milgate'

Putting aside themes of birth and rebirth, Lowell had begun what would be his last book, *Day by Day*, a collection concerned with premature aging, conscience and regret. He put a brave face on it in one letter, describing it as facing 'time and age without hysteria'. Yet, as the title suggests, last things were on his mind. There is the recurrent terror of the manic episodes ('Where you are going, Professor, / you won't need your Dante'—'Visitors'). *'Huic ergo parce, Deus'* (Therefore spare him, O God) one poem ends. To balance that, there is wry humour too, in poems to Jean Stafford and John Berryman.

Lowell's poetic masters had died: Roethke, Frost, William Carlos Williams, Eliot and Jarrell in the decade before, Pound and Berryman in 1972 and now his teacher John Crowe Ransom. What he said of one he might have said of all: they remained lying 'alive like a feather / on the top of the mind'. Lowell too was ailing, with a heart condition as well as the bipolar disorder. 'The doctors come more thickly' he wrote in another poem from the collection. The economic climate in Britain also made him uncomfortable. He wondered if the 'enormous problems and irreconcilables' it brought might not prompt their return to America, 'where I can earn, have friends, etc.'

He suggested to Elizabeth Bishop in October that Blackwood was having a nervous breakdown. The pressure may have prompted his own visit to a heart-specialist that month and in Boston in February 1975, where he had gone for the spring term to Harvard. He was again unwell, mixing alcohol with the lithium which held off the worst of the bipolar episodes. It heralded a year of manic behaviour, with spells in Greenways Hospital, Mount Sinai Hospital and Roehampton Priory. In between he prepared his *Selected Poems*. Then, with the aid of Bidart and editor Robert Giroux, he began collecting his prose writings. He also attended a poetry festival at Kilkenny with Seamus Heaney, before a little salmon fishing.

1976 began badly for Lowell. As he described it to Bishop in early March: 'I had a longish though not violently troubled stay in the hospital, and have been out a month—mildly depressed.... Mildly is bad enough. Though I can't make too much of it. I fear the frequency of these things, fear becoming something that must be categorized as a burden.' He still considered a return to America with the family, while feeling the difficulty of disturbed routines and houses. Years of abuse of alcohol and medicine were taking their toll. In 'To Frank Parker' he mused, 'What is won by surviving / if two glasses of red wine are poison?'

In April Lowell returned to New York City for a bicentennial production of his play, 'The Old Glory' (his trilogy from Hawthorne and Melville) finding the performance a disappointment. The city also failed to please him, now he had become accustomed to rural living in England. Better was a visit from Elizabeth Hardwick, in England for a PEN conference. He felt the three of them were reconciled. Lowell's honours continued, as did his problems. He attended Aldeburgh Festival in June to hear Benjamin Britten's cantata for his version of *Phaedre*. It was followed in September by Blackwood's decision to sell 'Milgate' because of rising costs. They were to travel to Cambridge, Massachusetts, but Lowell was first hospitalized. They spent Christmas in Scotland before he returned to Harvard in January 1977, being hospitalized for congestive heart failure before teaching again.

In his absence Blackwood had moved to an apartment in a stately home in Castletown, Ireland. Lowell flew over for Easter but their relationship was by now in grave difficulty. He wrote a number of poignant letters to her on the subject, including one of April 14th, 1977 which began 'I don't know what to say, our problems have become so many-headed and insuperable. Nothing like the sunshine of the years we had together—when it shone, as so often—so blindingly.' Caroline and Ireland ('all so far from home and help') both depressed his spirits. He wrote a week later 'I love you, am more dazzled by you, than anyone I've known, but can't I be your constant visitor?' Theirs was a relationship in which each by now exhausted the other:

> Will we always be
> one up, the other down,
> one hitting bottom, the other
> flying through the trees
>   – 'Seesaw'

With the end of the Harvard term Lowell moved back to Elizabeth Hardwick at 15 West 67th Street in New York, from where they made a ten day visit to Moscow as part of an American delegation to the Union of Soviet Writers. In May he received the Gold Medal for Literature from the American Academy of Arts and Letters. Although Blackwood attended the ceremony, their relationship now was too fraught. Lowell spent the summer quietly in Castine, Maine, with Hardwick. Later he visited Ireland to see his wife and son. There his restlessness worried Blackwood, who was anyway wounded by his return to his second wife. She left for London and Lowell curtailed his visit after a frightening night locked in the apartment alone. His free verse collection *Day by Day* had been published to better reviews, but his life was ending. He died of a heart attack in a New York taxi returning to Hardwick on September 12th, holding in his arms a portrait of Blackwood by her first husband, Lucien Freud, which he intended to have had valued.

The ironies would mount no higher. England had been a highly emotional retreat for Lowell. In the end he could not endure it and had returned to his former, settled life in New England. Even where the man failed, however, the artist survived. *Day By Day* ends with the wonderful 'Epilogue', a meditation on life and art and on the urgent need for recognition of our messy, transient lives: 'All's misalliance. / Yet why not say what happened?'

APPROACHING JAMES DICKEY: A CAUTIONARY TALE

> I remember how tremendously excited I was when I first formulated to myself the proposition that the poet is not to be limited by the literal truth: that he is not trying to *tell* the truth he is trying to *make* it.
> – 'Metaphor as Pure Adventure'

Reacting with something like horror to Edward Dowden's warts-and-all biography of Shelley, Matthew Arnold wondered, 'What has been gained by forcing upon us much in him which is ridiculous and odious?' Arnold had loved the poetry of Shelley. I had the problem of reading a life without knowing the work, being drawn into James Dickey's world by one poem, 'Hunting Civil War Relics at Nimblewill Creek' (just as I had earlier been drawn to his fellow Southerner and friend Robert Penn Warren, whose 'American Portrait: Old Style' I had greatly admired). For the reader, the poetry must always come first. I sent off for Dickey's collected poems, then the biography and the letters. First to arrive, though: the biography. I soon felt I had made an unwise investment.

For the record: Dickey was born into money in Atlanta, Georgia, in 1923. He had been a jock in high school and a night-fighter radar operator near the end of World War 11. Turning to literature, he graduated from Vanderbilt, taught at Rice Institute, Houston, and then had taken his family to Europe on a Sewanee Review Fellowship engineered by Allen Tate. Returning, he taught at the University of Florida before taking a job as an advertising copywriter for five years ('There is a medicine we take here to get rid of scruples: it is called money.'). After that his literary career took off. Dickey published widely, won prizes (including a 1966 National Book Award for *Buckdancer's Choice*) and began 'barnstorming for poetry' around the reading circuit, performing to great acclaim. A Consultant in Poetry to the Library of Congress (1966–8), he won greater fame with his novel *Deliverance*, which became a hit movie in 1972 (and in which he played a cameo role). He was eventually hospitalised with alcoholism, dying in 1997.

Having learnt this much, I opened Henry Hart's thorough biography, *The World as a Lie: James Dickey* (2000), only to find that his subject was a boastful scoundrel: lying habitually about his 'poor' background, his career, his womanising, his sportsmanship and war experience ('a high-school football star and a combat fighter pilot'—testaments somewhat glossed)—and even his poetry. Here was an athletic, aggressive, macho version of Ford Madox Ford with that profound disregard for facts.

Unfortunately, *The Whole Motion: Collected Poems* (1945–1992) was the last book to arrive. So I turned in exasperation to *Crux: The Letters of James Dickey* (1999) to find more of the same untrustworthiness admixed with moments of perverse bragging. Dickey admitted to James Wright, in a letter of February 1959: 'Humility is not my forte: I much more easily run to arrogance and insolence'. The letter continues with Dickey praising Wright's honesty and admitting he does not possess that quality himself. Then there are his routine trashing of other poets in the letters: William Carlos Williams, Robert Bly, W. D. Snodgrass, Robert Lowell, Elizabeth Bishop, Ted Hughes, Philip Larkin, and so on. He also has a habit of first picking fights with poets like Wright or Philip Booth before making acolytes of them.

By the time *The Whole Motion* arrived I was mellowing in *one* way. I saw that you could not fault Dickey's commitment to poetry. Apparently, although admired as a teacher, he believed—so he told Richard Howard in December 1963— that 'Though I am teaching poetry temporarily for a living, I deplore the increasing tendency to treat poetry as "a subject": that is, for "discussion and analysis."' Poetry existed to enjoy alone.

Now I needed to take a manageable amount of the collected poems to find the poet beneath the bluster. Here I had help from an American friend who, in grad. school, had been greatly influenced by Dickey's *Poems 1957–68*. So from my copy of *The Whole Motion* I determined to focus on those poems chosen by the poet for the earlier selection. It added up to most of Dickey's first four books—*Into the Stone* (1960); *Drowning with Others* (1962);

Helmets (1964); and *Buckdancer's Choice* (1965), plus a score of newer poems. As I read them, I continued to sample the letters from that part of his career and to push on with the biography, as well as to look elsewhere *un peu*. What follows is an account of my reactions to the poems.

* * *

Firstly, though, a little of the context: Dickey emerged at a time when the so-called Confessional Poets and the Beats were big game. He was one of those who offered a real alternative, fantastic in a different way from, say, the 'greenhouse' poems of Theodore Roethke, whom he admired, or the Freudian in Randall Jarrell, whom he did not. In his 'Paris Review' interview of 1976 he spoke of seeking 'poetic wildness': 'It's really a kind of madness I feel when I'm writing.' It is the madness of the Romantic. According to his biographer, Dickey aimed, like his friend Geoffrey Hill, 'for a powerful rhetoric that derived from Romantic visionaries like Blake and Coleridge, contemporary Romantics like Dylan Thomas and George Barker, and Fugitives like Tate.' Add to that the gothic taste of other Southern writers like Warren, plus his personal mythology, and the result can be highly stimulating—or just overblown.

It is controlled madness, of course. Dickey seems a technically restless poet. Early on he played down his experimentation with prosody when talking about his poetry ('I work by listening in the dark').When two collections were reissued as *The Early Motion* he wrote: 'these poems emerged from what I call a night-rhythm, something felt in pulse not word'. This he identified as an 'anapestic sound', a 'sound-before-meaning'. Soon though, he explained, 'I toned down the heavy bombardment of stress and relied more on matter-of-fact statement and declaration'. Eventually he would turn to very long lines, 'walls of words', with spaces punctuated for breath, and phrases which floated across the page.

With the early poems, the reader's task is to hear the roll of the rhetorical lines as much as to understand their sense. In *Into the*

Stone central Dickey themes *are* given shape nonetheless: his need for identification with the 'authentic' living world, usually untethered from civilisation, his wish to engage primal forces, to metamorphose into animal, into combative instinct. To Donald Hall he wrote in July 1957, 'I want a poetry… that gets me inside the world, in a new way, or in a way older than the world.'

Dickey remained eager to explore primitive myth and ritual. He wished, as he put it in another letter, 'to work at the intersection of the classic myths and everyday life'. So in the onanistic 'Sleeping Out at Easter' (*'In your palm is the secret of waking. / Put down those seeds in your hand'*) we have identification between fertile poet and risen Christ, and again in 'Walking on Water' and 'The Vegetable King' ('From my house and my silent folk / I step, and lay me in ritual down'). Dickey had taken courses on anthropology; it remained a vivid presence in his work.

He frequently returns to the formative loss of an older brother, Eugene, dead at six. In order to redeem that death, Dickey implicates it in the fertility myth of death and rebirth. The dead brother becomes an alternative self, or the living brother replaces him, or is empowered by the death. We meet him in 'The Other', which opens as quintessential Dickey, a vigorous fantasy in which the sickly brother, Orpheus, urges the poet to 'rise like Apollo / With armor-cast shoulders upon me'.

Animals invade Dickey's consciousness regularly. In 'Trees and Cattle', 'A bull walks forth, / And makes of my mind a red beast'. In another poem he writes, 'My animal eyes become human'. In the natural world one can feed on the instant, untroubled by entangling thought. There one can be most alive. As he wrote to William Carlos Williams, 'I know the supreme importance of the moment, and have a certain conviction that I may be able to feel more of it, to keep prolonging it, if I write about it.'

He claimed to James Wright that he wanted a 'kind of mindlessness, as though the world itself spoke in its sleep'. And yet that is not quite true since in Dickey's worlds the ego is protagonist, dialectically engaged with the natural world. He may desire, as he says in 'The Underground Stream', to be 'Timelessly smiling, and free / Of the world, of light, and of me', but actually he seeks symbiosis. He must not be subsumed in it, but share its instinctive behaviour, compete with its denizens. Then, enlightened, he will return home. While the poet's personae are many and witnessed from varied perspectives, they share one quality: they are all figures of action—swimming, hunting, fishing, questing.

If Dickey's poems are alive in the underworld of the psyche, they inhabit a recognisable world, also. The results are often equally disturbing, for violence is part of a world scarred by war. In the 1976 interview he noted 'most of my things depend on violence and length'. Poems like 'The Performance' and 'The Wedding' relive the war in the Pacific. He was to say of the experience that it influenced everything he had done since. And yet, returning to the war itself, it is almost always others' experiences he explores. His autobiographical contribution is the authenticating detail, the empathetic sense of being there, made memorable in 'The Performance':

> The last time I saw Donald Armstrong
> He was staggering oddly off into the sun,
> Going down, of the Philippine Islands.
> I let my shovel fall, and put that hand
> Above my eyes, and moved some way to one side
> That his body might pass through the sun

Here he envisions a nightmare scenario: the events of a beheading. Having seen the pilot clowning, we learn that the following day 'on an island beach to the south', he is decapitated by his captors. The poet imagines a grim replay of his last memory of Armstrong, now futilely, 'Doing all his lean tricks to amaze' his captors.

Dickey's ability to force moments of documentary realism into the otherwise surreal also catches the reader unprepared in 'Between Two Prisoners', where talk of prisoners held in a school room and a child's 'hacked hieroglyphics' on a school desk turn suddenly to:

> I watched the small guard be hanged
> A year later, to the day,
> In a closed horse stall in Manila

The title poem of *Drowning with Others* (again a Christ parallel) together with its opening poem, 'The Lifeguard', introduce the possibilities of self-mythologizing, whereas I was more attracted to poems like 'The Heaven of Animals' or 'A Dog Sleeping on My Feet', which engage with 'the hypnotized language of beasts' in an original way, or 'The Salt Marsh' with its beautiful image of sawgrass:

> And nothing prevents your bending
> With them, helping their wave
> By not opposing,
> By willing your supple inclusion
> Among fields without promise of harvest,
> In their marvelous, spiritual walking
> Everywhere, anywhere.

At times Dickey is the conduit between worlds. In 'To His Children in Darkness' he brings to the room of his sleeping children in their dreams his incarnation as God and beast. Even fear in the domestic poems can lead to a kind of rapture, a sense of being fully alive, as in 'In the Tree House at Night' which is a refuge he inhabits with his brothers:

> We lie here like angels in bodies,
> My brothers and I, one dead,
> The other asleep from much living

'Can two bodies make up a third?' he asks hopefully, concluding, 'I move at the heart of the world'. In 'The Hospital Window' the poet is similarly filled with joy. He descends 'six white floors' after a visit to his father and, crossing the street in traffic, turns to wave: 'I am not afraid for my father—/ Look! He is grinning; he is not // afraid for my life, either'.

Kin and the past are brought together in what is, for me, the finest poem from the collection: 'Hunting Civil War Relics at Nimblewill Creek'. It remembers the experience of the poet and his brother—his other, living brother; his 'one brother' he reminds us—working a 'mine detector' over the creek. The poem explores his emotions as they 'enter the buried battle'. For the brother the adventure is in 'his clapped ears', while for Dickey:

> underfoot I feel
> The dead regroup,
> The burst metals all in place,
> The battle lines be drawn
> Anew to include us
> In Nimblewill

So intense is the identification, he conceives of his brother's smile betokening an ancestor's, 'as if / He rose from the dead within / Green Nimblewill / And stood in his grandson's shape'. The poem ends with Dickey's accepting all the dead fathers as his own. In an essay, 'Notes on the Decline of Outrage', he had concluded 'the continuing power of the Civil War is not in these things [the relics] but in its ability to dramatize and perpetuate a feeling about a way of life'. In the moment of the poem it is the relics themselves, or the act of retrieving them, that restores a way of life and kinship, too.

If *Drowning with Others* suggests a strong sense of community, it is the community of the dead, of animals and spirits of the natural world. *Helmets* confirms this fixation with what is outside our comprehension but not out of imagination. The poet inhabits the consciousness of the horses in the opening poem, 'The Dusk of Horses', as he does with the trout in 'Winter Trout'. In that poem the focus then switches to the hunter, to Ulysses, and to the submerged gods 'attuning the world'. These gods—now the 'spirit of the place'—"Come to call us to higher ground' before the dam drowns the river in 'On the Coosawattee'. This is a benign rehearsal for Dickey's novel *Deliverance* (1970), although a place also violated: by the offal of a poultry processing plant. 'Fence

Wire' offers another image of the land in the grip of man. The endless, taut wire holds acres 'highstrung and enthralled'; for the animals it is 'defining their earthly estate'.

There is sadism, voyeurism and simple pain in Dickey's poetry—witness titles like 'The Scarred Girl' or 'The Poisoned Man'—though it sometimes resolves into a strange dream of unity, as with the former, where the girl whose beauty is gone into a smashed windscreen, looks to 'the seamless sunlight / And a newborn countenance / Put upon everything' except herself. And the poisoned man, rattlesnake-bitten, sees his 'bloodstream assume, // Inside the cold path of the river, / The inmost routes of a serpent'. A similar surrealism can be found in 'A Folk Singer of the Thirties', in the voice of a man martyred on a box car, or the weird 'Approaching Prayer'.

Dickey described 'Approaching Prayer' in his *Self-Interviews* (1970) as 'the most complicated and far-fetched poem I've written'. In this fantasy his persona dons his late father's identity. He puts on his grey sweater ('Like his gray body hair'); attaches his gamecock spurs (Dickey's father revelled in cock fighting); finally putting on the hollowed head of a hog he helped his father hunt. The speaker re-enacts the killing from the perspective of both hunter and hunted, propitiation in the hope prayer can be heard.

The two outstanding poems in this book are, I think, 'Cherrylog Road' and 'Drinking from a Helmet'. In the junkyard on Cherrylog Road—'In the parking lot of the dead'—the poet waits among the rusting hulks for his lover to slip her father and appear. Dickey recreates the rusted and overgrown mutilations and ghostly lives of the cars he waits among. That his girl is given a name, Doris Holbrook, adds a note of authenticity to their tryst. The event itself becomes an anecdote for the lover to recount: 'I held her and held her and held her, / Conveyed at terrific speed / By the stalled, dreaming traffic around us.'

It might serve as a memory of the young G.I.'s in 'Drinking from a Helmet'. Again Dickey, the Pacific airman, turns to the infantry to tell a tale, to take a terrestrial perspective which allows greater emotional immediacy (and evokes his dead brother again). Leaving his foxhole/grave on the island, a young man picks up the helmet of a dead G.I. to drink water from. He moves among 'the shelled palm-stumps' and dreams a landscape made whole again, so that he could 'call on the dead to strain / Their muscles to get up and go there'. He knows, however, that

> On even the first day of death
> The dead cannot rise up,
> But their last thought hovers somewhere
> For whoever finds it.

The young soldier imagines instead finding that 'last thought', then himself returning to the dead soldier's older brother in California to share his experience and—being also the dead G. I.—to 'tell him I was the man.'

The award-winning *Buckdancer's Choice* contains a number of poems which test the human spirit, poems like the fearsome 'The Firebombing', 'Pursuit from Under' and 'Slave Quarters'. Quieter poems like 'The Escape', 'Angina' and 'Mangham' celebrate that spirit in a more domestic way. The title poem concerns Dickey's mother, bed ridden by 'breathless angina' yet whistling an old fiddle tune, Buckdancer's Choice. Her heroic, vaudevillian whistling, evokes those other historical 'slaves of death' whom it summons up for the listening poet.

'The Firebombing' is another 'memory' from the war. It is a long poem which alternates perspectives between a WW11 airman on a raid over Beppu, Japan, with the domestic life his bombs destroy in the city below, a life he recognises as one that parallels his own. Literal distance creates detachment, as we witness when the pilot describes how 'some technical-minded stranger with my hands / Is sitting in a glass treasure-hole of blue light'. His mission involves the suppression of emotion ('One is cool and enthralled in the cockpit'). His payload is 'napalm and high-octane fuel', to 'make a town burning with all / American fire' in what he describes as 'Old Testament light'. The pilot's uneasy conclusion is ambivalent: 'Absolution? Sentence? No matter; / The thing itself is in that.'

Critics have claimed the poem glamorizes war. It does not, in my view. What it does do is dramatize the airman's state of mind as the poet intended ('a little worried a little too loud / Or too easygoing nothing I haven't lived with / For twenty years'). Dickey achieves his intention: to address the veteran's guilt, 'the guilt at the inability to feel guilty'.

Perhaps more controversial—even in its day—is 'Slave Quarters', a long poem which deals with miscegenation, a male fantasy on sex and race unredeemed by its consideration of the mind-set involved in slavery. In the poem the poet recounts how he looks from a ruined Georgia mansion 'at the low walls / Of slave quarters, and feel my imagining loins // Rise with the madness of Owners'. Here Dickey becomes master and slave, man and slave woman, and the father of a son whom he does 'not / Acknowledge, but own.'

In 'The Shark's Parlor' we meet another predator, this time in a free verse, tall tale of a tug-of-war between townspeople and a shark on Cumberland Island. Out hunting, the speaker and a friend create a 'pond of blood in the sea / Waiting for fins'. They subsequently fail to land the arriving shark by tying a rope to his porch-pillars, which give way. Finally they find 'the house coming subtly / Apart'. The tug-of war ensues until 'The shark flopped on the porch... driving back in / The nails he had pulled out'. Since the house is not absolutely wrecked, the poet determines to buy it as a memory 'against death', his own.

Poems 1957–1967 conclude with a score of new poems. 'Falling' with its 'exploration of the long, long broken line' is discomforting to read, an account of a stewardess falling from a plane. The tragedy, taken in slow motion, involves the young woman stripping in the course of her descent. According to Hart, 'As Dickey describes it, the stewardess's striptease in mid-air is a '"last superhuman act" that arouses the reproductive energies in the boys, girls, and fields of Kansas'. Despite the poet's concern about the real-life tragedy, it is hard not to read the poem as simply erotic and exploitative.

In his 1976 interview Dickey reckoned 'The May Day Sermon' to be his best poem, to date. The full title is 'May Day Sermon to the Women of Gilmer County, Georgia, by a Woman Preacher Leaving the Baptist Church', and it runs over nine pages of long lines. In this legend of 'rural blood lust and religion and sex and escape', according to the poet, 'God is neither more nor less than a combination of the Old Testament and a half mad Georgia hill farmer.' The poem is the text for a sermon 'telling the women of Gilmer County to throw off the shackles of the Baptist religion and enter into an older world of springtime, pleasure, love and delight'.

How the reader takes this tale is another matter. Its male eroticism connects it with 'Falling'. Another poem, 'The Sheep-Child', deals similarly with local legend, but with the more shocking taboo of bestiality. A similarly composite creature appears in 'For the Last Wolverine', a fantasy of ecological revenge where the wolverine, emboldened by an elk's heart, mates with an eagle to produce something 'gigantic legendary' that will attack the destruction we call progress. If the poem's angry rhetoric is strident, its metaphorical heart is in the right place and the creature's plea doleful (*Lord let me die but not die / Out.*').

In contrast, 'The Leap' and 'Mary Sheffield', 'Coming Back from America' and 'False Youth' are all poems which sympathise with the conventionally damaged, with 'Anyone who can wait no longer // Beneath the huge blackness of time' ('A Letter'). 'The Leap', for instance, is a memory of a school girl—once athletic in the playground—who leapt to touch a dance decoration as a young woman and later, as an unhappy wife, jumped to her death. The poem's last line ('I examine my hands') implies the poet's questioning his own behaviour and, perhaps, that of many men in their relationships with women. Vulnerability is also to be witnessed in 'The Bee', which also sounds the rare notes in Dickey, of humility and pathos. It is a poem in which the poet needs to rescue his son from 'the sheer / Murder of California' traffic. The boy is driven by fear of a bee, causing the poet to rush in a way which simultaneously brings to mind his old football training and the cynicism of his coach. Father, coach, son and bee all connect in the poem, and finally two are benched.

* * *

It is a long way from the world of Arnold and Shelley ('beautiful and ineffectual angel'), to the 'burly bravura' (in J. D. McClatchy's phrase) of James Dickey. After reading *Poems 1957–1967*, I remain ambivalent about the poems. Yes, his best are excellent. And yet, despite the fine war poems and others mentioned above, I find him too often a prey to masculine fantasies (with a sometimes tiresome mysticism). The problem with Dickey's poetry is that when not impressive it can at times be offensive…. Perhaps both our approaches were wrong.

MAXINE KUMIN'S TERRITORY

The arrival in March 2011 of Maxine Kumin's second selected poems, *Where I Live*, prompts this retrospective. Now, in two collections, the fortunate reader can take a fifty year journey through Kumin's fertile imagination, through memory and 'the mild hills of New Hampshire' from 1960—2010. One of the attendant pleasures will be the echoes of Thoreau, Frost, Moore, Auden and Anne Sexton. We have our own poets to honour, but in her 85th year we ought also to admire one who has contributed such a sustained, accomplished performance to American letters.

Maxine Kumin was born in Philadelphia in 1925. Although Jewish, she attended nearby Catholic schools and then Radcliffe. She wrote poetry from an early age, though the close friendship Kumin forged with Anne Sexton became the defining moment in her literary career, leading among other honours to a Pulitzer Prize. She has been Consultant in Poetry to the Library of Congress and held a number of residencies at American universities. In 1976 Kumin and her husband moved to a farm in Warner, New Hampshire, where they bred horses. They have two daughters and a son.

Selected Poems 1960–1990 gives the fruit of nine collections, taking us from Kumin's Jewish roots in Philadelphia in her debut volume, *Halfway* (1961), published when she was thirty-six, to *Nurture* in 1989. Corresponding with Peter Davison for *The Fading Smile* (1994), Kumin wrote of her meeting with Sexton in 1957 at the Boston Center for Adult Education. She revealed the continuity of Sexton's influence beyond her suicide in October, 1947:

> I think that I was able to grow much more personal in my poetry because of her shining example. The problem was talking about family, parents, personal considerations. That seemed very dangerous and very fraught with feeling, so that seemed very daring.

Kumin's poetic territory and voice established themselves in the opening verse of the title poem of her first collection:

> As true as I was born into
> my mother's bed in Germantown,
> the gambrel house in which I grew
> stood halfway up a hill, or down,
> between a convent and a madhouse.

There is a weaving of memory and imagination, with formal discipline. There is also an ironic tone, plus a conversational lyric style, the beginnings of collusion with the reader. Despite her private anxiety, Kumin seems to be the most centred of poets, finely balanced here both literally and psychically. However, for her as for many other poets—and particularly those of her generation awkwardly described as 'confessional'—the exploration of identity begins. This poem introduces the first of many self-styled 'tribal poems': poems about Kumin's cultural identity and family.

"On Being Asked to Write a Poem for the Centenary of the Civil War" deals with her Jewish great-grandfather who

> strapped needles up and notions
> and walked packaback across
> the dwindling Alleghenies,
> his red beard and nutmeg freckles
> dusting as he sang.

The poem ends with her observation that 'in a hundred years / all stories go wrong'. It is worth remembering at the outset that, although Kumin's generous voice is part of her attraction, the poet and her persona are not *exactly* one and the same. In an interview for the Interlochen Arts Academy, Michigan 1977, she made the point that 'the *I* is the persona that the poet is hiding behind...... Sometimes it can be very much a persona poem, and sometimes it can be quite an autobiographical poem.'

Alternatively, to create space between the *I* and the self is to create imaginative room for the poet to shape experience. Having said that, *The Privilege* (1965), seems to explore Kumin's cultural confusion quite directly. In 'Sisyphus' her burden is both pushing the legless man past the nunnery and failing to acknowledge her identity:

> He called
> me a perfect Christian child.
>
> One day I said I was a Jew.
> I wished I had. I wanted to.
>
> The basket man is gone; the stone
> I push uphill is all my own.

In 'The Pawnbroker', a conflicted elegy for her father 'comes again upon the desperate issue of autonomy'. According to the poet it follows, 'a strict rhyming pattern, a kind of enabling legislation to write the poem'. It opens with the words, 'The symbol inside this poem is my father's feet'. They are 'small white feet' bare as he lies awaiting cremation. They hint at something unused, unexpressed about his life.

Another facet of Kumin's quest for identity is the dream poem. Its significance she explained in a 1974 interview:

> Although I lived in a safe America my father's relatives were going into the ovens. I was a natural candidate for nightmares and I think we never outrun those early shadows. I tend to respect my dreams, perhaps overmuch, as I respect the unconscious and revere the things that arrive in the unconscious unbidden. Almost everything in my poetry in some way comes up through those pipes.

'Quarry, Pigeon Cove' is an early example ('The dead city waited, / hung upside down in the quarry'). Where it impresses is in the imaginative detail of its surreal perspective:

> A dog was swimming and splashing
> Air eggs nested in his fur.
> The hairless parts of him bobbled like toys
> and the silk of his tail blew past like milkweed.

Not every reader will find dream poems satisfying, however. 'The absence of any kind of touchstone', which Kumin notes in such poems, is the very reason. Dream poems have obvious symbolic significance, but they lack real experience. The title poem of her next collection, *The Nightmare Factory* (1970), is a case in point. The 'dream machines' offer a catalogue of nightmarish terrors, but takes us nowhere except to generalised fear.

The collection opens up into the fresh New Hampshire air with poems like 'Watering Trough', where a Victorian bath does animal service. As well as the utility of the move—of our forefathers being replaced by cows and horses—there is the comic sense in which the two are as one:

> let there be always
> green water for sipping
> that muzzles may enter thoughtful
> and rise dripping.

Poems set in rural New Hampshire increase in significance in the course of Maxin Kumin's career, being frequently among her most satisfying. They are life-affirming but not sentimental, always keenly observed. On and around her farm issues of identity are, if not resolved, then at least given perspective.

Up Country (1972) won the Pulitzer Prize, confirming her reputation. 'Creatures' gives us the poet as naturalist, immersing herself in close contemplation of pond species. More unusual in its arresting idea is 'Stones', where minerals are on the move, a nocturnal species ('The moving of stones, that sly jockeying thrust / takes place at night underground, shoulders first.') This imaginative perceptiveness modulates inevitably into dream and the honey mushrooms of 'The Dreamer, the Dream'. Infinitely more sobering is the poem 'Woodchucks', a meditation on human violence. Nominally about woodchucks ('Gassing the woodchucks didn't turn out right.'), our knowledge of Kumin's tribal sense alert us to the echo of mankind's barbarity to fellow human beings long before the last line confirms it.

House, Bridge, Fountain, Gate (1975) took its title from Louis Simpson's *North of Jamaica* in which the poet had written, 'it is as though things are trying to express themselves through us'. Kumin responded very positively to this because, as she explained, 'I believe so strongly in the naming and the particularizing of things.' The book features some of her most intense tribal poems. They recreate a lost childhood on the eve of war, full of poignant and pointed recollections. Kumin is encumbered by restrictions ('my queer pinched life'), but privileged. She must look elsewhere to the victims of the times:

> Warsaw will excrete its last Jews.
> My father will cry like a child.
> He will knuckle his eyes, to my terror,
> over the letters that come from the grave
> begging to be sponsored, plucked up, saved.
>   – 'The Thirties Revisited'

Why has the poet returned to this period? She tells us in 'Life's Work' that 'the midnights of my childhood still go on'. If the *House, Bridge, Fountain, Gate* is as strong a collection as Kumin has published, the bleak *The Retrieval System* (1978) is another fine one. Her unquiet dreams include the panic of a barn catching fire in which all the loved ones must first be imperilled before they escape. 'Angels' revisits moments where these eponymous figures fail to console, as with the suicide of Anne Sexton, which took place after a lunch with Kumin in October 1974. Her death reappears in 'How It Is':

> I think of the last day of your life,
> old friend, how I would unwind it, paste
> it together in a different collage,

> back from the death car idling in the garage,
> back up the stairs, your praying hands unlaced,

Also painful are the 'losses' of grown children, as they move away emotionally and geographically. 'Seeing the Bones' deals with this separation, the necessary adjustment to the absence of her 'European' daughter, caught very well in this unusual image:

> How many seasons walking
> on fallen apples like pebbles in
> the shoes of the Canterbury faithful
> have I kept the garden up
> with leaven of wood ash, kitchen leavings
> and the sure reciprocation of horse dung?

In 1982 Maxine Kumin published *Our Ground Time Here Will Be Brief, New and Selected Poems*. Here conviviality is laced with change and loss. A 'Family Reunion' ends with, 'So briefly having you back to measure us / is harder then having to let you go' and in 'Leaving My Daughter's House' the poet confesses, 'And no matter how hard I run I know / I can't penetrate my daughter's life'. Old thoughts intrude, old losses. 'Itinerary of an Obsession' and 'Apostrophe to a Dead Friend' return to Kumin's lifelong loss of Sexton:

> Soon I will be sixty.
> How it was with you now
> hardly more vivid than how
> it is without you,

'In Memorium P. W. Jr. (1921–1980)' is a poem in five sections, which deals with the wasting disease and death of a brother. It is elegy by way of fond memory, though typically it includes the unflinching acceptance, 'My whole childhood I feared cripples':

> Something entered people, something chopped,
> pressed, punctured, had its way with them
> and if you looked, bad child, it entered you .

The Long Approach (1985–6) refers in fact to the landing pathway preferred for the ease of horses in flight. The poems here travel, as does the mood since it comes to encompass global dread. Other poems return to Kumin's childhood and her mother:

> I give her back the chipped ruby goblets.
> I hand over the battered Sheffield tureen
> and the child I was, whose once-auburn hair
> she scooped up like gems from the beauty-shop floor.
>
> 'The Chain'

The final selection in *Selected Poems 1960–1990* is from Maxine Kumin's 1989 collection, *Nurture*. In the title poem she affirms:

> I am drawn to such dramas of animal rescue.
> They are warm in the throat. I suffer, the critic proclaims,
> from an overabundance of maternal genes.

The heart of the message in this selection is her affirmation of kinship with all other species. In 'Sleeping with Animals', for example, the poet keeps her 'covenant' with a pregnant broodmare:

> What we say to each other in the cold black
> of April, conveyed in a wordless yet perfect
> language of touch and tremor, connects
> us most surely to the wet cave we all
> once burst from gasping, naked or furred,
> into our separate species

The nine poems which precede it deal in different ways with our neglect, abuse, or wrongheaded treatment of the endangered: caribou, penguin, manatee (sea cows), whales and such. Man is a born meddler with species, 'who, sizing up the prospects of the few / in saving one, eradicated two' ('Homage to Binsey Poplars'). Kumin's concern for the environment and its life forms is, in my view, most successful when it is rooted not in tv documentaries or in her reading but in her daily experiences. Such is the case with her bear poem, 'Encounter in August' and with 'Custodian'. 'Custodian' is wonderfully alert, a poem which recounts her spotted dog's seasonal capture and release of frogs ('The ride untroubled in the wet pocket / of the dog's mouth'). It ends with 'Roberta Frost' humanism:

> Nothing is to be said here
> of need or desire. No moral arises
> nor is this, probably, purgatory.
> We have this old dog,
> custodian of an ancient race of frogs,
> doing what he knows how to do
> and we too, taking and letting go,
> that same story.

In its reluctance to draw a moral the poem is amusing, puzzled, large-hearted. Other poems in the selection deal with favourite subjects: time spent in Salzburg with her daughter and grandson, her past, Anne Sexton's reputation and—inevitably—old age: 'We are growing into one sex, a little leathery / but loving, appreciating the air of midday' ('Distance').

Where I Live New and Selected Poems 1990–2010 selects from the five volumes since *Selected Poems* 1960–1990 and adds twenty-three new poems for good measure. Kumin is nothing if not prolific. 'Credo', the first poem in the selection from *Looking for Luck* (1992) uses an old Kiowa legend in order to establish what the long-time reader of Maxine Kumin's poetry might have already concluded of her love of the land: that it has become increasingly spiritual over the years. Here she considers the legends and thinks of her relationship with horses:

> I believe in myself as their sanctuary
> and the earth with its summer plumes of carrots,

> its clamber of peas, beans, masses of tendrils
> as mine. I believe in the acrobatics of boy
> into bear, the grace of animals
> in my keeping, the thrust to go on.

In her later sixties, though one poem travels to Bangkok, another to Alaska, she is mostly nearer home, describing the birth of a foal (in 'Praise Be'), haymaking, giving an old neighbour's reminiscences and her own.

In *Connecting the Dots* (1996)—possibly a stronger selection of poems—the poet's old bachelor farmer neighbour, Henry Manley, breathes his last (fittingly in a monologue) and the children return home in the title poem, to visit and assess their aged parents:

> We're assayed kindly
> to see if we're
> still competent
> to keep house, mind
> the calendar
> connect the dots.

The Kumins have a clean bill of health, shovelling pine sawdust in 'Chores' and light-heartedly complaining of the farm's endless chores, or riding into the wonder of doe watching in the 'October dapple'. Much emotion is invested in the poems, 'Letters' and 'October, Yellowstone Park'. In the former, Kumin recalls a summer camp letter home to her mother. It is a longish poem which deals with their sometimes difficult relationship:

> Your laugh, your scarves, the gloss of your makeup,
> shallow and vain. I wore your lips, your hair,
> even the lift of my eyebrows was yours
> but nothing of you could please me, bitten so deep
> by the fox of scorn. Like you, I married young
> but chose animals, wood heat, hard hours
> instead of Sheffield silver, freshcut flowers,
> your life of privilege and porcelain.

There is a coming-to-terms in the course of this painful, confessional poem ('Little by little our lives pulled up, pulled even. / A sprinkle here and there of approbation'). Perhaps appropriately, Anne Sexton returns in 'New Year's Eve 1959' (a reminiscence of her lifelong friend dancing) and in 'October, Yellowstone Park', where Kumin is 'above a brace of eagles launched in flight', addressing the friend whose 'cigarette-and whiskey-hoarse chuckle' is always in her ear.

In 1998, Maxine Kumin was severely injured in a horse-riding accident, suffering 'a hangman's fracture' of the neck. Not surprisingly, then, *The Long Marriage* (2001) has one eye on oblivion, though its heart is in the natural world, woolgathering around her farm with Wordsworth and Marianne Moore, meditating on 'a rapture of blackest humus' in 'The Brown Mountain':

> What dies out of us and our creatures,
> out of our fields and gardens,
> comes slowly back to improve us

Only one poem makes reference to the accident. Yet others deal with man's inhumanity while the title poem, celebrating Kumin's personal good fortune, also fears for a future faced alone. Guilt stalks *Jack and Other New Poems* (2005). The selection opens with thoughts of the Vietnam War, prompted by extreme weather conditions in 'New Hampshire, February 7, 2003'. 'The Sunday Phone Call' brings back the poet's dead father, 'The Apparition' a pet dog:

> That night the old dog works
> his way back up and out
> gasping, salted with dirt
> and barks his familiar bark
> at the scribble-scratched back door.

Auschwitz returns in one poem, in another a hospice; a third deals with brutally discarded pets. In 'Summer Meditation' the poet tells us she wants 'to prepare / for death's arrival / in my life'. In the meantime there is the other guilt (in 'Jack') of allowing her 'big-nosed roan gelding' to be sold by a neighbour.

The poems that stand out in the selection from *Still To Mow* (2007) are again those that deal with Maxine Kumin's own experience: farm chores, memory, love:

> Marriage dizzied us. Hand over hand,
> flesh against flesh for the final haul,
> we tugged our lifeline through limestone and sand,
> lover and long-leggèd girl.
> 'Looking Back in My Eighty-First Year'

In these poems, her humanity shines clearly, more persuasively than in those poems that deal at second hand with public scandals. While her anger and frustration are perfectly justified prose might be a better medium for them. These poems—and there are a number of them—*as poems* lack what Henry James called 'felt life'; they belong to all our nightmares. Better to do what she tells us she did in 'During the Assassinations': 'I marched with other soccer mums. / I carried lemons in case of tear gas.'

Where I Live begins with the new poems, in two sections. The first tell us about her home, her dogs and horses, her dread ('another year, or not'). In 'The Taste of Apple' there is an affecting description of the death of her old horse:

> I poured
> a libation of apple juice for the earth to welcome his corpse—
> some drops spilled on his chestnut flank and some dribbled
> on his cheek and splashed onto his yellow teeth as he lay
> deep on one side and my hand shook—I could hardly see—
> rocking my grief back and forth over this kind death
> the taste of apple wasting in his mouth.

The second section returns to the world of poets, to reminiscences of Kunitz, Meredith, Miłosz and Auden. Then there are Kumin's beloved Victorians, Coleridge and the Wordsworths, particularly 'Dorothy who gave so much and got so little'.

Writing of herself in the third person, Kumin once noted: 'The poet would define these two themes—loss of the parent, relinquishment of the child—as central to her work.' Her readers would add the poet's lifelong exploration of her roots in nature. These have been her territory.

THE HARD LOSSES OF LOUISE GLÜCK

> Birth, not death, is the hard loss.
> I know. I also left a skin there.
>   – 'Cottonmouth Country'

1

The early poetry of Louise Glück takes its thematic tenor from Ecclesiastes 4, which opens with the oppressiveness of life and promotes the state of the unborn as the happiest. Birth is the first wound for Glück, 'the hard loss' from which we never recover. Intimacy is the second. Her voices constantly reiterate that message in a variety of ways, through broken narrative, enigmatic suggestion and moods of revulsion, suffering, guilt and grief. Her first four books—*Firstborn* (1968); *The House on Marshland* (1975), *Descending Figure* (1980), *The Triumph of Achilles* (1985)—and the absorbing essays collected in *Proofs & Theories* (1994) explore and illustrate uncomfortable perspectives with only the bleak beauty of her expression—except on rare occasions—to mitigate the darkness of the vision.

Frequently the early poems are energised by a disgust at life's sensuous processes which takes confession (think Plath, Berryman, Sexton) to Jacobean intensity. However, with Glück the personal is refracted through what Helen Vendler described as a 'posthumous tone', or by distancing voices—an increasing turning to The Bible, fairy tale and myth to deliver archetypal experiences (Glück's 'classicizing gestures', according to Rosanna Warren). The simple clarity of her expression and the urge to narrative paradoxically work against easy accessibility, because of the poet's unwillingness to fully disclose.

As Dave Smith noted, in the early work 'you find story, sharp and hacked'. Time and again in the essays in *Proofs & Theories*, Glück celebrates brevity, the unfinished, the unresolved, the 'reluctance to conclude'. For her 'The true has about it an air of mystery or inexplicability. This mystery is an attribute of the elemental'. In 'Disruption, Hesitation, Silence' she writes, 'I am attracted to ellipsis, to the unsaid, to suggestion, to eloquent, deliberate silence. The unsaid, for me, exerts great power'. For her it is art's role 'to harness the power of the unfinished'. Writing on George Oppen—a poet whose work is sympathetic to her vision—she explains:

> I love white space, love the telling omission, love lacunae, and find oddly depressing that which seems to have left out nothing. Such poetry seems to love completion too much... it lacks magnetism, the power to seem, simultaneously, whole and not final, the power to generate, not annul, energy.

This accords well with Glück's method of writing at that time. In 'The Dreamer and the Watcher' she says of her technique: 'For me, all poems begin in some fragment of motivating language—the task of writing a poem is the search for context.'

We are teased by the seeming openness of her diction and rhythm. Wendy Lesser noted in 'The Washington Post Book World' that 'Glück's language is staunchly straightforward, remarkably close to the diction of ordinary speech. Yet her careful selection for rhythm and repetition, and the specificity of even her idiomatically vague phrases, give her poems a weight that is far from colloquial.' The poems resist interpretation and thereby remain fresh. Hence Robert Hass could write of not being sure he entirely understood 'The Magi' (when offering Glück's poem to readers of his genial 'Poet's Choice' column) and Helen Vendler's laudatory 1978 essay, 'The Poetry of Louise Glück', is peppered with versions of 'if I read the poem aright'. She concludes: 'Glück's cryptic narratives invite our participation: we must, according to the case, fill out the story, substitute ourselves for the fictive personages, invent a scenario from which the speaker can utter her lines, decode the import, "solve" the allegory. Or such is our first impulse. Later, I think, we no longer care... Glück's independent structures, populated by nameless and often ghostly forms engaged in archaic or timeless motions, satisfy without referent.'

Lest one thinks of Vendler's words as some evasion of the responsibility to understand, it is at least worth remembering Susan Sontag's essay 'Against Interpretation' (1966) in which the essayist famously attacked criticism's obsession with meaning: 'interpretation is the revenge of the intellect upon art. Even more. It is the revenge of the intellect upon the world. To interpret is to impoverish, to deplete the world—in order to set up a shadow world of "meanings".'

11

For me, Louise Glück's more immediately personal poems are her most startling, the ones which deal with recognisable American lives, and *Firstborn* remains to this day a stunning debut. Everything appals the personas of these poems. The dominant response to experience is loathing. In the opening poem, 'The Chicago Train', one remembers the ugly parody of birth, how 'the kid / Got his head between his mama's legs and slept' and the speaker recalling the 'pulsing crotch… the lice rooted in that baby's hair'. Then there is the dysfunctional family in 'Returning a Lost Child', the mother whose 'thin / Arms, hung like flypaper, twist about the boy' and 'the father strung / On crutches, waiting to be roused'.

Self-loathing is equally pungent. With the many moments of sensuality and disgust, we are hardly far from Hamlet's urging Gertrude to avoid 'the bloat king' with his 'reechy kisses', 'paddling in your neck with his damned fingers'. In 'Hesitate to Call' we want to avert the ear:

> Lived to see you throwing
> Me aside. That fought
> Like netted fish inside me. Saw you throbbing
> In my syrups.

while in 'The Egg' it is the eye:

> The thing
> Is hatching. Look. The bones

> Are bending to give way.
> It's dark. It's dark.
> He's brought a bowl to catch
> The pieces of the baby.

'The Wound' offers another image of horror: 'The air stiffens to a crust'. Even quieter domestic moods are dysfunctional, as in 'Thanksgiving' where the popular sister sings 'a Fellini theme' and for the 'consoling meal' the speaker watches her mother

> tucking skin
> As though she missed her young, white bits of onion
> Misted snow over the pronged death.

The Fellini cast arrives in numbers in Part Two. These are Glück's damaged and resigned: sadistic male predators, victim lovers, the memory haunted, the faded 'queen', the cripple, the outraged nurse, the possessed and rejected. All is atmosphere. To the speakers in the poems perspectives are tightened. In 'Seconds' we have the neighbours

> Now huge with cake their
> White face floats above its cup; they smile,
> Sunken women, sucking at their tea...

In 'Letter From Our Man in Blossomtime' the wife is a revelation 'her white / Forearms, bared in ruth- / less battle with the dinner'. The collection's title poem, 'Firstborn', begins: 'The weeks go by. I shelve them, / They are all the same, like peeled soup cans'. The fact that the first poem invokes 'raw Botticelli' and the latter an onion 'Floating like Ophelia, caked with grease' has an absurdly reductive yet ambiguous power.

The photographer in 'Pictures of the People in the War' says 'one never / Gets so close to anyone within experience' as he did, but Glück takes another route. In her essay 'Against Sincerity' she has reminded us 'The truth, on the page, need not have been lived. It is, instead, all that can be envisioned.'

Art's 'truth' is not a matter of actuality, but of another order of authenticity.

'Cottonmouth Country' is the title of the third section and the opening poem introduces the notion of death as wooer. It ends with the collection's key lines (with their snakeskin image): 'Birth, not death, is the hard loss. / I know. I also left a skin there.' These poems, various in their speakers and forms, are the product of an imagination that acknowledges being oversensitive.

What we can take from this first collection is admiration for the poet's magnetic power, her ability to shake the usual domestic themes and turn up something rawly new. The same energy is to be found in Louise Glück's second collection *The House on Marshland*, though this and subsequent volumes better cohere. There is some difference in form between books, though brevity of line and poem are still favoured. The self-important initial capitals are missing, the effect less assertive. Beauty and quiet terror co-exist more resonantly and there are fewer 'others'. Grief has become a more dominant sentiment than revulsion, though when Glück writes, in 'For My Mother':

> And then spring
> came and withdrew from me
> the absolute
> knowledge of the unborn

we know we are still thematically connected to the 'hard loss', to the wounds of *Firstborn*. 'All Hallows', the book's opening poem, deals again in the corruption of childbirth. Helen Vendler read the poem as an allegory of birth and at its ending 'the child victim is sold into bondage, enticed into the world'. The suggestion of Halloween and the last crops of the year support this, since it is allegedly the time when spirits are free to pass between their world and ours. There is of course no option here: '*Come here, little one*', the voice croons, 'And the soul creeps out of the tree'; it needs no enticing from the wife in the window.

Pagan and Christian, Glück's draws these myths and fairy tales about her. Fear closes in. Gretel in 'Gretel in Darkness' yearns guiltily for her brother, 'we are there still and it is real, real, / that black forest and the fire in earnest'. The townspeople watch the wise men returning winter after winter in 'The Magi', probably (as Robert Hass suspected) with some irony for their route is now peopled—'cities sprung around this route their gold / engraved on the desert'—but what has happened beyond confirmation that this is the child-God?

This second collection also explores the wounds of intimacy. Tension comes from a chafing at commitment, at the intimacy experience involves. The domestic pleasure of a family photograph is ominously marred by sunlight in 'Still Life' so that, 'Not one of us does not avert his eyes.' The alternative to commitment is also loss. The child in 'The Apple Trees', at present in his crib, is bound some time to wander: 'I wait to see how he will leave me. / Already on his hand the map appears'.

All the love poems are spurred on by the fear or the experience of loss and rejection. Abishag's words apply to various speakers: *She has the look of one who seeks / some greater and destroying passion*. Poems begin with lines like 'You having turned from me'; 'There is always something to be made of pain'; 'Had you died when we were together'; 'I think now it is better to love no one'. In 'The Letters' dry leaves drift like the letters the lovers will soon burn. Beauty is above all perishable. The deer in 'Messengers', so beautiful in movement ('as though their bodies did not impede them'), resolve into 'dead things, saddled with flesh'. Even the beautiful calm of a house at dusk in which a woman carries roses and a man lifts his head from his work reveals 'a form / of suffering', because creation, for the writer, involves intruding upon lives ('Poem'). Glück's 'house' is built after all on marshland; there is no security.

Descending Figure—Glück's favourite of her first four books—explores the same themes. Intimacy is literally described as a 'wound' in 'The Return'. Love will not stem the bleeding; momentary beauty is our only distraction; even the dead are uneasy. 'World Breaking Apart', another poem that locates meaninglessness in the failure of intimacy, meditates on pain:

> Like the winter wind, it leaves
> settled forms in the snow. Known, identifiable—
> except there are no uses for them.

'The Drowned Children' is almost ineffably sad, opening with a quiet rationalisation that is heart-breaking: 'You see, they have no judgment. / So it is natural that they should drown'. 'The Garden' offers images of birth, life and death stunned by the fear of loss and yet offering no alternative in death: 'Admit that it is terrible to be like them, / beyond harm.' The landscape of loss is without support:

> How far away they seem,
> the wooden doors, the bread and milk
> laid like weights on the table.

Glück captures the paradox of birth into death in the title of her poem 'Pietà', which inverts the normal iconography taking the Italian definition 'pity' literally, presenting us with a pregnant Mary and a fatherless Christ reluctant to be born.

Such fear comes closer to home in the title poem 'Descending Figure'. In her essay 'Death and Absence' the poet has described it as being 'saturated with a mother's grief and fearfulness and a haunted child's compulsive compensation'. The poem deals obliquely with the death of the poet's elder sister, Glück's lifelong sense of guilt, her debilitating attempt at substituting herself as 'compensation', and her recognition after giving birth herself how 'appalling' maternal love can be, hedged in by terrifying fears for the child':

> Long ago, at this hour, my mother stood
> at the lawn's edge, holding my little sister.
> Everyone was gone; I was playing
> in the dark street with my other sister,
> whom death had made so lonely.

Glück's love poems carry similar anxiety. 'Night Piece' introduces the growing child to his own monsters: 'He cannot sleep / apart from them'. 'Aubade' fixes on the image of a gull, expressive of 'the unexhausted / need of the body'. In 'Epithalamium' (another ironic title) intimacy cannot assuage such need; 'the terrible charity of marriage' leaves one unprotected:

> *Here is my hand, he said.*
> But that was long ago.
> *Here is my hand that will not harm you.*

Admiration of male beauty in 'The Mirror' turns to horror when the man's shaving becomes bleeding. In 'Rosy', the crippled dog seeking further self-harm is likened to the lover being rejected. Even in the contented waking scene of 'Happiness' it is the shadow of the 'the burning wheel' which 'passes gently over us'. Suitably the collection ends with the four part poem 'Lamentations', Glück's version of the creation myth. The man and woman who have become parents with 'no authority above them', have also discovered in their sin and nakedness, 'white flesh / on which wounds would show clearly / like words on a page.'

The last of Louise Glück's early books—before the poet moved more to narrative sequence—is *The Triumph of Achilles*, winner of the National Book Critics Circle Award for poetry. This collection takes her further into her characteristic mythologizing and into fears of intimacy. The first two poems, 'Mock Orange' and 'Metamorphosis', plus others like 'Winter Morning', 'Summer' 'The Mountain', 'Legend' and 'Morning' confirm, for me at least, the feeling that Glück's more immediately personal poems are her most satisfying.

'I know / intense love always leads to mourning', Glück writes in the poignant 'Metamorphosis', a poem addressing a dying father. Everything fails in time and especially optimism. Glück's 'The Reproach' opens:

> You have betrayed me, Eros.
> You have sent me
> my true love.

'Morning' concludes with the virtuous bride, so different from the mother who cried at her wedding, happily innocent of time:

> Never has she been further from sadness
> than she is now. She feels no call to weep,
> but neither does she know
> the meaning of that word, youth.

In 'Mock Orange' the odour of this fragrant white flower with its virginal associations merges with the odour of sex to repel the speaker, since the sex act is 'humiliating' and the post-coital 'split into the old selves, / the tired antagonisms' so desperate. Such images of relationships are predominantly negative. In 'Hawk's Shadow' the momentarily fusing of predator and prey, mirrors the lover and beloved. Uncomfortable, too, is the final poem, 'Horse', in which the husband believes his marriage is exhausted, his wife wedded now to dreams of fulfilment through escape.

Relationships sour. 'Marathon', a poem in nine sections, reflects on such failure. After the elemental force of lovemaking, happiness is offered as pre-natal oblivion. 'Once we were happy, we had no memories', the voice tells us, and again further on:

> Sooner or later you will call my name,
> cry of loss, mistaken
> cry of recognition, of arrested need
> for someone who exists in memory: no voice
> carries to that kingdom.

Finally we learn that in the world accessible only to dreams 'the bond with any one soul / is meaningless; you throw it away'. 'Summer' remembers the days of 'our first happiness' and then the lovers losing their way, drifting as on a raft in their bed:

> And in each of us began
> a deep isolation, though we never spoke of this,
> of the absence of regret.

The poem ends with the hollow freedom of 'artists' left to continue their journey. The seasons change but one is never whole because, as the teacher illustrates in 'The Mountain' (contrary to her intention): the Sisyphean labour is never really attained. Even standing at the top 'the rock has added / height to the mountain'.

Louise Glück's poetry clearly addresses both a stark recognition of loss in the self and a need in her readers. Perhaps it is as she wrote in 'Death and Absence':

> When you read anything worth remembering, you liberate a human voice; you release into the world again a companion spirit.
>
> I read poems to hear that voice. And I write to speak to those I have heard.

Part Two: Poets in America

CZESŁAW MIŁOSZ IN EXILE

> Fame will pass me by, no tiara, no crown?
> Did then I train myself, myself the Unique,
> To compose stanzas for gulls and sea haze,
> To listen to the foghorns blaring down below?
> Until it passed. What passed? Life.
>   – 'A Magic Mountain'

On balance, America proved more generous to Czesław Miłosz (1911–2004) than he was to it. By turns it tolerated, rejected, ignored and lionised him over half a century, while he endured his time there with incomprehension at its values. Perhaps he felt a lingering gratitude. France, on the other hand, offered a decade's refuge and an impoverished living. Although he preferred Paris, California ultimately won out because Miłosz badly needed a more comfortable exile, a teaching exile, in order to thrive on the rigorous self-examination which lay at the heart of his work. For both countries he remained the 'reformed communist', a writer on politics whose poetry was at best undervalued and, being in Polish, generally ignored.

Yet Miłosz was one of the finest poets of the twentieth century, a survivor of two World Wars and the Cold War, his majestic poems are preoccupied with history, conscience and ethics. Of the three, it is probable that he will be chiefly remembered as the first hand witness to a savage century, in such poems as 'Song on Porcelain' (1947):

> Rose-colored cup and saucer,
> Flowery demitasses:
> You lie beside the river
> Where an armored column passes.

Miłosz lived as a controversial figure for much of his life, especially with the Poles whom he was felt to have deserted after the war. Denounced for his supposed communist sympathies, he was compromised by his post-war enlistment in the diplomatic service of Soviet-controlled Poland. In 1957 he acknowledged this: 'Representing a country that was turned into the province of a totalitarian foreign state was wrong and degrading, which I feel ashamed of today.' Then again, a thorn in the side of the Soviet-Polish authorities, he remained ardently pro the Polish people and their arts. As he wrote in *Native Realm: A Search for Self-Definition* (1968), 'Many were amazed at my cunning or my insensibility to totalitarian atrocities; they saw my stance as the height of hypocrisy. But it was not, perhaps, hypocrisy.' He needed to keep silent, he argued, not from cynicism. He did not want the pre-war social-economic order in Poland, but also he wanted 'a considerably better fate than that of a Stalinist province'.

On a personal level Miłosz seems to have been somewhat difficult. Exploring the difference between his infamous image and his self-image in a late piece, 'Hatred', he sketched in the portrait of a man without patriotism, a man on the make: inordinately lucky, materialistic and untrustworthy even in his personal life. He contended that in actual fact he felt himself to be 'a tangle of reflexes, a drunken child in the fog'. If the first part of the likeness is unfair and the last 'poetic', the ambition, arrogance and over-sensitivity he also noted seems to have fitted the man.

Then again, Miłosz's life illustrates the old Russian proverb that to live a life is not to cross a field. Born a subject of the Tsar's in Lithuania—to landed gentry at Szetejnie near the Polish border—his father worked as a Polish civil engineer, while his mother came of a noble family. The child and his younger brother, Andrzej (later a journalist and documentary film maker) were raised Catholic and spoke Polish. In *Native Realm* he remembered,

> My first awareness came with the First World War. Peeping out from under my grandmother's cloak, I discovered horror: the bellow of cattle being driven off, the panic, the dust-laden air, the rumbling and flashing on a darkened horizon. The Germans were arriving in Lithuania.

The war drove them to Wilno (the Polish name for Vilnius). Miłosz later studied law there and, in 1931, visited Warsaw where he was also to study briefly. He was already publishing poetry as a student in socially involved magazines ('The only criterion for evaluating a piece of art is its social role', he wrote in 1931) and constantly revising his intellectual positions. As he remembered later, 'What drove me toward the Left, which was rather fluid and heterogeneous, was not Marxism but my resistance to nationalist obscurantists, or perhaps destiny hidden within the cells of my body.' Three years later he argued against a radical position: 'I have had enough of sucking up to plebs, by telling myself that we occupy the same level. I hate these primitive people, as well as the plebeian traits within myself.' This aggressive reaction served as a way of preserving his poetry's 'living springs'. He did not want to be a political poet, nor a poet of social protest. He felt driven to address his inner needs, as a poet of spiritual yearning—and a restless one.

Miłosz first visited Paris in 1931, where he met a different world of paved rather than cobbled streets, of daily routines with the 'smoothness of civilised life'. He and his friends had come from the drab East to the exciting West, albeit at a time of great unemployment. His 1980 poem, 'Bypassing Rue Descartes', remembered the Paris of his youth with clarity:

> Bypassing rue Descartes
> I descended toward the Seine, shy, a traveler,
> A young barbarian just come to the capital of the world.

and

> I had left the cloudy provinces behind,
> I entered the universal, dazzled and desiring.

Graduating from Vilnius University in 1934, he won a scholarship to return to 'the capital of the world' to study for a year. He did not feel mature enough to exploit it, however, being by his own admission 'filled with inhibitions, bashful, frustrated at every turn'. At the time he produced poetry he later considered 'blocked', overloaded with imagery, poems such as 'The Gates of the Arsenal' ('A tempestuous noise, the din of waves, the soughing of pianos / Resounds from the abyss.')

If life in Paris had its tensions for him, it also held inordinate attraction: 'The wilderness of Paris, the mythical image of Paris, was always connected with a vision of debauchery or something of the sort.' Miłosz lived first in a student hotel and then in a *pension* near the Panthéon, before joining a Polish friend at a hotel across from the Ecole Polytechnique. At the time he met few French people, though he studied the language, gaining a diploma. His chief point of contact, his distant cousin Oscar Miłosz, introduced him from time to time to French writers. This Miłosz, a well-respected Lithuanian poet writing in French, influenced Miłosz greatly (as did the philosophers Simone Weil, Jacques Maritain, with his view on spiritual transcendence, and Catholic theology in French).

Oscar Miłosz had begun as a Symbolist poet before turning to mysticism ('Speak. Tell / Unsparingly what your soul has seen / In the blind, wandering and forsaken cosmos'). A visionary poet as well as a writer productive in various literary genres, he was appointed *chargé d'affaires of* newly recognised Lithuania in 1920, taking citizenship a decade later.

His poetry alone did not influence Czesław Miłosz, though that has a certain power:

> It will be exactly like this life. There will be
> The poor voices, the voices of winter in old slums,
> The glass mender singing his own duet,
>
> The broken grandmother under a dirty bonnet
> Crying out the names of fish, the man with the blue apron
> Who spits into a hand worn by the wheelbarrow
> And yells nobody knows what, like the Angel of Judgement.
> – 'Symphonie de Novembre'

Miłosz remembered not understanding 'all his mystical pursuits and prophetic writings at the time'. Oscar really influenced the younger poet more in his feelings about the vital role of poetry in capturing the spiritual dimension of man together with the material. According to Edward Hirsch (in 'The New Republic') this involved showing him 'a new kind of spiritual thinking. Poetry must be aware of its "terrible responsibilities"—it is not purely an individual game—but it could also blend historical with mystical concerns. Milosz's poetry would seek an "eternal moment" lifted from the river of time. It would try to understand our human relationship to the divine.' Czesław Miłosz always credited his cousin's influence, writing of him often, though he also blamed him privately for 'spoiling my life by filling me with exaggerated spiritual yearnings'.

When he returned to Wilno Miłosz found increasingly tedious occupation working on literary programs for Polish Radio. He published his first significant collection, *Trzy zimy* (*Three Winters*) in 1936 (a small collection had appeared in 1933 with some critical success). Having been fired for his leftist views, he took a trip to Italy, then settled in Warsaw where he met Janina (Janka) Cękalska working at the radio station.

Miłosz's literary circles continued to expand as his reputation grew, but Poland's survival became jeopardised with the invasion by Hitler's and Stalin's forces in September, 1939. During the conflict, by a necessarily circuitous route Miłosz returned to Wilno and then to Warsaw to reunite with Janka. He scraped a living in the town saving university books from the rubble, continuing clandestinely with the poetry. He took refuge in a kind of classicism: 'What really interested me was poetry ... from the stress of daily tragedy for millions of human beings, the world had burst and fallen to pieces. All previous forms had become meaningless.' Although Miłosz's war experience was honourable, he did not join in the uprising, feeling the need to survive as a poet to the nation. Others he found reckless:

> The twenty-year-old poets of Warsaw
> Did not want to know that something in this century
> Submits to thought, not to Davids with their slings.
>   – 'A Treatise on Poetry'

At the war's end Miłosz joined the Writers' Union, translated others and published his own work, such as *Ocalenie (Rescue)*. Eventually he joined the diplomatic service in an effort to return to Western Europe. Good fortune and good contacts led to his being appointed cultural attaché at the Polish embassy in New York. He arrived there inauspiciously in January 1946 on board a small cargo ship. He and Janka were met in New York by an old friend from Polish Radio. In truth, America had fascinated him even as a bookish child who loved nature:

> America is for me the illustrated version
> Of childhood tales about the heart of tanglewood,
> Told in the evening to the spinning wheel's hum.
> – 'A Treatise on Poetry'

As an adult Miłosz did not remember his first experience of America negatively. In *Native Realm* he wrote, 'The air in America, even summer in Washington with its 98 degree humidity, it did not make me lethargic. It exhilarated me. The air in Poland is always oppressive; one breathes in elements of melancholy there that constrict the heart.' Soon, however, Miłosz became privately scathing of what he saw as an intellectual void in the nation, the natives suffering a 'cow-like existence'. Firstly he noted the highly unsettling fact that he had moved from devastation to what appeared, in contrast, decadence: 'The gigantic city itself was an outrage, because it stood there as if nothing had happened—it had received not a single notch from a bomb'. Then, as he got to know Americans, he decided that 'The spiritual poverty of millions of the inhabitants of this country is horrifying... These unfortunate American puppets move like *chocholy*, with a depressing inner stupor.'

At the peril of reading into the poems, in 'Greek Portrait', written in Washington D.C. in 1948, we have perhaps an inscrutable, tight-lipped self-portrait:

> I have left behind
> My native land, home, and public office.

> Not that I look for profit or adventure.
> I am a foreigner on board a ship.
> My plain face, the face of a tax collector,
> Merchant, or soldier, makes me one of the crowd.
> Nor do I refuse to pay due homage
> To local gods. And I eat what others eat.
> About myself, this much will suffice.

To Miłosz privacy became paramount. At the consulate where he worked he took exception to 'the constant lying of my colleagues and superiors', to their 'half-wittedness and innocence'. Yet his commitment to the work continued: unflagging, inventive and recognised. He outwardly conformed. In October 1946 he found himself promoted to the position of cultural attaché at the Washington Embassy. Unfortunately, to him 'the Embassy was a dog collar, a waste of time'.

Although he found the international intellectual community fascinating—meeting profitably with *some* American literary intellectuals—he felt generally unhappy with his relations with the Polish émigré community, which he felt generally backward-looking. Consequently Miłosz, his wife and son led a quiet, solitary life. When not working hard to promote Polish arts via the embassy, or studying American literature, he took holidays into the country ('Splash of a beaver in the American night. / The Memory grows larger than my life.' 'A Treatise on Poetry'). As he remembered in *Native Realm*:

> Most of all I got to know the American countryside, which restored me, after a prolonged interval, to my boyhood. Like all Europeans I had painted for myself a false picture of technology's reign in America, imagining that nothing was left of nature. In reality her nature was more luxuriant even than the wooded regions where I grew up.

He may have 'ceased to be a foreigner' in its wilderness, but Miłosz nevertheless found urban America impossibly capitalist.

He felt they had suffered 'a loss of the sense of history and, therefore, of a sense of the tragic, which is only born of historical experience'. On one trip he visited the West but arriving at length in California—his future home—he dismissed Los Angeles as 'a small hell-hole with no imagination, consisting of palm trees and nothing'. Later he wrote:

> I did not choose California. It was given to me.
> What can the wet north say to this scorched emptiness?
> Grayish clay, dried-up creek beds,
> Hills the color of straw, and the rocks assembled
> Like Jurassic reptiles: for me this is
> The spirit of the place.
> – *The Separate Notebooks*

His view of the land and its inhabitants, then, did not improve with familiarity. Visiting Poland briefly in 1949 he talked a lot to a friend 'about the lack of intelligence in Americans'.

In contrast, Miłosz loved Paris. Recalled to the Polish embassy there because of fears he might be at risk of defection in America, he defected in Paris instead. He left the embassy, spending three and a half months in hiding in Maisons-Laffitte, a Parisian suburb and home of the Polish émigré press, 'Kultura'. The official announcement of his defection came on the 15th May 1951. Impoverished, separated from his family, depressed, he began to be condemned by politically correct Polish writers as a 'pen mercenary'.

Failing to gain immediate re-entry to America, Miłosz made a sort of living writing for the 'Kultura' journal. He forged links with anti-Soviet French intellectuals (notably Albert Camus), especially after he published *The Captive Mind* in 1953, his study of the Soviet influence on intellectuals. Further complicating his situation, he found a supportive, romantic relationship for a time with the Swiss philosopher, Jeanne Hersch, who persuaded him to write fiction, a medium he was uncomfortable in but which produced the award winning political novel, *The Seizure of Power* (and *The Issa Valley* in 1955). Ironically, it earned him enough money to bring Janka and the two boys to France.

Reunited, the family lived a penurious life in one, then another small village outside Paris, where he kept a low profile. Miłosz feared being kidnapped and sent back to Poland. He and Janka married in 1956. While he felt 'very much at home in France' his opportunities were restricted by the uncertainty of freelance journalism. His income occasionally rose with royalties from foreign editions of his work or articles for the BBC. Although poor, the family managed holidays to the coast and to Italy. Miłosz travelled for 'Kultura' to London and to West Germany, contributing to France's tempestuous intellectual life. Janka, who had been desperate to stay in America, still urged their return, but Miłosz's feared the country did not want him (at a time of McCarthyism), that living there would erase his poetic impulse or deny his sons the opportunity to develop the 'intellectual passion' that had been so much a part of their parents' youth. Instead he continued to publish prose and poetry in Paris. His reputation grew slowly through the decade in France but as a political writer, a frustration that caused him to finally make peace with the idea of a return to America.

Having turned down an academic offer from the University of California at Berkeley in 1959, Miłosz relented on its renewal the following year. He became a visiting Lecturer in the Department of Slavic Languages and Literature, then shortly thereafter a tenured professor, a role he was to play through eighteen, largely lonely years. As Andrzej Franaszek wrote in his convincing biography, *Miłosz* (2017), 'Perhaps Californian reality seemed too amorphous for him, too detached from history and culture'. It also lacked the rhythms of the seasons. The further problem remained that Miłosz continued to be valued as a political writer, 'a reformed communist', but ignored as a poet. Worse, he felt exiled from his Polish language and readership, a 'ghost', although ironically, as he explained, his roots were Lithuanian and he had no direct family ties with Poland: 'I was not born in Poland, I was not brought up in Poland, I do not live in Poland, but I write in Polish.' He had ever been its critic. Even before the war he had been sceptical about the government, becoming 'a Marxist writer by reflex-reaction'.

Increasingly the publishing pressure in Soviet-controlled Poland to conform to 'socialist realism', as well as his feeling of being an 'inner émigré', contributed to periods of depression. His European sensibility also clashed with the ideology of American intellectuals. He saw them as materialists who were 'remarkably well supplied with worldly goods. Their conformism is so far advanced that they are sometimes reminiscent of Pantagruel's sheep.' As Pankaj Mishra noted in a piece for 'Bookforum' (autumn 2017):

> [His] unillusioned realism made Miłosz immune during his long decades in America to the usual temptations of exiles: to over-valorize one's refuge (as Nabokov did...) or to absurdly idealize, like Solzhenitsyn, the lost homeland.

Despite the fact that in his first twenty years in California he published five collections of poems, for many years he remained frustrated, unsociable, feeling as a writer and man (if not as a teacher) 'mute'. He explored the contradictions in the 'California variety' of contemporary civilisation in his essay collection *Visions from San Francisco Bay* (1969). Privately, that view continued to be negative, bordering on the tragic.

In *Conversations with Czesław Miłosz*, first published in Polish in 1983, he replies to Ewa Czarnecka's question whether America has remained a land of loneliness as follows:

> There is no question that for someone raised in our extremely gregarious society typical of the countries in our part of Europe, where there is great warmth and closeness between people, there's a feeling that something is missing here. It's the loneliness of Anglo-Saxon society that makes it alien to us... And also it shouldn't be forgotten that my revolt against capitalism ran very deep.

It ran deep enough to appear and reappear in his work. 'Ill at ease in the tyranny, ill at ease in the republic, / in the one I longed for freedom, in the other for the end of corruption', he wrote in the poem To Raja Rao'. And yet the despondency seemed not totally incapacitating. As a professor he was well appreciated by students and colleagues, despite feeling initially, in his words, like a cow joining the ballet. He taught Polish literature from notes, in an interdisciplinary way, careful to relate his teaching to current events while avoiding repetition by offering courses on prose and drama, translating and film. He was also sympathetic to students during the anti-Vietnam years.

Eventually he made his peace with his supposed Californian anonymity. In his 1975 poem 'A Magic Mountain' Miłosz considered his Berkeley home in light of another's remark that without seasons 'so little changes you hardly know how time goes by'. If a magic mountain, he concluded, despite being bypassed by fame (as he continued to believe) he would say yes to the life there: 'One murky island with its barking seals / Or a parched desert is enough.' However, he ended his book-length 'conversation' with Ewa Czarnecka by describing how he felt uncomfortable about continuing to be labelled a historical poet because 'the proportions are distorted'. He referred to poems like 'From the Rising of the Sun' or *The Separate Notebooks* as capturing another self:

> the meditative poet, which I find more comfortable and suitable. That's a far cry from the poet of action, the poet actively involved in history. I never wanted to be involved in history. Everything we've been talking about may be reducible to my discomfort when my image is too noble.

Actually, interest had been gradually growing as perspectives on Miłosz's poetry gathered subtlety. If he avoided promoting either himself or his poetry in English, he had not shied from allowing it to be translated. In California he had turned increasingly to theology as the one real subject of study. It influenced his poetry. Hitherto Miłosz had judged that, bedevilled by historical events, he had had to deal with the political as 'a faithful chronicler of our times', the witness who could say, '"I see, I describe", nothing else.' Yet in his later poetry others saw, as his biographer Franaszek explained, that there was room for human uncertainty: 'the voice steeped in great ideas will abate, allowing more prominence to human whispers'—to whispers, to autobiography and even to humour.

If America heard complaints over the years, it hardly took offence. On his retirement Miłosz was made Professor Emeritus. His reputation thrived. There had always been those who supported his work in Europe and then in the English-speaking world. The increasing focus from critics like Donald Davie and Helen Vendler helped his cause. Also Poland began to feature in the world spotlight with the election of Cardinal Wojtyła as Pope John Paul 11, as well as through the emergence of Solidarity, the first independent trade union in the Soviet bloc. Miłosz had become fashionable again. In 1976, on a trip to Paris, he was moved, he confessed, that a younger writer could recite his poems from memory: 'I never expected you people in Poland to know my poems by heart. I thought I was *persona non grata*.'

Far from it now. In 1980 Miłosz was awarded the Nobel Prize for Literature, which transformed him overnight into a world poet, welcomed even in Poland where he returned in 1980 for his first visit in thirty years. By then a widower, he took America to his heart at last in in 1992, when he married an American academic, Carol Thigpen. They moved to live in Krakow the following year and that is where he died in 2004. The realist whose declared aim was to 'to seize hold of fragments of reality' had written his own epitaph as a poet in the poem 'Blacksmith Shop', from a 1991 collection: 'I stare and stare. It seems I was called for this: / To glorify things just because they are.'

TIME AWAY: LOUIS MACNEICE'S AMERICA

> Time was away and she was here
> And life no longer what it was.
> The bell was silent in the air
> And all the room one glow because
> Time was away and she was here.
>   – 'Meeting Point'

In his projected *Countries in the Air* Louis MacNeice had been keen to explore 'the corroborations and refutals of my myths, the frustrations and illuminations I have found in various travels'. His American experience provided much fertile ground for this. MacNeice's brief working visits there, while successful professionally, led to something of an attenuated romantic disaster. His relationship with Eleanor Clark, the American writer whom he met in New York in 1939, overshadowed his engagement with the country. It did, however, inspire some fine poetry and in his letters a vivid self-portrait of a poet conflicted by love and duty on the eve of the war.

MacNeice's life until that time had been one of public success and private heartbreak. He was born in Belfast in 1907, to a clergyman father and a mother he lost in 1914. Prep school in England led to a Classical Scholarship to Marlborough College and subsequently Merton College, Oxford, from which he gained a first in Classics. He published his first collection of poetry, *Blind Fireworks*, in 1929, the following year marrying and taking a post as an Assistant Lecturer in Classics at Birmingham University. Although his marriage had produced a son, Dan, in 1934 he divorced two years later. MacNeice moved to Bedford Women's College (London University) where he taught in the Greek Department. He published regularly throughout the decade: fiction, a translation of *The Agamemnon of Aeschylus* (1936), *Letters from Iceland* (1937) with Auden, his entertaining *Modern Poetry: A Personal Essay* (which drew Orwell's scorn upon his generation of poets) plus a second poetry collection, *The Earth Compels*, in 1938.

After a visit to Barcelona in December of that year, MacNeice turned his attention the writing of *Autumn Journal*, to his study of Yeats and to America.

To that end he asked T.S.Eliot's help in organising a short reading and lecture tour for the spring of 1939. Letters went out to a number of prestigious institutions. Writing to Wellesley College, Massachusetts, Eliot described him as 'one of the best of our younger poets, whose work is I am sure known to you'. MacNeice left immediately at the end of Easter Term at Bedford College, being met in New York by his ex-wife, Mary, and her husband, their one-time lodger. His first lecture, at the state college in Pennsylvania was well-received, he remembered in his unfinished autobiography, *The Strings Are False*. His host told him, 'They gave you a big hand. They usually only do that for an orchestra.' Other readings at Princeton, Harvard and Wellesley, although successful, failed to underwrite his expenses. Nevertheless the trip provided useful academic introductions, as well as a reunion and reading with Auden and Isherwood.

At a 'Partisan Review' party MacNeice met Eleanor Clark, a twenty-five-year-old left-wing, Vassar-educated writer, divorced from one of Trotsky's secretaries. In contrast to Clark's political commitment, although also left-wing in his sympathies, MacNeice was too sceptical, too much of a lifelong outsider to embrace Marxism, Communism or any ideological constraint. As he expressed it in a later letter:

> I am trying to develop [a world-view] but I am damned if I am going to swallow Marx or Trotsky or anyone else lock stock & barrel unless it squares with my experience or, perhaps I should say, my feelings of internal reality.

Returning from the tour on board the Queen Mary on Friday 21st April, 1939, MacNeice initiated three years of correspondence with Clark when he wrote breathlessly, 'So few people have both beauty & intelligence & a conscience & gaiety but you seem to, darling.' Clark on her part endeavoured to keep some distance between them emotionally, though MacNeice bombarded her with lengthy letters which attempted—festooned with 'darlings'—to erase it. He was also keen to breach the 'Hindenburg line… which you were very reluctant to stop defending'. This physical aspect became a leitmotiv of his letters, just as his worry about 'suffocating' her in his effusions (while continuing to do so). He did not completely lose his senses, however. He was, for instance, wary of sharing her commitment to revolution, wondering about the 'internal capacity for revolt' of the 'lower classes'.

Arriving home, he reported 'several painful scenes & been made to feel very conscious of moral irresponsibility etc.' There would be disapproval if he were to return to America, he knew, and he cited the experience of Auden and Isherwood as a warning. Still, he confessed himself 'sick of this place' by early May. To alleviate his 'American fixation' he asked Eliot's help again, this time in obtaining a semester's academic appointment, although later MacNeice stood in two minds about a lecturing job ('They all work so hard that I am not sure I shouldn't prefer hanging about and living by visiting lectures and journalism'). Subsequently he was offered a 'Special Lectureship in Poetry' at Cornell University from the 12th February to the 3rd May (for $2000), with added lectures elsewhere. The offer enhanced his emerging reputation after the publication of *Autumn Journal* in America in January 1940. The dust cover of *Poems 1925–1940*, published by Random House, referred to him as 'one of the leaders among England's younger generation of poets'.

MacNeice defended England when Clark wrote that the country was 'doomed'. He felt not at all convinced by the prospect of war and anyway, as an Irish citizen was exempt from conscription. What worried him had more to do with the endgame:

> I do hold that morally the British Government ought to check Hitler, there will be so little morality in it by the end of it that I don't feel very inspired to have my legs shot off to bring about that a Europe which is now say 80% rotten should be 85% rotten, supposing H. is checked, instead of say 89% supposing he isn't.

To his mentor, Professor E. R. Dodds, MacNeice wrote on the 13th October, 1939, '"Destroy Hitlerism" but what the hell are they going to construct?' He was sure of one thing: that a trip to the United States was necessary 'in order to clear myself up emotionally. Three months would solve the question of E. one way or the other'. The following month he vacillated, writing to Dodds, 'I am beginning to think this may be my war after all.' Despite the fact that 'there is plenty wrong with the British Empire & especially India', he hoped perhaps that events would right wrongs even if the government lacked the will.

In December MacNeice's other option closed. He had held hopes at the prospect of appointment to the Chair of English at Trinity College, Dublin, his application supported by T.S. Eliot and Professor Dodds, (later to be his executor). When he heard that he had not been chosen for the post, MacNeice turned his attention back to the burning issues of romance and responsibility. Christopher J. Fauske put the matter bluntly in *Louis MacNeice: In a Between World* (2016), 'He would return to the States in January 1940 motivated by an intense ambivalence about the war, an inability to find permanent refuge in Éire and a desire to see and seduce Clark.' In his autobiography MacNeice addressed his prevarication as follows:

> I felt I was not justified in supporting the war verbally unless I were prepared to suffer from it in the way that the underprivileged must suffer. But I was not yet prepared to do this, so I had made use of certain of my privileges to escape for a little to America. I had an especial reason for wanting to return to America, but apart from that I thought I could think things out there, get myself clear before I went back into the maelstrom.

The 1940 trip turned out to be starred with ill-luck, though the lectures went well. Their subjects included Yeats, Eliot (at Vassar), as well as the poems of Auden, Spender and himself. He also lectured on 'Since the Victorians' at Skidmore College and 'The Younger English Poets' at Bennington, where he was paid $25 for a talk which necessitated an arduous journey involving two buses and a train.

Disaster struck in July when MacNeice had to be hospitalised in Portsmouth, New Hampshire. He endured an emergency operation for peritonitis, followed by a near fatal infection. Recovering, he was taken to Clark's mother's house in Roxbury, Connecticut, to convalesce. There he stayed for several weeks. In mid-August he wrote to his ex-lover, Nancy Coldstream, of perhaps migrating to the USA 'unless there is a social revolution in England which makes everything new'. He had grown attached to America, he decided, though that attachment would weaken as his relationship with Clark failed to develop.

Meanwhile he began 'pouring out poems in an unprecedented state: five ballads, 'Jehu', 'Picture Galleries', 'Plurality', 'Autobiography' and 'Province' among them. No wonder he wrote giddily to Clark, 'I have written ELEVEN since coming here; what do you think is wrong with me?' *Plant and Phantom*, published in 1941, collected these American poems with others. For the reader, the reward of MacNeice's American time is to be found in the poems he composed there, poems which reflect his feelings about the cost of neutrality, the fate of love, the coming conflagration of the world order.

One was 'Bar-Room Matins', written in a 5th Avenue New York apartment. It imitates the tough-mindedness of hard drinkers, its prayer satirising the hypocrisy of everything from church to media, then ending with rather harrowing foresight: 'Die the soldiers, die the Jews, / And all the breadless homeless queues. / Give us this day our daily news.' 'Refugees'—written around the same time—shows insight into the lot of immigrants arriving in New York. The poem is informed by MacNeice's compassion, as it is by his recent experience of fellow passengers at sea:

> Thinking, each of them, the worst is over
> And we do not want any more to be prominent or rich,
> Only to be ourselves, to be unmolested
> And make ends meet—an ideal surely which
>
> Here if anywhere is feasible.

Something or nothing may turn up, but for these refugees the known world has gone. As he neatly concludes, 'they still feel / The movement of the ship through their imagination / The known and the unheard-of constellations wheel.' 'Exile', another poem of 1940, seeks to hide the 'inhuman night' after such recognition:

> Knowing that in Europe
> All the streets are black
> And that stars of blood
> Star the almanac

'Picture Galleries' reminds us 'of what we always / Would rather forget —that what we are or prefer is conditioned / By circumstances, that evil and good / Are relative to ourselves who are creatures of period'. And this is not the time or place for lasting love. The fine poem, 'The Closing Album', from August/September 1939 ends:

> And why, now it has happened,
> Should the atlas still be full of the maps of countries
> We never shall see again?
>
> And why, now it has happened,
> And doom all night is lapping at the door,
> Should I remember that I ever met you—
> Once in another world?

Neither can the bucolic pleasure of neutrality, of an 'Evening in Connecticut', hold the world and its war away:

> The lawn a raft
> In a sea of singing insects,
> Sea without waves or mines or premonitions

Despite the beautiful September and the katydids, Nature is no guarantee of continuity. The coming fall evokes not quietness but, 'the fall of dynasties'. 'Only the shadows longer and longer', the poem ends. As with 'Jehu', the mood is prophetic of 'the flood tide' coming. And consequently in 'Cradle Song for Eleanor' (which 'reads like a valediction as well as a benediction' as Edna Longley noted) MacNeice's protective injunction is to

> Sleep, my darling, sleep;
>   The pity of it all
> Is all we compass if
>   We watch disaster fall.

The best that can be done is to slip the moment, to take time out of the coming war, as MacNeice and Clark do in the famous 'Meeting Point', which he wrote in late April 1939. It is 'a kind of love poem in the third person', he told Clark and, transmuted into art, the expression of MacNeice's feelings is highly seductive. In the reality of his letters, the romantic immediacy is raw. That of May 21st, 1940, written from Ithaca New York, is the most revealing, most devastating of MacNeice's side of their correspondence. Certainly sexual frustration plays a part in his defence of his supposed 'awful lack of curiosity about the world': 'once again you seem to forget the distracting effect sex has on one (in situations like mine at the moment)'. In this angry letter MacNeice attempts to dispel 'this little pixie myth about me' Clark was supposed to share with her sister: the belief that he has been sheltered from the world while keeping himself aloof from others.

In fact, an ironic reserve does seem to have characterised MacNeice. His friend John Hilton later wrote: 'Meeting people face to face he was apt to make too clear that he was treating them—head thrown slightly back, eyes quizzically narrowed—as specimens, bearers of the potentialities of the race'. Hilton generously interpreted this watchfulness as self-protection.

In that letter to Clark, MacNeice presents himself as a 'peasant who has gate-crashed culture'. He is, in his own words, able to identify with common people, being one of them. He is aware that he may give the impression of being standoffish, of being 'inhuman' but

> I couldn't keep on feeling on behalf of other people. And so I got this detachment or aloofness or whatever it should be called but if you think I am aloofness to the core & can't see behind what was only a protective crust, you are, darling, more short-sighted than I should have expected.

The letter may have cleared the air, but their relationship was doomed. Christopher J. Fauske concludes that, 'Ultimately, she was less interested in him than in what he stood for, and he was more interested in her than in what she stood for.' Yet what MacNeice might have stood for was the nub of the problem for Clark. When he wrote: 'The trouble (& the glory) about being in love with you is that I see you against the world', she replied, 'I don't see you that way.' She was beginning to find it difficult to see him in any way. What he offered was the wrong kind of commitment.

Returning to England in November 1940, MacNeice ultimately dedicated himself to the war effort, taking a position with the BBC's Features department, which he was offered partly due to family connections. He wrote to Clark explaining that 'the BBC, though deplorable, does leave some loophole for intelligence & individual decisions'. The following month he reported that he did have misgivings about his war work, knowing it was propaganda, 'vulgarisation', but that it had 'its excitements & (what was less to be expected) its value'. It also had its dangers. He gave her his Oxford address to write 'as one never knows how long a London one will last'.

At least now MacNeice felt he had a role. As he told Dodds's wife, 'We play Rummy here every night. It occurs to me that even playing Rummy in London now is a kind of assertion of the Rights of Man, whereas in America it would be nothing but playing Rummy.' Although he informed Eleanor Clark about the possibility of his brief return to America for the BBC, it did not materialise. Their letters continued until MacNeice effectively severed the connection with a brief one in early July 1942, which tells her he has got married to someone, 'but not to anyone I had mentioned to you before'. He hopes they will continue to write 'without post-mortems'. (Clark was to marry Robert Penn Warren in 1952 and to receive the National Book Award for *The Oysters of Locmariaquer* in 1964.)

MacNeice was by no means done with America after that, principally because the country remained vitally important to Britain's war effort. Indeed, to the BBC part of his attraction lay in the fact of his recent experience and budding reputation there. He had written at length to his father in the summer of 1939 after his first visit that there were a lot of popular misconceptions about America, enumerating some of them. He had also explored his familiarity with American manners and customs for his readers in *The Strings Are False,* where he celebrated it as a congenial place where people could 'evade the rigours of caste'. Also, on his return to England, MacNeice had written five 'London Letters' to the American periodical 'Common Sense', to describe the war on British cities.

In 1941 his first programme for the BBC, 'Word from America', took the form of an anthology of American poems and songs, which was followed by 'Cook's Tour of the London Subways', a fifteen minute play for an American audience. The following October MacNeice's play 'Christopher Columbus' was broadcast on the Home Service to mark the 450th anniversary of Columbus's discovery. In 1943 *Meet the US Army* was published, his pamphlet commissioned by the Ministry of Information as a tool for teachers to explain to schoolchildren the culture of our allies.

There were to be later visits to the United States. In 1953 MacNeice embarked on another American lecture tour, this time alternating with a recital of song and verse with his wife, the English singer, Hedli Anderson. The following year he returned on a visiting lectureship at Sarah Lawrence College, New York. It is hard to believe that MacNeice might ever have wanted to remain in America. He was not at home there. Then again he was not really at home anywhere. As he had written to his fellow Ulsterman, Dodds, at the war's end, 'I wish one could either live in Ireland or feel oneself in England.' Perhaps it was only in his work that MacNeice was at home. There time was away and somewhere else.

DYLAN THOMAS ROARS ACROSS AMERICA

> Now I am a man no more no more
> And a black reward for a roaring life
> – 'Lament'

He may not have known where he was exactly, or even really cared: beery, hands blue with cold, arriving late, the audience restive. He may have put a little extra weave in it, but he had finally arrived drunk at Mount Holyoke, a venerable college for women in South Hadley, Massachusetts. The evening's reading did not promise well. Yet subsequently Professor Joseph McG. Bottkol recorded in his diary, 'Dylan Thomas here to read. Hour and a half late. Tight as an owl and the most powerful reader I've ever heard. A ludicrous party afterwards—the poet using very plain language, and making drunken love to all the lady professors of whatever age.' This was Thomas in America: unreliable, outrageous, occasionally offensive, and generally—when it counted—spellbinding.

He charmed America even as he scandalised it. The greater part of the substantial income earned from four visits there, he—or he and Caitlin—left in innumerable bars and otherwise frittered away. America had a negligible effect on both the poet and his poetry, partly because the poems bound tightly in their own somatic and sonorous preoccupations, partly because Thomas noticed only the gruelling distances of the continent. There may have been a darker reason: the question of the decline of his lyrical gift.

In *Dylan Thomas: The Biography* (1977/1999) Paul Ferris noted, 'Thomas lived in Laugharne [South Wales] for four and a half years before his death in November 1953, writing only six complete poems in that time.' (These included favourites like 'Lament', 'Poem on his Birthday' and 'Do not go gentle into that good night'.) This covered the period of Thomas's four American tours. The country's contribution to the Thomas legacy lay not in the poetry but in *Under Milk Wood*, his 'play for voices', a good deal of which was written there. And it was the Americans who pressed him to complete—in his last months—a stageable version.

America's contribution to the legend, on the other hand, has been enormous. As Adam Kirsch wrote in the 'The New Yorker' in 2004, 'the glamour of Dylan Thomas has always been peculiarly potent in the United States, because the last acts of his tragedy were played out here, in Manhattan'. This implies an unwarranted innocence, for America fostered the outrageous, the bad boy image for its own titillation. The writer Elizabeth Hardwick once explained, 'There was a certain amount of poison in our good will.' Audiences came for the poetry, the voice, but also for the scandal, the frisson of the dramatic: 'Would he arrive only to break down on the stage? Would some dismaying scene take place at the faculty party? Would he be offensive, violent, obscene? These were alarming and yet exciting possibilities.'

No poet embraced his roaring image with more readiness. Born in Swansea in 1914, Dylan Thomas left the grammar school where his father taught, to briefly join the 'South Wales Daily Post'. Although encouraged by his father's own literary aspirations, he grew hard to live with, a sickly schoolboy, an errant adolescent. To Ferris, 'Poetry was the reality he lived by, an end in itself, an excuse for everything. To beg, borrow, steal, dodge, pretend and prevaricate was included in the poet's licence.' Thomas gathered about him the affectations he imagined in the poet's calling, a bardic role inherently destructive.

After publishing poems here and there, he made the first of a number of moves to London and back, publishing his critically successful collection *18 Poems* in 1934, followed by the earlier *Twenty-five Poems* two years later. By then a good part of his oeuvre had been completed. Thomas would have another twenty years of gathering fame before his death. His singular vision, what Caitlin thought its 'snail's-eye view of his world', offered an alternative to the more politically engaged 1930s poetry of Auden, MacNeice and company. Thomas might be a socialist himself, were it not for being sunk in his own circumstances, and therefore 'not a man to dislike becoming a pillar of the Establishment so long as his warm heart was not affronted' as William Empson, who knew him, judged.

He turned to radio in 1937, a medium in which he excelled plus a frequent source of money over the coming years for the catastrophically penurious Thomas. In that same year he married Caitlin Macnamara, a disturbing force in his drunken, disorganised life, yet his one true love. They moved to Laugharne where they were to live most of their married life. In one of his warmest letter—an invitation to the American poet John F. Nims and family in July 1950—he described it with his characteristic over-abundant comic energy as offering: 'beds, couches, cots, playpens, fish, cockles and mussels, flat warm Welsh bitter beer, affection... sea and river, are all yours in this arsehole of the universe, this hymnal blob, this pretty, sick, fond, sad Wales.'

In 1939 came the birth of the first of three children, shortly followed by two more books, *The Map of Love* (with seven stories and sixteen poems) and a short story collection, *Portrait of the Artist as a Young Dog*. 1946 brought recent poems with the title *Deaths and Entrances*. In his remaining years, aborted projects for television and films were to follow. In 1949 the Thomases moved into the Boat House at the generosity of a friend—their most settled address. In that year he agreed to the first of the American trips. His popular *Collected Poems* appeared in England in 1952 and in America the following year, where *Under Milk Wood* assured an even brighter fame—and where he died.

In the years of Thomas's American tours his mostly self-inflicted worries coalesced: his relationship with the 'unshockable' Caitlin, money, drink, and poetry. As Ferris suggested, Caitlin was 'Always the stronger partner, she was the fixed point in his life. But he treated her badly... she retaliated with anger and contempt that he may have deserved but couldn't endure. In that sense she helped to break him.' They cheated on each other, she brazenly as she increasing felt asphyxiated by life in Laugharne, tied to the upbringing of her children and failing to make ends meet in the frequent absence of her husband.

Money worries crippled their chance of happiness. Thomas petitioned for financial help repeatedly as the years passed, from publishers, editors, the Royal Literary Fund, the BBC, friends, to pay tax collectors and local tradesmen for rent, coal, for bread, for his son's school fees, for holidays, even for cigarettes. Yet compared to many of his countrymen, Thomas had been frequently well paid.

Carelessness with money passed as flamboyance. His disorganised life became a life of taxis. He told one correspondent that he tried 'never to live below the imagined standard I had set myself', while his inventive begging letters are full of apology and cunning. Thomas also became adept at mortgaging unwritten work and re-selling rights. His income was certainly erratic, but good times were never banked. The first American tour raised nearly £3000, for example; the *Collected Poems* sold 10,000 copies in the English edition and in American even more.

Inevitably the drinking exacerbated Thomas's health issues, while contributing to his poetic licence. Close friends and biographers saw fear there, too: fear for his health, fear for the eclipse of his lyric talent. His American sponsor, John Malcolm Brinnin, suggested in *Dylan Thomas in America* (1956) that they were both aware by 1950 that 'his great work was finished'. Perhaps Thomas foresaw audience tastes changing, with the stirrings of what would be The Movement in England and The Beat Generation in America. This should not be overstressed, however. As Charles Tomlinson remembered it, at the end of the 1940s 'Dylan Thomas was still the voice which sounded in one's ears as one sought for a contemporary style or, quite literally, if one switched on the BBC.'

For multiple reasons, then, America seemed to offer him the time to breathe. Money would be the glittering prize, while consideration of his poetic direction could be temporarily shelved. Rob Gittins, in *The Last Days of Dylan Thomas* (1986), stressed another incentive, respite 'from the grinding and endless friction with Caitlin, from the increasingly oppressive demands of family'. So, when Brinnin—director of the Poetry Center in New York— approached Thomas in 1949 with an offer of a three-month tour of arts centres and campuses, with fees of $150–500 dollars per appearance, he leapt at the idea. This would be a chance at fortune and fame. ('The idea of the States puts the fear of Mammon in me' he observed, amused). To Caitlin, Thomas said, America was only either Hollywood or Senator McCarthy, but then she was shrewd enough to sense what the country could do to Thomas, let alone to his ego.

The truth is that as early as 1939 Thomas had written of wishing to leave Britain for America, returning to the subject in letters near the war's end. He would settle for temporary employment, as he explained to the anthologist Oscar Williams in 1942, as he would 'love a little ladleful from the gravy pots over there'. He described what he had to offer in characteristically humorous terms: 'How could I earn a living? I can read aloud, through sonorous asthma, with pomp; I can lecture on The Trend of Y, or X at the Crossroads, or Z: Whither? with an assurance whose shiftiness can be seen only from the front row'. Besides, American poetry had always appealed to the poet. His Boat House studio contained portraits of Walt Whitman and Marianne Moore (the latter hardly read in England at the time). Later he would encourage younger poets like Theodore Roethke and Robert Lowell by offering readings of their work to the BBC 3rd Programme.

The plan went ahead for a three month tour (February 21st–May 31st, 1950) with two provisos. Thomas announced his willingness to accept any fair fee from Brinnin, though he would need funds almost on arrival. Secondly, he preferred to read the poetry of others with his own. Before travelling to America he compiled an anthology and varied his reading choices each performance. He included poems by Hardy, Binyon, E.Thomas, Owen, Eliot, Auden, Yeats, MacNeice, Sitwell and Lawrence among others. As Thomas explained, 'I far prefer reading other chaps' work to my own: I find it clearer.'… At the mere thought of reading only myself, I begin to feel hunted.'

In his biography, *The Life of Dylan Thomas* (1965), Constantine FitzGibbon neatly sums up the poet's behaviour abroad: 'Dylan in New York was not essentially different from Dylan in London. He toddled about the bars and bookshops, asked women to take him to their beds, talked to other poets and behaved outrageously at literary parties.' Here he became the celebrity actor in alien territory. As FitzGibbon noted, Thomas treated his American time as he did his English, but in New York there were no hiding places and no old friends to support him. There was no Caitlin, either, a circumstance not intended in the initial planning. Brinnin, who had organised the tour in great detail, turned out to be no substitute for Caitlin, no match for the wayward Thomas, as he came to realise: 'There was a seam of primal innocence at the core of him that caused judgment to be obliterated, accusation to dissolve in mid air.'

Nevertheless things began well. His first appearance, before an audience of a thousand, took place at the Kaufmann Auditorium of the Poetry Center in New York. Although Thomas suffered terribly before his readings, in performance he could be enchanting, as Brinnin memorably described: 'at the appointed time he walked on to the stage, shoulders straight, chest out in his staunch and pouter-pigeon advance, and proceeded to give the first of those performances which were to bring to America a whole new conception of poetry reading'. (There is some irony in the fact that, according to Brinnin, Thomas 'had an obsessive antipathy to poetry as a public forum activity'). He knew how to charm an American audience with his majesty and self-deprecation, his talks delivered in what Kingsley Amis once described as his 'clear, slow, slightly haughty, cut-glass Welsh voice'.

The tour took off from there, by car, by train and by plane, taking in approximately forty venues from coast to coast and from Vancouver, British Columbia (where he met Malcolm Lowry) to Gainesville, Florida. Being constantly in the company of academics—in auditoriums, at cocktail parties, and always as his hosts—proved uncomfortable for Thomas. Their eager solicitousness or their literary talk, he deflected as best he could. As Theodore Roethke (another roaring boy of poetry) reckoned shortly after Thomas's death, 'Any kind of social pretentiousness disturbed him, and particularly in academia. The bourgeois he did not love.'

Thomas tended to rebel, therefore, against social niceties. His letters home, which naturally hide the extent of his drinking, his profligacy with fees, his attempts at womanising, illuminate the culture shock. He writes of the enormous quantities of food on offer, including 'a T-bone steak the size of a month's ration for an English family'. He describes America as a dystopia: 'It's nightmare, night & day; there never was such a place; I would never get used to the speed, the noise, the utter indifference of the crowds, the frightening politeness of the intellectuals, and, most of all, these huge phallic towers, up & up & up, hundreds of floors'. Warming to his theme of a 'cancerous Babylon', he reports, 'I have been driven for what seem like, and probably are, thousands of miles, along neoned, jerrybuilt, motel-ed, turnbined, ice-cream-salooned, gigantically hoared roads of the lower region of the damned, from town, college to college'. Then again, as he acknowledges, 'I am no globe-trotter, no cosmopolitan, I have no desire to hurl across the American nightmare like one of their damned motorcars.'

The root of Thomas's negativity seems to have been this arduous travel. He complained to Caitlin of 'hardly living', of being 'just a voice on wheels', though he also conceded that '*Everything* is not terrible here. I have met many kind, intelligent, humorous people, & a few, a very few, who hate the American scene, the driving lust for success, the adulation of power, as much as I do.' Finally, though, Dylan Thomas found an American dream. He reported to Caitlin, 'But, oh, San Francisco! It has everything… The wonderful sunlight there, the hills, the great bridges, the Pacific at your shoes. Beautiful Chinatown'. What's more, he had a possible job at the University of California at Berkeley with the Department of Speech, teaching the oral interpretation of literature. In Hollywood he stayed with Christopher Isherwood and dined with Charlie Chaplin (who had he kindness to telegraph Caitlin of the amazing fact).

So it went. In the end Thomas had much to be forgiven for, though mainly the drunkenness with the bad or rude behaviour that came with it, especially the abuse of his hosts' generosity. Some of this was encouraged—the drinking—to conform to his image; most of it was forgiven. It did not seem, as Caitlin was to contend, that lacking a ruthless streak he was eaten alive by the Americans. He had been 'loudly lost for months', but the tour had been a brilliant success—except in its central purpose ('I made money, and it went, and I returned with none'). He came home with so little he would have to go back 'peddling and bawling to adolescents the romantic agonies of the dead'. Debts continued to 'batter' him. The Inland Revenue required £1,607 as tax on the disappeared earnings of the tour. He soon petitioned Brinnin to have him 'imported' again, being 'so deadly sick of it' at home.

From January 20th–May 16th, 1952, Thomas undertook a second American tour, which would turn out to be the longest, with forty-six engagements. Rumours had crossed the Atlantic, so this time Caitlin insisted on accompanying him. Their spirited, drunken public spats only stoked the legend. Brinnin remember Caitlin, after a Boston University reading, responding to being asked how she liked the country with "I can't get out of the bloody country soon enough.' Her rudeness, variously on show, had something to do with her lesser role or the feeling that the Americans both overpraised and exploited Thomas.

To Brinnin, their only relatively happy time on the tour had been in the anticipatory few hours after their disembarkation from the Queen Mary. A planned respite in Flagstaff, Arizona, later in the tour certainly contributed to sour moods when the Thomases, staying with Max Ernst and his wife, found themselves out of money. According to Thomas, 'We stayed here, absolutely penniless, for 8 days, being unable to buy our own cigarettes, to post a letter, or stand with a beer at Sedona's cowboy bar, or even to wire [Brinnin] again.' It is difficult to sympathise with a man who, back at home, wrote to Oscar Williams (who sold work for him on the sly), 'Here, as you know, we are not as we are in the States, where we don't think or care about what we spend. Here, we have nothing to spend, and think and care about it all the time.'

Unsurprisingly, in April 1953 Thomas needed to return alone to America for a third tour of six weeks. In March he complained to Brinnin that Caitlin declared, '"You want to go to the States again only for flattery, idleness, and infidelity". This hurt me terribly. The right words were: appreciation, dramatic work, and friends.' She could be mollified only by the promise of a three winter month holiday to Portugal with sun and servants. Thomas continued to dream of their going to California, where he would spend a month with Stravinsky on a proposed collaboration. Most significantly, on this tour Thomas performed a version of *Under Milk Wood*, his play for voices, at first solo, then with a cast.

Although Caitlin warned that a fourth American trip would kill him, Thomas returned to New York on 20 October 1953 for another potentially lucrative visit. His final days were spent instead in illness and on alcohol. He appeared in public for the last time at a lunchtime reading at City College on the 29th. His doctor was summoned on the 4th November to relieve chronic symptoms of alcohol, gout and gastritis. The half grain of morphine injection has been judged to have created the breathing difficulties that led to his coma and lingering death. News travelled fast but inaccurately. According to Robert Lowell, in a letter to Elizabeth Hardwick of November 29th, 'The details are rather gorgeously grim. He was two days incommunicado with some girl in some New York hotel. Then his wife came, first cabling "eternal hate," and tried quite literally to kill *and* sleep with everyone in sight. Or so the rumors go in Chicago and Iowa City.'

Being so much talked about, Dylan Thomas had always been partly the creation of others. He became wholly so in death. To Lowell he had lived a 'short and shining' life. To Empson, 'he ought not to be regarded as the Marvellous Boy who could not grow up' but a writer on the brink of a theatrical career. Yet the poetry counted more. To friends he had lived the life of a desperate man. John Davenport reckoned that, the lyrical gift gone, Thomas had been left with only the public role he despised. It is perhaps near the mark. He summed up this situation himself, in a letter to Princess Caetani in November 1949, not long before his first American trip:

> I do not like reading my old poems; because I *am* not working on new poems; because I must earn my living by bits and pieces of forced prose, by exhibitionist broadcasts, by journalistic snippets; because, nowadays, I can never spare the time to begin, work through, and complete a poem *regardless* of time; because my room is littered with beginnings, each staring me accusingly in the eyes.

In the absence of poetry Dylan Thomas had elected the lucrative path of celebrity. Where better than America to fashion a roaring legend?

CHARLES TOMLINSON & AMERICA

> Different places on the face of the earth have different vital effluence, different vibration, different chemical exhalation, different polarity with different stars: call it what you like. But the spirit of place is a great reality.
> – D. H. Lawrence, *Studies in Classic American Literature* (1924)

Charles Tomlinson acknowledged a great debt to America. Its poets influenced and encouraged him; its landscapes offered countless opportunities to explore Lawrence's famous insight. Tomlinson's poems focus on the individuality of places and on the way we see and understand them, a relationship in which the clarity of our perception comes by diminishing the ego.

Tomlinson identified with American landscapes almost as keenly as he did with Wotton-under-Edge, Gloucestershire, where he lived with his wife Brenda, or Italy's Bay of Lerici which, he said, confirmed him as a poet. He also learned greatly from modernist American poets, who offered him encouragement and their friendship. These were reciprocated. For the American poet George Oppen, 'it is [Tomlinson] and Basil Bunting who have spoken most vividly to American poets'. In a 2015 Guardian obituary, Michael Schmidt quoted Oppen before continuing, 'Tomlinson bridged the vast gulf between old and new world poetry, and was an heir equally of Dryden and Williams, Coleridge and Pound.'

Born in 1927 in Stoke-on-Trent (the 'Potteries', Staffordshire), he went in due course to Cambridge. According to his own account Tomlinson picked up a selection of Ezra Pound's poetry in 1944, at seventeen, fascinated by his inability to scan the lines in the conventional way, by the 'prosaic phraseology' and 'a sense of cleanliness in the phrasing'. Then he found Michael Roberts's *Faber Book of Modern Verse* the following year, which brought Wallace Steven to his attention, a poet of 'evocations', a poet 'whose imagination warms to the cold' in his loneliness before the natural scene.

Tomlinson married in 1948. He first taught primary school then, after travel and work in Italy, pursued the academic life, his poetry and painting. Unfortunately, as he testified, 'The 1950s were an unpropitious time to write the kind of verse that interested me, and England an unpropitious place in which to publish it.' Since the poets who influenced him were largely unobtainable in England, his work lacked context. It was not until 1955—with the intercession of his former Cambridge tutor and then friend, Donald Davie—that Tomlinson's booklet *The Necklace* appeared. He began teaching at Bristol University. A positive review by the Canadian critic, Hugh Kenner, appeared the following year in 'Poetry' (Chicago) which led to continued encouragement by its editor. It was in America that his first full collection, *Seeing is Believing*, appeared in 1958. The following year he travelled there on a fellowship, meeting formative influences Marianne Moore and William Carlos Williams.

Tomlinson's prolific career as a prizewinning poet, translator and artist had begun. There were to be a number of visits to the country. In the 1962–3 academic year, for instance, he became Visiting Professor at the University of New Mexico, where new friendships included a number of other poets whose work influenced his own: the 'Objectivists', Louis Zukovsky and Oppen, and the 'Black Mountain' poets, Robert Duncan and Robert Creeley. In 1967 he met his first modernist hero, Pound, in Italy at the Spoleto Festival.

In 1976 Tomlinson gave a reading tour in America, visiting New Mexico again and then again four and five years later, while a Visiting Senior Fellow at Princeton. The University of New Mexico conferred an Honorary Doctor in Literature on the poet in 1986, the year after Oxford University Press published his *Collected Poems*. He became an Honorary Fellow of the American Academy of Arts and Sciences, as well as a member of the Modern Language Association. More collections were to appear from Carcanet Press, the last, *Cracks in the Universe*, in 2006. By the time of his death Charles Tomlinson had established an impressive international reputation.

He publicly recognized the major influence of American poets, commenting that through the 'tonality' of its 'distinguishable

American presences' his work sounded American, but he was keen to make it clear that they themselves had a debt, to 'Wordsworth and Coleridge and their exploration of how the self arrives at knowledge and identity, and of how mind and senses contribute to this process'. Then there was the influence of art, Tomlinson's own paintings and 'the sort of visual and literary discipline' he learned from Ruskin, which involved a combination of acute observation with exploration of ways to articulate it.

Asked what had first drawn him to America, in his interview with 'The Paris Review' (1998), Tomlinson replied, 'All bits and pieces, to begin with. A monochrome reproduction of a Georgia O'Keeffe in a book that was a twenty-first birthday present (we were to meet her in New Mexico)'. He then spoke of the American poets his Cambridge education had failed to prepare him for. His *American Essays: Making it New* (2001) includes *Some Americans: A Personal Record* (1981), a memoir of Tomlinson's early times there and his friendships with those poets. *American Essays* opens with the words, 'I found my own voice as a poet by learning from four Americans, a woman and three men—Marianne Moore, Wallace Stevens, Ezra Pound and William Carlos Williams.'

Marianne Moore's poems captured his imagination with their originality: their cunning syllabics, their use of prose rhythms, their idiosyncratic logic and, of course, their content. To Tomlinson her best poems offered 'resolutions of tough moral elegance'. To him they were not necessarily as warm, as intentionally cherishable as the popularity of that eccentric poet might suggest. Moore herself was. After he was introduced to her through Kenner in 1959, they exchanged books and letters. His poem 'Ship's Waiters' is dedicated to Moore, while a snatch of their first conversation surfaces in 'Over Brooklyn Bridge':

> 'I do not live in town
>   I live in Brooklyn.
>   I was afraid
>   you wouldn't like it here—
>   it's gotten so ugly.'

Tomlinson began to read William Carlos Williams seriously in 1956. He 'helped make clearer the inherent rubato of speech. Furthermore, I liked his ability to deal with phenomena unegotistically—a piece of paper blowing across the street, a yellow chimney emitting smoke, all the miscellany and detritus of what just lies around'. The following year he adopted the three-ply cadences that Williams used in the two books of his that Tomlinson had read. He produced 'Letter to Dr. Williams' and 'Sea Poem':

> A whiter bone:
>   the sea-voice
>   in a multiple monody
> crowding towards that end.

If he had hoped for a more enlightened response from editors, Tomlinson would be disappointed. He received the same puzzled reception to his work in England: 'When I began imitating Williams's measure and applying it to the cadences of an Englishman's English, I was still finding it difficult to place poems in my native country.' Their layout seemed too unusual. Again Hugh Kenner came to the rescue, first with promoting his manuscript, *Seeing is Believing*, secondly by directing Williams to his poetry. In a letter to Tomlinson thanking him for the poems which had appeared in 'Spectrum' (a student magazine from the University of California with which both Kenner and Davie had connections) Williams wrote, 'Anyone who is influenced by a verse form which liberates English verse is my friend.' Although Tomlinson did not subscribe to Williams's belief that the pattern of his verses was distinctly American, he nevertheless greatly admired the poet, gaining confidence from his support at a time when he felt excluded from the British scene and alienated from The Movement poets.

On that same 1959 travel grant tour Tomlinson visited the ailing Williams in Rutherford, New Jersey, on two occasions. Thereafter they exchanged affectionate letters (until his death in March 1963) in which Williams encouraged Tomlinson's poetry.

As Tomlinson remarked in *Some Americans*: 'Moore, Williams, [Yvor] Winters, and Henry Rago ['Poetry' editor] are all dead. They cemented a bond of affection for America I could never have anticipated at the time of my earliest poems.' He acknowledged admiration for other American poets over the years, including Lorine Niedecker and Elizabeth Bishop, on both of whom he wrote.

Although American subjects surface in *A Peopled Landscape* (1963), Tomlinson began working with his American experience more systematically in *The Way of a World* (1969). Timothy Clark observed, in *Charles Tomlinson* (1999), 'It is the moment-to-moment quality of a place as a space of habitation that concerns Tomlinson.' The possession of place shades into his other great, allied preoccupation with perspective in Tomlinson's well-known 'Swimming Chenango Lake'. This poem, set in New York State, opens *The Way of a World*:

> There is a geometry of water, for this
> > Squares off the clouds' redundances
> And sets them floating in a nether atmosphere
> > All angles and elongations: every tree
> Appears a cypress as it stretches there
> > And every bush that shows the season,
> A shaft of fire

Place and perspective are twinned, for 'space' is what 'the body is heir to'. The section 'Western Pieces' from later in the collection introduces us to the manners and rituals of the Southwest: the Honda's driver playing cards with a passenger while driving; the farmer whose revenge on a mountain wolf turns out to be misinterpreted; ritual dancing in San Antonio and at Zuni in New Mexico. In 'A Sense of Distance' the landscape of the Southwest combines with the poet's imagination on his return to England in 'the kingdoms of possibilities'.

American Scenes and Other Poems (1966) explores contrasting place within America. In a 1975 interview Tomlinson said, 'there's a lack of myth in my poetry because it usually arises directly from something seen. I want to register *that* in all its clarity or in all its implications. The nearest I come to myth is that word 'Eden', which I can't seem to get rid of and that fits what I'm doing with its implication of primal things, fresh sensations, direct perceptions unmuddied.' So it is landscapes and cultures, rather than their potent myths that preoccupy him. His favourites were the Southwest (New Mexico) and Mexico, which he views in his poems, in Clark's words, from the perspective of a 'sympathetic foreigner'.

'American Scenes' is the second part of the collection, gathering nineteen poems from Tomlinson's travels in the Southwest and New England. These marvel at what he sees of the desert states. They hear the silence, imagining the subterranean in 'Arizona Desert', where 'Eye / drinks the orange ground' and:

> Villages
> from mud and stone
> parch back
> to the dust they humanize
> and mean
> marriage, a loving lease
> on sand, sun, rock and
> Hopi
> means peace

The poems relish the desert with its big skies, which match the endless land 'whose space outpacing sight / recede as speechless and as wide as death' ('A Death in the Desert'). Its harshness is underscored with references to bleached cow skulls, shallow graves, desiccated villages, decaying shacks, locked churches, ghost towns:

> Clear
> of the weight of human
> meanings, human need,
> gradually
> houses splinter to the ground
>   – 'Two View of Two Ghost Towns'

The land is peopled by tough descendants of Native American tribes and pioneers, some of whom Tomlinson encounters. There is humour even here, as in 'Old Man at Valdez' and 'Las Trampas USA', which records with wry amusement conversations that attend the poet's visit to the Spanish-American church village in this northern New Mexico village, while the subjects 'Mr Brodsky' and 'Chief Standing Water' are eccentric representatives of this unusual culture.

The America of the 1960s is evoked in poems like 'At Barstow', concerning that unattractive Californian truck town ('Nervy with neons, the main drag / was all there was. A placeless place'). Its 'execrable conjunction / of gasoline and desert air' is a short step to 'Arizona Highway', which also befuddles the mind while it saps the energy and deceives the imagination:

> The windshield drinks
> the telegraphed desert miles,
> the tarmac river: tyranny,
> glass identity,
> devouring and dusty eye,
> pure duration, all
> transition, transformation.

In stark contrast to that 'orange ground', Tomlinson is introduced to New England. In the poem 'In Connecticut' all is white, clean and clear in the village church during a first snow. It is a world of 'shadowless conviction'. In the more anglicized culture of New England, Tomlinson savours Longfellow's study, with

> the busts of
> Homer, Aeschylus
> and Sophocles still
> pedestalled where
> they ambushed Hiawatha

while in Dickinson's 'square cool mansion' the poet retreats even from her letters. Tomlinson also offers 'A Garland for Thomas

Eakins', for that supreme realist whose self-portrait reveals the 'anguish' at the enormity of his unheralded task. A similar artistry of the eye is there in 'Maine Winter', a snow landscape which proves the death of a fox who 'flaringly goes / with more of the hunter's caution then / of the hunter's ease' but is torn apart by ravenous crows. The poem is reminiscent of Winslow Homer's painting of 'The Fox Hunt'.

Part three of *American Scenes* constitutes ten Mexican poems, again products of Tomlinson's travel. Recurrently these cinematic poems consider the Catholicism and eschatology of the natives, through moments of Día de la Constitución (the anniversary of the 1917 constitution), with a straw Christ, old buses, poor churches or peasants with their butchered saints ('They / are in paradise now / and we are not'). The most successful of the poems focus on the most unusual scenes. 'The Well' captures the whisperings as the turbulence of history. The well endures in an old Mexican convent, riddled with revolutionary history

          the standing
shaft of water
sends its echoing up
Catching, as it stirs
the steady seethings
that mount and mingle
with surrounding sounds
from the neighbouring
barrack-yard

The old slogan 'We have served the revolution' ('Hemos servido / lealmente / la revolución') ends a fine poem. A memorable oddity is 'On the Tlacolula Bus', which concerns an absent driver—one Lukenbac—who 'flew for the Fuehrer', as he boasts on his vehicle in Gothic script. The Nazi becomes a goat observing the bus—passing into history like the man—with 'its narrow stare, looking / like Lukenbac in exile'.

Tomlinson returned to America and Mexico in *Notes from New York and Other Poems* (1984). The city seems almost eerily devoid of its citizens, as the poet is absorbing the geometries of light and shade on the buildings. His view begins in the air, overlooking the 'mathematic of the suburbs'. What holds his attention are the clouds over the City, how 'they intensify for one that sense of things always moving, disintegrating, re-forming—the sense of a world which is never quite *there* because light and time have changed it' ('Sight and Flight'). It is, then, the fascinating 'double mystery' of sight that 'haunts the mind'.

The first poems deal with the arriving jet ('The map of land, the map of air'). The poet's perspective changes as he leaves behind the plane and his consideration of the Iroquois construction workers ('Above Manhattan'). He descends to the streets of beggars, to the smells of food. To Tomlinson 'The view in space become a view in time', in 'At the Trade Center' and in 'Crossing Brooklyn Ferry'. Even at ground level, however, the poet looks at the city as an architecture of light and shadow. Like another poet and painter, Derek Walcott, Tomlinson seems preternaturally attuned to the play of light:

> All afternoon the shadows have been building
> A city of their own within the streets,
> Carefully correcting the perspectives
> With dark diagonals, and paring back
> Sidewalks into catwalks, strips of bright
> Companionways, as if it were a ship
> This counter-city.
>   – 'All Afternoon'

'The Mirror in the Roadway' (punning on Stendhal's description of the effect of the novel) is one of Tomlinson's bravura successes at capturing the shifting planes of perspective in the reflections of a piece of furniture standing in the street. He is amused at such local rituals as this, as at the hero sandwich, the football game, eating ice cream (consolation for missing Washington's house). However, light and its play on the urban landscape have intrigued him even more.

At the end of *Notes from New York*, the poet returns to Mexican subjects: the duty shells of grasshoppers; the ghostly house of

Trotsky (though it is Europe that 'seems a distant planet'); the poor churches with their beggars ('both prologue and epilogue / to each gold interior'); the dead gods of Teotihuacán.

Tomlinson returned frequently to America, in life as well as for inspiration, with such collections as *The Return* (1987) and *Annunciations* (1989), where the 'tri-toned whistle of the night rain' on 'The Santa Fe Railroad' summons the following response:

> The desert has no need
> To declare itself by fanfare. It is itself indeed
> As you and I might be only in Eden.

His essentially romantic view of America continued to work on into his last collection, *Cracks in the Universe*. Here, in 'Above the City', he wishes to be walking rooftops, marvelling at the pigeons with their 'airy acres' and from the 'travelling eye' of a car, in 'New Jersey-New York', witnesses 'The merging of cars, the chains of light / Announcing bridges, intersections'. Always it is the poet-painter's eye that thrills by what it sees in movement, light and shadow. Surprise is Tomlinson's medium. It is that surprise which comes from momentary recognitions of the workings of the world. It is the reward of a profound sensitivity to place.

MICHAEL MOTT: DELVING INTO THE SHADOW

(I wrote the following essay a decade ago. The book has not yet appeared, for various reasons. I include it, anyway, as a glimpse of Michael's excellence as a poet, and with great affection for the man himself.)

One of the privileges of friendship is to enjoy a copy of a collection still in preparation. What follows is a consideration of Michael Mott's as yet unpublished new book, *Conspiracy*. Most of the poems from this have appeared in magazines on both sides of the Atlantic, from the 'The Sewanee Review' to the 'TLS'.

My intention here is not to review as such, but to illustrate some of the current preoccupations of an insufficiently appreciated poet. There is a reason for this 'neglect', one Robert Nye identified when writing of Michael Mott's 2005 collection: '[Mott] is an unassimilable poet—considered English in America, American in England.' He then went on to write, 'The poems about his childhood in *The World of Richard Dadd* prove that in fact he belongs as naturally to our common language as Frost or Auden; a true poet.'

English readers, at least, have failed to track the career of a poet who, though he went to live in the USA in the 1960s, has retained an English sensibility in his work and who is still, in his late seventies, producing excellent poems.

By way of background: Michael Mott was born in London in 1930. His father was a solicitor, his mother a sculptor from Denver, Colorado. He grew up in Hampstead, but was evacuated to America during the war, returning to London (and the V—Bombs) in 1944. After extensive travel and a stint of National Service and at Oxford University, he became a writer. Four novels followed, including the best seller *The Notebooks of Susan Berry* (1962) and the *succès d'estime'*, *Helmet and Wasps* (1964). After working briefly as an art editor for Thames and Hudson, in 1966 Michael was invited to teach at Kenyon College, where he became poetry editor of the 'Kenyon Review'. He published a best-selling biography, *The Seven*

Mountains of Thomas Merton, before retiring from teaching in 1992. However, Michael Mott is firstly a poet and over the years has published eleven collections of poetry, including *Absence of Unicorns, Presence of Lions* (1976), *Corday* (1986) and a selected, *Woman and the Sea* (1999) before the prize-winning *The World of Richard Dadd* (2005) [and, most recently, *Pyder Hundred (The Natural History of Harlyn)* (2013)].

The keys to *Conspiracy*, are conspirators, landscapes and games, nouns which feature in the section headings. The conspirators are in one sense ourselves, colluding at the complicating of our lives. The landscapes are the landscape of that life and the games the sometimes grim hand life throws us. As Michael himself says, 'There is an understanding in my poetry that, whatever the landscapes of our life, we are haunted by the ghosts of ourselves.' The metaphysical truth of this may be allied to his epigraph from Richard H. Popkin's work on the history of scepticism, 'unless per impossible, all information available to us could somehow be part of a conspiracy to lead us astray'. The combination of the two is mindboggling, but has resulted in an oeuvre that challenges complacency.

Charles Taylor, in *Sources of the Self* (1989), writes of 'the ideals and interdicts of this identity—what it casts in relief and what it casts in shadow.' Michael Mott's poetry delves into the shadow.

The first section of his *Conspiracy* opens and closes with two poems that address Michael's private life. This is uncharacteristic, since he is not a poet who overtly addresses his autobiography, his life experiences being typically mediated through masks. Numbers of his poems have first person voices, but generally they are those of historical or imagined figures. The opening poem, 'The Blanket', is shaped as an address, however:

> Grandfather, of all the things
> I inherited from you, having
> had no time to know you,
> this fawn coloured blanket
> with the Greek key pattern
> has worn best

What the poem revels in is the military paraphernalia that came down to an eager boy (and later, national service officer) from his grandfather. He admires the decorations, bayonet, toy soldiers, the sword—but its source is a pride in the contribution of a relative whose war service, 'north of Troy' (at Gallipoli), ties the generations to a great theme of western history.

'Ship Burial, Isle of Man', the poem that closes the first section, is a heartfelt yet restrained elegy, prompted by a close friend's death. The poet comes across the site of a Viking barrow whilst he is walking with his grief:

> Before your ashes are scattered,
> our friendship of fifty years,
> I'd want more than one morning
> to build your boat for you—
> white ribs, grey sails.

The poem, which opens in a 'sparrow-fierce morning' and ends in the 'thousand-year grief of the gale', exposes emotion and the elements to the poet's eye. Ultimately, the friend and the Viking settler both 'steer for an island / beyond islands', Hamlet's undiscovered country. This introduces a note of heroism, appropriate in the farewell to a long-time friend.

Between these two personal poems we meet a number of public figures—Descartes, Saenredam, Bruno, Turner, Duchamp and others. Two of my favourites—Haydn and de Sévigné—illustrate Mott's skill at reclaiming lived experience, whilst imbuing it with controlled poetic craft. 'The Shawls' has a contemporary celebrating Haydn's triumph with 'The Creation' in a letter to a friend. The composer himself is close to death; his frailty spurs the attentiveness of the audience and the old man is given shawls for his trembling. At Haydn's departure, we learn

> That Creation simply dissolved into air, Prager.
> When Haydn was gone, things went back to emptiness:
> the room, the singers, musicians, everyone
> and in place of everyone a pile of shawls.

The shawls here are as evocative as the earlier blanket on a personal level. Figuratively they resonate as a symbol of mortality. The composer, his great creation, are living—they inhabit the room, the heart—and yet weightless. At least 'The Creation' is not evanescent. One remembers that Haydn's work ends with the choir joining the soloists in thrilling praise of the perfection of God's new world.

'Madame De Sévigné Writes to Her Daughter' metaphorically condenses the famous seventeenth century letters by the artifice of the Claude Glass (the slightly convex tinted mirror which shaped a large scene into a neater, mellowed view), much as Mme de Sévigné herself reflected the gossip of court intrigue, family and artistic matters and national affairs. Not only is there life in her letters, but her letters are life itself. They can exhibit the kind of nuances that the 'great talkers' cannot, for they are not enslaved by rhetoric but enfranchised by truth: 'It is our art to know the borders of a leaf. / Half singing is the breath. Unstressed the details.' In Mott's poem, Madame de Sévigné claims 'I see as in a Claude Glass all of France, across this moving / like waterboatmen on a sepia lake, the postboys'. Her urge is constantly for news from her much loved daughter: 'Your absence is too much compelling. / Your absence is the passion of my life.'

Yet given the vagaries of the postal system, the rhythm of their correspondence has been upset ('first you were cured, after fell ill'), which allows de Sévigné to illustrate Michael's point that, with love and parental concern, acceptance is finally a prerequisite of distance:

'I rest content. Continue where we paused, my daughter.'

In 'Bruno in Prague' he introduces another theme that interests him: the dangers inherent in belief. Here the 'heretic' Bruno is pursued by Papal agents across Europe ('each hiding place more obvious than the last'), his philosophy, his cosmology destined to lead him—if the 'logic' of the chief defender of the 16th century church, Bellarmine, has his way—to the stake, with its 'air too hot to breathe'.

Painting has always been a subject of deep interest for Michael, given his mother's sculpture and his father's art collecting. A number of his poems, unsurprisingly therefore, deal with paintings and artists, including 'Not-So-Secret Lives: Homage to Tissot', which begins ideally with the fated words, 'Talented to the point of no return'. Here the artist's demise, however, is a result of infatuation. The poem perfectly captures the 'storm in tea cup' *haut monde* tattle that was occasioned by Tissot's affair with one Mrs. Newton. His foreigner's indiscretion is evident in his rashness:

> Her sensuality is veiled, but not at all uncertain.
> It was a secret she but hinted at, yet he reveals it.
>
> To paint his love was one thing. To exhibit her, another.

The poem perfectly captures the narrow world of 'envy', the erotic frisson of its being. What interests the poet—aside from the satiric possibilities, the ironic edge to his delivery—is his recognition that somehow the finished work transcend the hubbub that sank it socially: 'Then what power translates them / a little beyond storms, his talent and her beauty?' 'Not-So-Secret Lives' becomes, finally, an oblique study of what we may call perspective, or time.

Part two of the draft of Michael Mott's *Conspiracy* attends to 'Landscapes, Innocent and Implicated' and I preface my comments on it with one of the poet's own:

> Many of my poems begin with questions that test my surroundings. My "haunted landscapes" (of Cornwall, the American Civil War, etc.) are redolent of battle, the repercussions of a crime or an atrocity remain to disturb and threaten. It may be a small disturbance or a fully developed threat. Something is wrong here. What is false? Camouflaged? Unjust? What has been deliberately excluded and why?

Mott relies on the resonances of language to help him and his readers to puzzle out answers. This finds an echo in the epigraph, 'wrongly attributed to Cicero', where a crime scene is interrogated in terms of its security. The disturbing mood is established immediately with 'Land Left Over, Subsicivus', in which a perfectly ordinary pool scene is made ominous by rendering the sight of surveyors' flags in bullfighting terms; they become the banderillero's decorated darts.

In 'Too Much Blood on the Sidewalk of the Via Paternostro', the poet wanders Palermo and watches as

> They re-staged a mattanza, whole tunas rose
> white eyed, twisting as if on a wire
> running in blood. Not this blood.

Given the dreadful deaths of these huge fish, the word 'mattanza' has entered the Italian vernacular as 'massacre'. The poem's ambiguous ending invokes past crimes—the mafia? the allied invasion of 1943?—especially given the earlier reference to wrought iron balconies as 'witnessing' and washing hanging, 'like hanged men, women'?

In Michael Mott's poetry the contemporary world has only an illusory calm. Beneath it are the ghosts of yesterday. This is again apparent in another Sicilian poem, 'Torre Salsa', which uses Montale's memories and makes reference to the Furies who once 'had strung the air / with screams like wires.' This is a beautiful, rough landscape indifferent to the grip of a violent past:

> Things other than amphoras spilled
> what ran into sand like wine
> and went underground
> to gurgle in the gutters
> of dreams, one generation
> after another.

The cuttlefish bones (ossi di sepia) are both the scoured bone on the beach in Mott's poem and also the title of Montale's first collection (1925). It is no souvenir for listening to the sea:

> Is it sensible to ask
> after the crucified slaves,
> the kidnapped women,
> the more recent dead,
> if the Furies
> have opened their talons,
> released their grip
>
> on this particular landscape?

Here he has entered empathetically a dialogue with a poet who suffered with 'the more recent dead' and had turned to the landscape in admiration of its power to remain unmoved at human folly and loss though possessed of 'too much passion / to be contained for ever'.

Travel, for Michael, releases a strong appreciation of beauty, also, and results in some poems that testify to his descriptive gifts. 'Villa Capo Above Sciacca', for instance, is highly evocative of the Sicilian scene, ending with the delightful:

> and the wind blows
> over pot marigolds,
> their colour, rooftops
> of the encroaching city.

Closer to home is the delicacy of 'The Quay', with its pun on 'catspaws' which both captures the water ripples and the potential deceptions in relationships:

> In the white gloom
> we rest our elbows on the railing
> and talk to our reflection on the water.
> Little the risk at this late date
> of catspaws in our friendship
> however the rain distorts
> and jiggles that double portrait

The two friends have turned their backs on the town, but clearly not on each other. At times, to the observant, nature provides the entertainingly surreal. In 'Powder Mountain' beetles are 'drops of metallic ink'. In the Netherlands, 'A View of Alkmaar' reveals the following:

> A boy stands midway on a bridge,
> the bicycle he leans on
> leers back in giant spectacles

Another characteristic of Michael's poetry is his willingness to explore a thought that seems fanciful, but proves to have an inner logic. At such times his tone adds the requisite gravity to balance it. In 'Birthplace'

> A slab or two
> might speak of Kafka if it were the habit
> of masonry to guide, repeat the same ideas
> over and over—'we very stones, exactly,
> were here, exactly, when Austria—Hungary held
> the Old Town Square, and there was born, exactly…'

The repetitive exactness of bricks is their 'nature', but here they contrast with the bewilderment of Kafka's protagonists, just as their sturdiness is the antithesis of his characters' tenuousness. (One might add the thought that a mischievous reference to the little tyranny of tour guides is also being suggested by the adverb 'exactly'). This same seemingly rational tone is heard in 'Enclosures', where

> The canal is a matter of maps.
> You accept it for what it is
> even on silent afternoons,
> confirmed by the different bitterness
> of bryony and woodsmoke,
> a stench of backwater.

The reasonableness of the first two lines here is subverted by the 'bitterness' and 'stench' that follow. It may be a fact that one cannot access the canal from 'here', but exploration is frustrated anyway.

Attempting to unravel a mystery—another kind of frustration—is the effect of a longer poem, 'Postcard from Pougues-Les-Eaux', which is intrigued by a very old picture postcard that has come into the poet's possession. He is fascinated by the view, by what can be seen at the meeting of streets, 'simply a view with two vanishing points'. Despite the 'simply', it is the perspective that provides the figurative conceit in the poem: the Sartrean choice, Oedipus at the crossroads. The poet puzzles over other aspects of the old photo: the hotel, the coach, the woman with a parasol. He attempts to read into the body language of the woman, into the coach's movement; he attempts to explore shadows, the weather. Ultimately though, it is what is missing that stimulates regret: the unused roads are, by analogy, the failure of experience, for the owner, 'never wrote on the back, / never posted the postcard'. The postcard from Pougues-Les-Eaux, however intriguing its view, is ultimately a quiet tragedy, since it represents the unlived.

'Serious Games' is the title of part three of *Conspiracy*. Here there are six longer poems, the longest of which is 'The Glass Soldier', which is based on two ancient Roman board games, involving glass pieces and dice. In Mott's poem fourteen, twelve line stanzas of irregular length enact the game initially to the accompaniment of children's voices. In the course of reading we inhabit the world of the glass soldiers, their fragility being an image of war. The games are played as military exercises and consequently cruelty is their medium. In board games actions are decisive, results merciless. One soldier is 'Taken':

> I stammer number,
> rank and name.
> The same two fetch a hammer,
> bag of nails.

Another returns through Rome's old southern gateway, 'Porta Capena', to its dilapidated present where he remembers, 'the room above that once / kept quiet about our love'. Cynicism is the vernacular of veterans. So, a third articulates the connection between board games and the rule of empire, a fourth philosophises: 'At the end /of the day, eh, Marius? / You have only your wounds to show.'

There are moments of rest, too, moments of brotherhood and beauty. In the twilight in the park in 'Exchange of Prisoners':

> Look, I will let you
> take back your pieces
> for old friendship's sake.
> One memory for another.
> Ah, between trees of the avenue
> in the still pale panels
> go Tanagran figures,
> women I loved.

If there are shades of David Jones in the poem, there are also moments of Browning; the wistful regret here is reminiscent of 'A Toccata of Galuppi's'. And then it is back to war and the non-coms in a harrowing image:

> Every mother's son
> will be replaced alright
> by one night's mattress bashing
> in the slums.

The glass soldiers are not without their ghoulish side. In 'The Gleamers':

> Scavengers work the field
> bending over the dead
>
> for the whitest teeth
> for the loveliest laughter.

Finally, however, 'The Glass Soldiers' are not soldiers but instruments of wars throughout time—Marathon, Austerlitz, Gettysburg—and 'The Gaming Board' takes us to 1949 and Michael's own national service stint, to the deserted barracks square at Shorncliffe Camp.

Another of Mott's preoccupations is evident in 'Ricordo' (Memories): his traveller's fascination with an alien community. The poem is a meditation on the passage of man through time, via the sepia photographs that once decorated Italian railway carriages. Here sepia portraits of cathedrals, straw-hatted figures and horse drawn vehicles were testament both to tradition and to the technical innovation of the camera. As photographic portraits

> Their light, embalmed in Egypt,
> never was corrupted; flesh was frail
> and marble, as if the mice had eaten
> dark veins of gorgonzola.

After this fantastical simile, the poem ends by redeeming experience, by forging a link with past and present, when Michael imagines some 'sun-quarried village on a distant hill', where these rites of passage still take place and are recorded, 'as one late generation more settles in amber'.

For his imagery alone Michael Mott would be a poet worth searching out, but there are clearly other reasons. In 'Making One's Peace with the Place' he writes:

> Open to enormous spaces, of skies, of the sea:
> not limited to these, you feel proportionate ache,
> beginning with arthritis, but not limited to this
>
> in wild old age, when joy flies pirate colours, all
> the excitement over things

One does not have to have the pleasure of knowing Michael to enjoy his 'excitement over things'; reading his verse would be enough.

***

With Michael's permission I end with one of my favourite more recent Mott poems:

Flavia

Twenty mouthfuls of halibut
or else red mullet
rolled in porcini dust.

Flavia shakes the seas out
between Etna and Vesuvius
or south of Hekla.

Her guests have the best
and freshest, scaled
in stones, a feast and
a marine mosaic

with an amphora
of old, well stoppered
sea cold Chian.

TED HUGHES IN BOUNDLESS SUBURBIA

> You were a new world. My new world.
> So this is America, I marvelled.
> Beautiful, beautiful America!
> – '18 Rugby Street'

To Ted Hughes what was marvellous about America was Sylvia Plath. The country itself depressed him with its conformity and consumerism. Aside from the serious impetus given to his career with the publication there of *The Hawk in The Rain* (1957), America made, arguably, no impact on his poetry at the time of his residence (June 1957 to December '59). That is to judge from his second collection, *Lupercal* (1960). In his last book, *Birthday Letters* (1998), America did surface, but then rather as contexts for his brief life with Plath.

I said 'arguably' above because on December 3rd 1959 Hughes wrote of the state of mind that had produced *Lupercal*, 'this type of exile has driven me to nostalgic themes, and altogether I feel as if my brain had been bound up in sewn leather. Most of the poems are metaphors for this state of psychic hibernation.' There is no real evidence, I think, that American 'exile' actually drove Hughes to nostalgic themes, even though the book was written almost exclusively in New England. Nor is Hughes's 'psychic hibernation' evident from reading the poems. In fact 'hibernation' rather gives it away as being an intuition regarding the natural world.

Probably, his comment had been a way of underlining Hughes's disenchantment with his experience of Massachusetts, with the American way of life. Inevitably, however, the alien circumstances of a new 'home' and the homesickness attending it contributed to the intensity of *Lupercal*. This is entirely consistent with the poet's 'exile' and a desire to identify with his rural Yorkshire past. In *Lupercal* Hughes stood metaphorically on home ground, in living among the themes that would always excite his imagination, ones that put him in touch with earlier or alien sensibilities. What is unarguable is that although America was for Hughes, he was not for it.

The story of how he came to be there is now as much legend as a Hughes poem; in fact, it is a Hughes poem. He met Plath, an American on a Fulbright Scholarship to Cambridge to read English, at a party given to inaugurate the 'St Botolph's Review' on the 25th February 1956. Plath, an academically high achieving Bostonian with a late professor-father and some early publication credits ('Seventeen', the 'Christian Science Monitor') was recovering from a breakdown. Hughes, a working class, Yorkshire Grammar school boy and then Cambridge graduate, had grown up with a special feeling for the myths of the Upper Calder Valley, where he was born.

The two married four months later. Plath spent time trying to promote her husband's poetry (while working on her own stories), sending out the manuscript of *The Hawk in the Rain* and other American submissions which, by the end of July, had resulted in acceptances for Hughes at 'Poetry' (Chicago) and 'The Nation'. In January 1957 'Poetry' also printed six of Plath's own poems, 'The Atlantic Monthly' her poem 'Pursuit' (Hughes as panther, she as prey) and 'Granta' a story, 'The Wishing Box'.

Plath's intention, as she told her mother, Aurelia, that same month, was to teach. Hughes had no real interest in being an academic, she said, whereas she had a 'need to get a self-respecting teaching job in America'. Plath ideally wanted to prove herself before returning to Smith, so she attempted to obtain posts with other American colleges, but her *alma mater* was the one that finally made an offer. She would teach three sections of Freshman English each term for a salary of $4200 a year.

In late February they received word that *The Hawk in the Rain* had won the New York Poetry Center competition and would be published that summer by Harper. 'I am so happy *his* book is accepted *first*,' Plath declared selflessly. Her focus turned to the teaching. In July she was to write 'I need very badly to work: to feel I can, and can teach.' Hughes was more circumspect about their plans. He wrote to Plath's mother and brother, Warren, five months before they sailed: 'Sylvia reads out your long fascinating letters. I'm getting a very definite idea of America—of your America from them.' He did not of course indicate whether favourable or not. Their plan, anyway, involved spending a year there before moving on to Italy. Hughes became aware that the prospective move raised his status in England. To his older brother, Gerald, he confided in May 1957: 'America is waiting with arms open... Over here one or two literary nabobs are saying very flattering extravagant things about me, seeing that America has as it were snatched me from under their nose. This is very different from the life I led a year or more ago.'

In June 1957 Plath completed her B.A. at Cambridge University, after which they sailed on the Queen Elizabeth 11, arriving in New York on the 25th June. In Wellesley, Greater Boston, Plath's mother held a reception for them, her wedding gift a seven week vacation in a cottage at Eastham, Cape Cod. Hughes arrived at a good time, as leading periodicals on both sides of the Atlantic were taking his poems: 'The Spectator', 'The TLS', 'The Nation', 'Poetry', and 'Harper's'. He had already learnt that *The Hawk in the Rain* had been chosen as the London Poetry Book Society autumn choice.

It should have been a massive incentive. On Cape Cod they were living in 'a little wooden house in a Christmas tree forest', writing in the mornings, cycling to the beach in the afternoons, reading in the evenings. Somehow, though, the world seeped in as an irritant. Criticisms of what Hughes perceived to be the American way regularly appeared in his letters. To Gerald, he wrote late in June of the rat race there, of his feeling that success depended on superficial sociability. On the other hand he supposed, 'It's good for me to be surrounded by a world from which I instinctively recoil. I mightn't waste quite so much energy here.' Even then he conceded liking a fraction of his experience. Typically it involved firstly the wildlife, but then he admitted 'the real American phenomena is the kindness of these folk'. He even included the literary reviews, which he felt less snide than the British.

In August Hughes returned to criticism in a letter to his sister, Olwyn, 'This is my main impression of America—it is a temporary expedition... And everything is a temporary fixture.' Again he qualified himself, acknowledging that it might be different for Americans in this 'boundless suburbia'. His attitude had not been helped by his feeling that they were living at someone else's inflated expense. In late August he admitted: 'At first the cost of the place $70 a week so got on my nerves that I couldn't do anything. A too-costly article paralyses my appreciations. It paralysed Sylvia too.' They idled, then suffered 'a black week' or so.

Although Plath admitted to feeling 'a bit blue' on Cape Cod, her problem involved frustration with her own work rather than American culture. On July 17th 1957 she wrote, 'if I am not writing, as I haven't been this last half year, my imagination stops, blocks up, chokes me, until all reading mocks me'. As she had Hughes to delight in, such moods came and went. She did have a clear sense of her problem: 'The prose is not so easy to come into maturity as the poetry which, by its smallness & my practise with form, can look complete. The main problem is breaking open rich, real subjects to myself.' The prospect of teaching seemed both her fear *and* salvation. It would give her 'a sense of reality', much needed because 'I have had the most unfortunate hap: the bright glittery youth from 17 to 20 and then the break-up and the dead lull while I fight to make experiences of my early maturity available to my typewriter.'

The start of Plath's academic term had taken them to accommodation at 337 Elm Street in Northampton, Massachusetts. Again Hughes felt uncomfortable, not liking the 'provincial' nature of the town. With Plath teaching, he told his friend Lucas Myers in October 1957 that he had never experienced such difficulty in writing: 'I sit for hours like the statue of a man writing'. American life had disturbed his balance. Two years would be their 'stretch' there.

Plath found teaching initially difficult while always wearying. Added to that, eventually, were her suspicions about Ted's behaviour around the Smith girls, despite his dismissal of them as 'Chromium dianas'. Plath, who naturally individualised them, came to like the girls she taught, though the pressures at Smith undermined her health. Her journal entries testify to this. On Feb 5th 1958, for instance, she writes, 'Am I living half alive? I am so tired, after last night, & the mound of dishes, after the pressure-cooker of patchwork last minute preparation.' Teaching involved endless preparation, as well as sixty-five papers to correct every other week. Ill with pneumonia for the last week of the fall term, she determined she would not seek employment for a second year.

In November Plath wrote of living in Boston the next year as a housewife. In February 1958 she noted in her journal, 'I want all my time, time for a year, the first year since I was four years old, to work and read on my own. And away from Smith. Away from my past, away from this glass-fronted, girl-studded and collegiate town.' All this confirmed Hughes's feelings about their American lives. They would go further away. They would take their friend W.S. Merwin's advice to return to England, away from academia, into the arms of the BBC and the literary magazines.

Although Hughes had quickly soured on America, he recognised that things were relative. As he explained in a letter to a friend in early 1958: 'You are right about England. It is a vicious doghole for the most part.' He would concede that 'America is about as insufferable as England, but there are possibly more compensations.' One was some employment for his cynicism. He had engaged to teach a half year (fourteen weeks) at the University of Massachusetts, knowing 'the money will get us back to Europe nicely next summer'. He began at the end of January with a 'Great Books' course, with two classes three times a week and a class of freshmen twice a week, a heavy load like Plath's, though he enjoyed teaching Milton.

They moved into a Boston apartment in September for their second year. They were determined, Hughes reported to Olwyn, to live off their savings and whatever came in from their writing ('I'm going to waste no more time on employers'). Their fifth floor apartment might be small, but had two bay windows at which they could work, with views of the Charles River, the park, and Louisburg Square on Beacon Hill. Plath also took part-time employment as a secretary at Massachusetts General Hospital, then at Harvard University. She audited Robert Lowell's poetry writing course at Boston University, returning to therapy with Dr Ruth Beuscher, her psychoanalyst from McLean Hospital.

In late summer Hughes was writing optimistically of putting Northampton behind them and of loving Boston. His teaching had been 'amusing', his wife 'unique to live with'. Early in 1959 he even declared, 'I think I've finally got my day into shape.' This may have been connected in some way with their decision to leave the country. Although he wrote of the calm life there, according to his first biographer, Elaine Feinstein, who knew the poet, 'When Ted recalled their life in 9 Willow Street, Boston, he remembered their closeness as more destructive than supportive. They were entering a difficult period of their relationship, in which Ted, for all his sympathy, had begun to feel that Sylvia's desperation to write, and her inability to cope with rejection, was too much for him.' And even worse, 'While he admired what Sylvia was struggling to achieve, he was beginning to fear that she shared the oppressive American urge to conform, which he so disliked.'

Still, there were idiosyncratic poets to enliven their time. Hughes reported that Robert Frost 'talks continually, & very amusingly'; Marianne Moore is 'delightful', 'engaging', though 'the worst reader alive'; Robert Lowell, as well as been their best poet under fifty and subject to manic attacks, is 'about the most charming & likeable American I've ever met'; the 'chipper' Allen Tate 'has wasted his gifts more or less on whisky & criticism—though his criticism is quite interesting'; John Crowe Ransom is 'a little whimsical gentle-man' who in the wholeness of his poetry resembles Shakespeare; William Carlos Williams has: 'an intense unique flavour when he's good… His irreverence for poetic tradition is a bit like the pig in the palace, though'.

These poets were exceptions. Generally Hughes felt that, 'poetic language is getting to be more or less consonant with HEP [hip] talk over here. I can't describe the terrifying lack of inwardness about America.' Poetry seems to have disappointed him in this period, as he wrote vividly in June: 'Most poetry, particularly modern poetry, is quite without…wholeness—men make their whole style out of one filament of the thick rope of human nature.'

During the summer, the Hugheses bought a $65 tent and an air mattress. Borrowing Plath's mother's car, they took off for an American adventure, their nominal destination Aunt Frieda in California. They intended a national parks trip, taking them first to Ontario and then back across the border through Michigan, Wisconsin, South Dakota, Montana, Wyoming, Utah and on to California. They returned via Arizona (the Grand Canyon), Louisiana, Tennessee (a visit with Myers's family) and Washington DC. Their brief visit to Yellowstone National Park, Wyoming, had resulted in some scary bear adventure (and later a Plath short story) which involved one ransacking the Hughes' car, for biscuits and oranges.

Then, from 9 September to the 19th November, they were guests at Yaddo, the artists' colony in Saratoga Springs, New York, where Plath completed *The Colossus* and Hughes *Lupercal*. After Yaddo the Hugheses had Thanksgiving with Plath's mother before returning to England on the SS United States. Plath had decided she too was happy to return to England. 'The fastness & expense of America is just about 50 years ahead of me', she offered by way of explanation.

With the help of the Merwins, they found a small flat at 3 Chalcot Square, close to Primrose Hill. Plath shortly after gave birth to their first child, Frieda. In the following year, after *Lupercal*, her collection *The Colossus* would appear. During Hughes's absence his reputation had continued to grow, such that on his return he declared: 'I found myself really quite famous and was deluged by invitations ... the B.B.C which I had been trying to penetrate for years, suddenly received me as a guest of honour.'

Yet it had come at a significant cost to his sense of mental well-being. He had written to Daniel Huws, in that letter of December 3rd, 1959: 'Another year in America would have worked a permanent petrification on my glands'. The poems written over there, he described to Huws as being 'all gravely crippled by the awful emotional dryness I've felt'. The 'emotional dryness' he charged America with inducing presumably contributed to the creation of Hughes's distinctive poetic voice, since with *Lupercal* he produced his most intense collection. It would be fanciful to see the poet as akin to 'the frozen one' in the book's last poem, 'Lupercalia', which invokes the intercession of a deity on behalf of fertility:

> Maker of the world,
> Hurrying the lit ghost of man
> Age to age while the body hold,
> Touch this frozen one.

There is poetic fertility enough in the book. What comes out of *Lupercal* is an older pre-Latinate world—an older northern England largely—mediated through the vision prompted by that fertility festival of ancient Rome. The collection reeks of brute power in its subjects (recurrently hunting and husbandry) and in the telling. According to his biographer, Jonathan Bate, Hughes later reflected that in the poems 'View of a Pig', 'Pike' and 'Hawk Roosting', 'his distinctive poetic voice, with its "broad inclusive concentration" on the facticity—the intractable condition—of the world, truly emerged'. These are poems of the natural cycle of predators ('Killers from the egg: the malevolent aged grin'; 'I kill where I please because it is all mine') and their prey.

Although there are American moments in *Remains of Elmet* (1979) and *River* (1983), we come more fully back to the biographical Hughes and America in *Birthday Letters*—the book of Plath—in which he put aside his mask of impersonality. Published just months before his death in 1998, it contained upwards of twenty poems that deal with their time in America, about a fifth of the collection.

These poems show us a Hughes fated by an early blindness: 'In those days I coerced / Oracular assurance / In my favour out of every sign'; intimidated by his first sight of America ('the weird shameful pain of uncrumpling / From wartime hibernation'); and trapped in his thought-world ('Sitting at a book—a strange prisoner, / Pacing my priceless years away'). We see Plath as besieged by doubts at her teaching: ('What a furnace / Of eyes waited to prove your metal.'); also trapped, even in her writing year ('Freed from school / For the first time in your life, this was the cage / Your freedom flew to'); and painfully sensitive to rejection ('You wept / And hurled yourself down a floor or two / Further from the Empyrean'). America is caught in snatches: 'The cindery air, / A waft of roasted iron'; 'the scabby humped pelt of the prairies; 'a landscape / Staked out in the sun and left to die'; 'the bats in the Karlsbad caves, / Thick as shaggy soot in chimneys'.

This terminal collection proved a sensation when it was published. Elaine Feinstein astutely noted that 'Part of the determinism of *Birthday Letters* comes from the sense, with hindsight, that the service of poetry had to take some of the blame for what happened to their love.' We see it directly in the poem 'Flounders', which recounts a 'tiny' symbolic adventure—being almost lost at sea—which reverberated in their marriage. The poem ends:

> It was a visit from the goddess, the beauty
> Who was poetry's sister—she had come
> To tell poetry she was spoiling us.
> Poetry listened, maybe, but we heard nothing
> And poetry did not tell us. And we
> Only did what poetry told us to do.

Ted Hughes and Sylvia Plath did what poetry told them to do. In December 1959 it told them to leave America. Inspiration and worse lay back in England.

Part Three: Critics here & there

ALEXANDER HERZEN IN LONDON

> Decembrist blood! We are taxed
> for their visions. The earth
> turns, returns, through cycles
> of declamation
> — Geoffrey Hill, 'Scenes with Harlequins'

> There is no town in the world which is more adapted for training one away from people and training one into solitude than London. The manner of life, the distances, the climate, the very multitude of the population in which personality vanishes, all this together with the absence of Continental diversions conduces to the same effect.
> — Alexander Herzen

'Copperfield is Dickens's *Past and Thoughts*.' So wrote Alexander Ivanovich Herzen (1812–1870) of his brilliant, tidied memoirs and the comparison holds to a degree. A revolutionary socialist and feared publicist, Herzen also turned out to be an exact contemporary of our great novelist. Like Dickens, Herzen was indefatigable in his pursuit of social progress, a writer of great skill if a man personally disappointed in life. For twelve years the two shared London, but while Dickens memorably explored its nooks, crimes and idiosyncrasies Herzen remained aloof. His great cause remained the Russia from which events had exiled him. Nevertheless in London, between 1857 and 1867, Herzen made his most important contributions to the political climate of Russia, firstly through his newspaper Kolokol ('The Bell'), then with *My Past and Thoughts* (1862).

In the words of his contemporary champion, Isaiah Berlin, Herzen was 'the rarest of characters, a revolutionary without fanaticism'. Herzen's hard-won political philosophy still has relevance in the populist mayhem of Europe today: we must not sacrifice the present in the name of the future. 'That suspicion of pat solutions, millennial goals and providential ends continues to offer a secular liberal vision whose watchword is reason.'

It had been a long, for the most part grim journey for Herzen. The illegitimate son of a Russian nobleman and a German mother, he was raised as a valued child—hence the surname given him ('herz'/'heart')—though soon sensitive to his circumstances while out of sympathy with his unapproachable father's treatment of the serfs. With his lifelong friend, the poet and activist Nikolay Ogarev, Herzen grew to venerate the memory of the aristocratic, reformist victims of the Decembrist Revolt of 1825 ('those brilliant young men who emerged from the ranks of the Guards, those spoilt darlings of wealth and eminence who left their drawing-rooms and their piles of gold to demand the rights of man, to protest, to make a statement for which—and they knew it—the hangman's rope and penal servitude awaited them'). Herzen ascribed his feeling for human dignity and his political awakening to those victims of the autocratic Tsar Nicholas 1.

At the age of seventeen he entered Moscow University, intent on studying the natural sciences as well as philosophy and literature. Herzen's scientific training turned out to be crucial in teaching him a disciplined methodology, one without a narrative of universal design. It proved curiously life-affirming for the young man. 'We must be proud of not being needles and threads in the hands of fate as it sews the multicoloured cloth of history', he later wrote. With others he hotly embraced radical ideas founded on German romantic idealism, on Hegel, Goethe, Schiller and on the Utopian socialism of Saint-Simon and Fourier, though these ideas had no practical outlet, given the strict censorship of the time. Nor were the influences completely assimilated: 'We preached everywhere and all the time. What precisely we preached, it's hard to say. Our ideas were vague, we preached the Decembrists and the French Revolution, then we preached Saint-Simonism and the same revolution, we preached a constitution, a republic.'

Unlike the Slavophils who proclaimed a conservative, anti-Western philosophy for Russia and an Orthodox faith, Herzen counted himself among those radicals who admired Western ways, who wanted to follow a democratic, secular path. He also idealised the Russian peasant, seeing in his self-organizing village communities the hope of socialism. Eventually he steered a course between the liberal gradualism that attracted sometime friends like the novelist Turgenev and the violent anarchism of his lifelong friend Bakunin ('Artillery, on the whole, was apt to excite him').

In preparation for the day he would inherit his father's large fortune, Herzen intended to take the necessary course of joining the civil service. However, association with other compromised radical students brought his name to the attention of the authorities, resulting in his being exiled from Moscow to Viatka (Kirov), to Vladimir, and finally, after injudicious remarks in a letter to his father, to Novgorod on the orders of the Tsar.

In 1838 he had secretly married his devout cousin, Natalie Zakharina. Their marital troubles, terminated pregnancies and two affairs (his casual, hers intense) ultimately accelerated her early death. In 1842 Herzen, allowed to return to Moscow, again threw himself into intellectual circles there. 'Bakunin and Belinsky stood at their head,' he remembered, 'each with a volume of Hegel's philosophy in his hand, and each filled with the youthful intolerance inseparable from vital, passionate convictions.'

At the death of his father in 1846, the brilliant but now unfocused Herzen petitioned for foreign travel which was granted the following year. He, his wife and family left for Western Europe, where he would remain despite being ordered home. At first Europe greatly appealed to Herzen, now a writer and journalist freed from the asphyxiating censorship of his homeland. He travelled in both Italy and France. Being a realist, he also managed, with the help of Baron Rothschild, to have most of his money brought out of Russia. As he wrote in *My Past and Thoughts*, 'It would be stupid and hypocritical to affect to despise property in our time of financial disorder. Money is independence, power, a weapon.'

The abortive 1848 revolutions in Europe caused him to re-evaluate his faith in socialist movements, which had failed liberty and justice. For Herzen Russia had nothing to lose, while Europe was reluctant to risk what it had gained: 'The liberals are afraid of losing their liberty—we have none; they are nervous of interference by governments in the industrial sphere—with us the government interferes with everything anyhow; they are afraid of losing their personal rights—we have yet to acquire them.'

The revolutions also influenced his view of human nature. He came to expect a little less of his fellow man. Now he began to believe that 'if people would sooner or later get the idea of saving themselves rather than saving the world, of liberating themselves rather than liberating humanity, how much they would do towards saving the world and liberating mankind'. As Lesley Chamberlain wrote, in her first-rate philosophical history, *Motherland* (2004), 'He matured as a reformer rather than a revolutionary.'

Personal unhappiness further depressed his spirits when his mother and his second son drowned and Natalie died of tuberculosis. Unpopular with the French authorities, Herzen arrived in England at daybreak on the 25th August, 1852 with his son Sasha and the Austrian General Haug, having left his two younger children in Paris with friends. London did not appeal to Herzen at the outset, except as a respite from intimidation. On his arrival and for some time after he was, by his own account, grieving for his late wife, frustrated, weary and humiliated. London, he soon felt, catered perfectly for the lover of solitude since the weather drove people indoors, which suited his mood. The frequently dense yellow fog—an invasive paste of fish smell and sulphur—led the wife of one German associate to urge her husband to carry a revolver. When Herzen did venture outdoors it would be simply to walk, to linger on Thames bridges, to read newspapers or 'stare in taverns at the alien race'. He might have been one of Dickens' loiterers in *Bleak House*: 'on the bridges peeping over the parapets into a nether sky of fog, with fog all round them, as if they were up in a balloon, and hanging in the misty clouds'.

Tedium and anonymity were on offer in London; Herzen felt grateful for them. Having taken a sculptor's house near Primrose Hill, then 'one of the remotest parts of the town', he began his 'hermit-like seclusion'. He remained, as he always would, an outsider, observing but never in anyway intimate with the English, never speaking the language well. Yet even distant familiarity bred some insight. He would write of the country in contrary moods: 'Life here is about as boring as that of worms in a cheese. There is not a spark of anything healthy, vigorous or hopeful' (1855). And then, 'England, with all the follies of feudalism and toryism which are peculiar to it, is the only country to live in' (1857).

Part of the attraction to a man much hounded by the authorities in his own country was the English tradition of liberty, which surprised him even as London beggary appalled. He was shrewd enough to see that 'The Englishman's liberty is more in his institutions than in himself or in his conscience', and fascinated with the extremes of free speech allowed by the British. Yet according to Isaiah Berlin 'he could not altogether like them: they remained for him too insular, too indifferent, too unimaginative, too remote from the moral, social and aesthetic issues which lay closest to his own heart, too materialistic and self-satisfied'.

Sometimes respite is all that is needed. Gradually Herzen 'came to love this fearful ant-heap', this brutally uncaring city. Even the policeman who would once have roused his anger, now 'only adds a feeling of security'. No doubt his adjustment to London hastened his decision to bring over his family in 1853. To provide for them Herzen rented a large house in Euston Square. In May Olga (2½) Tata (8) accompanied by their nurse joined the 13 year old Sasha. Herzen hired a German tutor, Malwida von Meysenbug (herself having fled from Prussian revolutionary associations).

Whatever intimacy he might achieve outside the family would be with émigrés. Initially the resting revolutionary had little positive to say about his fellow exiles, these actors in the 1848 revolutions who suffered their privations with pettiness, commemorating their glory days, defending their actions, and fundamentally lacking direction. 'Dead men burying their dead', he described them in a letter of 1855. Nevertheless, these were to be his associates. Over the next few years he gradually gravitated toward circles led by other internationally famous dissidents like the Italian revolutionary activist Giuseppe Mazzini and the French socialist, Louis Blanc.

The Poles proved to be the first to draw Herzen to a public platform, in November 1853, to commemorate their 1830 insurrection. ('In all their actions and in all their poetry there is as much of despair as there is of living faith', he wrote). Given the English tolerance of the period, he felt welcomed again at an 1855 event, albeit that England and Russia were at war in the Crimea. This commemorated the failed revolutions of 1848. Ultimately Herzen's alliance with the Poles would not serve his reputation abroad with Left or Right, given the anti-Polish feelings in Russia after the January rising of 1863, which resulted from the Russian imposition of land reforms and conscription.

Herzen turned to publishing in Russian to live 'in the atmosphere of Russia'. In his memoirs he acknowledged that: 'Three years of life in London had fatigued me. It is a laborious business to work without seeing the fruit from close at hand; and as well as this I was too much cut off from any circle of my kin. Printing sheet after sheet with Chernetsky and piling up heaps of printed pamphlets in Trübner's cellars, I had hardly any opportunity to send anything across the frontier of Russia. I could not give up: the Russian printing-press was my life's work.'

In April 1856 the poet Nicolay Ogarev, Herzen's lifelong friend, arrived in London with his second wife, Natalie, and they soon settled into a *ménage à trois* at Herzen's. The two men had shared a youthful promise to see the Decembrists' goal of freedom for the serfs realised. A year later they began publishing 'The Bell' (Kolokol). According to his account, Herzen's thinking had been as follows: 'A book remains, a magazine disappears; but the book remains in the library and the magazine disappears in the reader's brain and is so appropriated by him through repetition that its seems his very own thought.'

'The Bell' appeared at a critical time in Russian history (1857– 67) which saw the death of the autocratic Nicholas I, the emancipation of the serfs and the accession of the more liberal Alexander II. The paper, which was mostly smuggled into Russia, provided a platform for much needed liberal thought. It offered essays, investigative reporting, news items, letters and poetry, utilising the talents of such writers as Herzen himself, Proudhon, Garibaldi, Michelet, Mazzini, Lermontov and Bakunin. 'The Bell' became highly influential for a time. Herzen even cited an anecdote in which Russia's Secretary of State had grumbled to the Empress, 'Complain to the Tsar, do what you like, write to The Bell, if you must'. He announced himself proud of the fact that 'we were the fashion, and in a tourist's guide-book I was mentioned as one of the curiosities of Putney'. Yet Herzen had no illusions about fashion knowing, after the emancipation of the serfs in 1861, his newspaper would lose some of its impact. He judged that 'Seven years of liberalism had exhausted the whole reserve of radical aspirations.'

His other main claim to our attention is *My Past and Thoughts*. This epic, personal history was the product of sixteen years of labour, parts being published here and there in Russia (1854) then subsequently in France, Germany and England. According to Herzen's Soviet editors, his commitment to the project had been inspired by his desire to justify his conduct to posterity, especially in light of his behaviour over his wife's affair. The claim to fame of *My Past and Thoughts* lies partly in the telling and partly in its relevance. As a work of literary art it benefit from an engaging style. With uncharacteristic modesty, Herzen explained that unlike the elevated expression of mandarins, 'We simply talk; for us writing is the same sort of secular pursuit, the same sort of work or amusement as any other.' Fortunately for the reader, the charismatic Herzen was always a renowned talker.

As to the pragmatic value of *My Past and Thoughts*, Herzen explained in an article in his earlier paper, 'The Polar Star', that 'the publication of contemporary memoirs is particularly useful for us Russians. Thanks to censorship we are not accustomed to anything being made public, and the slightest publicity frightens, checks, and surprises us.'

The London Herzen remained highly influential for a time, therefore, his work admired by great Russian writers like Tolstoy, Dostoevsky and Turgenev. Then, beset by critics and mellowing with age, his influence slowly declined. Towards the end, he became more critical of his initial utopianism and of his belief in the potential of the Russian people, nor did he rely on the rationality of any group or nation. 'It is not enough to despise the Crown,' he wrote on one occasion, 'one must not be filled with awe before the Phrygian Cap'; on another, 'Whatever rubbish peoples demand, *in our century*, they will not demand the rights of a grown-up.'

After London, he moved to Switzerland and to France. On the 22nd January, 1870 Turgenev wrote from Baden-Baden to a mutual friend that he could not hold back his tears at the news of Herzen's death: 'I suppose everyone in Russia will say that Herzen should have died earlier, that he had outlived his usefulness. But what do these words mean?' Turgenev was aware that certain ideas cannot go out of date, like the ones referred to in Herzen's preface to his son, in *From Another Shore*: 'I give my blessing to your journey in the name of human reason, of individual liberty and of brotherly love!' Charles Dickens might have coined the epitaph for Herzen and his generation when he wrote, 'The men who learn endurance are they who call the whole world brother.'

NOTE:

For the interested reader Alexander Herzen is the subject of several brilliant books beside his own (abridged) masterpiece, *My Past and Thoughts* (1982): Isaiah Berlin's *Russian Thinkers* (1978), E. H. Car's *The Romantic Exiles* (1933) and now Aileen M. Kelly's biography, *The Discovery of Chance: The Life and Thought* of Alexander Herzen (2016). (It is a route Tom Stoppard took to produce his flawed but fascinating theatrical trilogy, *The Coast of Utopia*.) Berlin and now Kelly have done more than anyone to secure the continuing relevance of the tireless Russian polemicist, but here the last word belongs to him. Educated and bruised by a lifetime of struggle on behalf of his fellow countryman and his wayward family, Herzen offered this memorable poetic vision, 'Art, and the summer lightning of individual happiness: these are the only real goods we have.'

THE SHELF LIFE OF ROBERT BROWNING (1812–2012)

> Such, British Public, ye who like me not,
> (God love you!)—whom I yet have laboured for
> – *The Ring and the Book*

Of all popular poets Browning was and is one of the least popular and, of great poets, the most controversial, condemned by his voluminous lesser work, his difficulty, his facility with blank verse, his clotted style, his facile optimism (Chesterton described Browning as 'the only optimistic philosopher except Whitman') as well as the overestimation of his peers, which led to the launch of the Browning Society in 1881 dedicated to a study of his 'teachings' in religion, philosophy and science. Even his personality has been called into question, for as a social being Browning could be loud and windy. That heroic diner-outer Henry James first met Browning in 1877, finding him 'chattering and self-complacent', and wrote of 'a kind of vulgarity'. Later, James posited the idea of two Brownings in his short story "The Private Life" (1892): the sensitive artist and the conventional social hearty.

There is some truth in the above allegations. However, Browning stands as one of our major poets because his best verse—and there is enough of it—is vigorously accomplished and more relevant to our sensibilities even than it was to those of his own time. As a precursor of Modernism, he bookends the late Victorian world with psychological realism, as surely as Sir Walter Scott did the early nineteenth century with his influential romanticism. In Browning's case the influence could be said to be twofold. Firstly, as Modernists Ford and Pound recognised, he brought the brash and sometimes buckled idioms of man into poetry as surely as Wordsworth had. The poet himself flaunted his "hip to haunch" openness, as he does in *The Ring and the Book:*

> Do you see this square old yellow Book, I toss
> I' the air, and catch again, and twirl about
> By the crumpled vellum covers,–pure crude fact

Secondly, in his exploration of human motivation he learned from his master, Shakespeare. His monologues turn soliloquy into narrative. He is novelistic in an era of novelists. As an early champion, the author of *Browning's Message to His Time* (1890), Edward Berdoe noted:

> Browning is always subjective, and probably will never appeal to any great extent except to the class of mind which delights in the analysis of our motives.

It was a small class even in the poet's own day. At the height of his fame in the 1880s Browning earned about £100 a year for his poetry, whereas Tennyson earned in the region of £5000.

Yet Browning has the power. As with Shakespeare, so with Browning; the lines read aloud brilliantly: the dramatic ('I am poor brother Lippo, by your leave! /You need not clap your torches to my face'–'Fra Lippo Lippi'); the intimate ('But do not let us quarrel any more, / No, my Lucrezia; bear with me for once: / Sit down and all shall happen as you wish'—'Andrea del Sarto'); the humorous:

> Where a friend, with both hands in his pockets,
>   May saunter up close to examine it,
>   And remark a good deal of Jane Lamb in it,
> 'But the eyes are half out of their sockets;
> That hair's not so bad, where the gloss is,
> But they've made the girl's nose a proboscis:
> Jane Lamb, that we danced with at Vichy!
> What, is not she Jane? Then, who is she?'
>   – ('A Likeness')

Browning has a genius for dramatic intimacy in his characterisation. We see it in 'My Last Duchess' or 'The Bishop

Orders His Tomb at Saint Praxed's Church' ('Vanity, saith the preacher, vanity! / Draw round my bed: is Anselm keeping back? / Nephews—sons mine… ah God, I know not! Well—'). His preoccupations create wonderful atmospheres, evoked by fine detail. In "Meeting at Night", for example, we have 'A tap at the pane, the quick sharp scratch / And blue spurt of a lighted match'. Browning was also capable of shrewd aphorisms ('incentives come from the soul's self; / The rest avail not.') and could produce the perfect image:

> All we have gained then by our unbelief
> Is a life of doubt diversified by faith,
> For one of faith diversified by doubt:
> We called the chess-board white,—we call it black.
> – ('Bishop Blougram's Apology')

Familiarity might stale them, but that should not detract from their brilliance. With all this there is the musicality, the great virtuosity with metre and rhyme in such poems as 'A Toccata of Galuppi's' (1855):

> Oh Galuppi, Baldassaro, this is very sad to find!
> I can hardly misconceive you; it would prove me deaf and blind;
> But although I take your meaning, 'tis with such a heavy mind!

Where Browning might fall foul of contemporary taste is in his treatment of women. That may be why there seems to be a current swing toward Tennyson amongst students. Tennyson is warmer, more conventional, more mellifluous and melancholic, more cinematic. Browning's women tend to be the enigmatic or the abused (like Pompilia Comparini in *The Ring and the Book*, the last Duchess, the lover of Porphyria). Where they are sexualised, it is with what is described, nonsensically, as the 'male gaze'. There is upper and lower class eroticism:

> Your soft hand is a woman of itself,
> And mine the man's bared breast she curls inside.
>
> > So! keep looking so—
> My serpentining beauty, rounds on rounds!
> —How could you ever prick those perfect ears,
> Even to put the pearl there! oh, so sweet—
> > – 'Andrea del Sarto'
>
> Saint, forsooth! While brown Dolores
> Squats outside the Convent bank
> With Sanchicha, telling stories,
> Steeping tresses in the tank,
> Blue-black, lustrous, thick like horsehairs
> > – 'Soliloquy of The Spanish Cloister'

Matthew Arnold wrote to his mother on June 5th, 1869, hopeful of posterity's indulgence: 'It might be fairly urged that I have less poetical sentiment than Tennyson, and less intellectual vigour and abundance than Browning; yet ... I have perhaps more of a fusion of the two.' Arnold was wrong about being 'likely enough to have my turn, as they have had theirs', as far as the poetry was concerned. Browning, loved or unloved, has come down to us with *some* force intact, at least that of his dramatic monologues and a handful of lyrics. In his meditation on Browning, after the great poet was buried in Westminster Abbey, (a secretly contrite?) Henry James judged him to have captured the interests of the English:

> His voice sounds loudest, and also clearest, for the things that, as a race, we like best -the fascination of faith, the acceptance of life, the respect for its mysteries, the endurance of its charges, the vitality of the will, the validity of character, the beauty of action, the seriousness, above all, of the great human passion.

Some of these 'interests' have fallen away since 1890, but the vitality remains. Browning's is the perfect voice for this age of leak, twitter and tweet. To celebrate his bicentenary, take him down off the shelf. You may like him yet, '(Marry and amen!)'.

MATTHEW ARNOLD LECTURING AMERICA

> I proceeded to Chicago. An evening paper was given me soon after I arrived; I opened it, and found under a large-type heading, '*We have seen him arrive*,' the following picture of myself: 'He has harsh features, supercilious manners, parts his hair down the middle, wears a single eye-glass and ill-fitting clothes.' Notwithstanding this rather unfavourable introduction, I was most kindly and hospitably received at Chicago.

While Americans may have needed a really good five cent cigar at the end of the nineteenth century, they did not need Matthew Arnold. According to Lionel Trilling, 'He was culture, and he was suspicion of democracy; he was amenity, urbanity, the Church of England and aristocratic manners.' They were therefore ambivalent about his coming, 'eager to learn from him', but fearing 'that this great exponent of criticism would—criticize.' Americans had every reason to be wary. Arnold's preconceived notions of the country had been unfavourable.

At the time of his lecture tour (October1883 to March 1884) Arnold remained a presence in English letters, though the great work lay behind him. Far behind were the melancholy poems of his first incarnation, collected most recently in *New Poems* (1867). Of more immediacy were his elegant but hard hitting *Essays in Criticism* (1865/88), *Culture and Anarchy* (1869) and the influential religious criticism of *Literature and Dogma* (1873). Arnold had been Professor of Poetry at Oxford, still worked as a school inspector and was always in need of money. Incorruptible, however, he remained a cosmopolitan who loved to lecture his countrymen on their failings from his classical eyrie, one quite open to doing the same to Americans, whom he considered transplanted middle class Englishmen.

He had in fact used them as a negative example while berating his own countrymen, the three failing classes he judged Barbarians (the aristocracy), Philistines (the middle class) and the Populace (the working class). In an 1860 essay, 'Democracy', Arnold wrote of his fears for England, that in the absence of the guiding hand of an engaged aristocracy, the time would come when the middle class will rule for a while and 'will certainly *Americanise* it. They will rule it by their energy, but they will deteriorate it by their low ideals and want of culture'. Privately he had confessed on another occasion, 'I have not much faith in the nobility of nature of the Northern Americans.'

Yet all in all, Matthew Arnold's lecture tour would turn out to be a success. Educated Americans liked nothing more than a good lecture (except perhaps a sermon) while the press enjoyed having a controversial celebrity to alternately valorize and vandalise. Besides, there were two Matthew Arnolds in America: the critic and the man. As Trilling judged of the man, 'Arnold handled himself very well. He was simple and sweet-tempered and never let himself be rattled; and indeed there was, on the part of the Americans, always an overplus of courtesy, friendliness and admiration to reassure him.'

The idea for the tour developed at a London party in 1883 where Arnold delighted Andrew Carnegie, the Scottish business man who had made a fortune in iron in Pittsburgh. His invitation to the Arnolds to stay in his New York hotel provided a catalyst to the enterprise. Since money had always been a pressure on the critic, in that year he had reluctantly accepted a Civil List Pension. As he told the M.P. John Morley, he felt troubled at the prospect of taking a further £250 a year on top of his salary of almost a thousand. He was correct in recognising 'there will be murmurs, and that I shall lose something of the "benevolentia civium," of which I have not too large a stock to begin with'. His American critics were among those who detected a mercenary note in this behaviour (The Chicago Tribune had made 'a violent attack on me for lecturing for "filthy lucre"', he reported).

Arnold had other cause for trepidation about the lecture tour, acknowledging to one correspondent that he hated the idea of going to America and to another that he disliked lecturing and 'living in public'. Nevertheless he now had an agent, Mr Richard D'Oyly Carte of the Savoy Theatre, and seventy speaking engagements to attend to with, as it turned out, very little in the way of free time. His itinerary involved New England cities and campuses in November and December, then Philadelphia, Washington, Richmond and Baltimore. In January he was to travel to Madison, Chicago and St Louis and return through Toronto, Ottawa, Montreal and Quebec, to sail from New York on March 8th 1884. Fortunately, everything had been comfortably arranged.

He would later joke that he felt like an actor, because he and his family travelled at reduced fares with tickets that had printed on them *Matthew Arnold Troupe*. Sometimes he would leave his wife, Flu, and elder daughter, Lucy, to the delights of a city and their hosts, while he journeyed to lectures. Despite the separation, he could report that 'My travelling is done in great comfort, as the agents send a man with me (a gentleman), who finds out my trains, takes my tickets, sees to my rights, and saves me all trouble.' He wrote to his younger daughter, Nelly, that whereas the others 'had both got tired of knocking about. I was used to the sort of thing in my old inspecting days, and bear it pretty well, but there is more of it than I expected'.

The only real discomfort for the family had attended their passage out. They had sailed on the steamship *Servia* from Liverpool to New York on October 13th, first having to endure a gale on the Atlantic, before they could settle into a voyage which ended on the morning of October 22nd in New York City, when they were driven to The Hotel Windsor on 5th Avenue at 46th Street.

Eight days later Arnold gave his first lecture, 'Numbers', to an audience of almost 2000. He received an ovation, though the truth was his voice did not carry and some left Chickering Hall perhaps ruing the dollar admission charge. He had the same problem reading his poetry at Harvard on November 12th, but had already determined on a course of action. He told his sister, Fan, that on the first occasion although being 'badly heard' his reception had been warm: 'There is a good deal to be learned as to the management of the voice, however, and I have set myself to learn it, though I am old to begin'. By December he was telling another correspondent that the English papers made too much of his early inaudibility, which 'never really endangered my success' and that the elocution teacher had been a professor interested in his work, who took him to the empty hall, giving him advice against dropping his voice at the end of sentences, 'which was the great trouble'.

To read Arnold's best essays, as Stefan Collini neatly explained, 'is to find oneself in the company of a mind of such balance and sympathy that we come, without really noticing, to see experience in his terms, and, unusually, to think the better of ourselves for it'. This is generally *not* the case with the American lectures or the related essays that followed. There are convincing moments—as in his assessment of Emerson or at times in 'Numbers'—but when he turns to America as subject, Arnold can be as nonsensical as profound. He is observant on American manners, but the conclusions he draws are hammered to fit his English model.

'Numbers' is actually a reflection on its subtitle 'The Majority and the Remnant', where Arnold is considering 'the prospects of society in the United States'. His argument, via examples of the Athenian and Jewish states, is that the judgment of the majority is eternally unsound but that throughout history there has been too small a 'remnant' of the right thinking to guide it. With larger states the remnant is, of course, larger, but again it may not be in a position to save the nation. In France, for instance, a certain licentiousness has undermined the enterprise.

Turning at last to his hosts he worries 'that in a democratic community like this, with its newness, its magnitude, its strength, its life of business, it sheer freedom and equality, the danger is in the absence of the discipline of respect; in hardness and materialism, exaggeration and boastfulness; in a false smartness, a false audacity, a want of soul and delicacy'. He concludes on a note of wary optimism nevertheless, putting his faith in the size of the remnant, its moral, German ancestry, its Puritan discipline and 'unbounded' size.

On a personal level Arnold reported himself impressed with 'the way in which the people, far lower down than with us, live with something of the life and enjoyments of the cultivated classes'. For example, as a celebrity he had caught the attention of the hotel staff, barbers and the like. His peers were not always as approving of him. One view, quoted in Park Honan's biography, came from the naturalist John Burroughs: '[Arnold's voice is] more husky, more like a sailor's, I thought... When he talks to you he throws his head back ... and looks out from under his heavy eyelids, and sights you down his big nose—draws off, as it were, and gives you his chin. It is a critical attitude, and not sympathetic. Yet he does not impress one as cold and haughty.'

In fact he could be quite sociable. Arnold came to enjoy the experience of lavish homes (one belonging to 'a Delano married to an Astor') and 'immense' receptions, as well as cosier visits with people the family had known in England. Whatever the milieu, Arnold's critical faculties remained alert. The lifestyle of a professor and widower he observed, albeit in a 'small way', was better than in England: 'Still, what we call a gentleman has a tremendous pull in the old world—or at any rate in England—over the gentleman here.'

In Boston Dr. Oliver Wendell Holmes, who introduced his lecture, told Arnold 'he had never seen such attention and interest'. New England proved highly hospitable, as he wrote to his sister: 'The strength of the feeling about papa, here in New England especially, would gratify you; and they have been diligent readers of my books for years.' He had been persuaded that 'Literature and Dogma had certainly done good here in New England; at a critical moment it has led many back again to the study of the Bible, and has given reality to the study of it.'

Arnold gave his 'Literature and Science' lecture at Princeton on November 20th, the following day in New Haven, Connecticut, repeating it in Newport, Rhode Island, then at venues in Massachusetts, including Salem. The essay begins again in the classical world, with Plato's disdain for working trades and professions, before turning to 'the needs of modern life' and to whether science is the key. He proceeds with a favourite device of quoting some misinterpretation of his ideas, on this occasion by Thomas Huxley, which he then clarifies and, in effect therefore, revitalises. Arnold's famous reference to literature as a 'criticism of life' had been read by Huxley as referring to *belles lettres* alone when, actually, Arnold explains, he was referring to 'all knowledge that reaches us through books' which includes—and he spells the names out for the purpose of this lecture—'Copernicus, Galileo, Newton, Darwin'.

Having earlier established his relative ignorance in specific matters of science, this is meant to suggest his credibility as an informed commentator on more general issues. His conclusion is that the student of the natural sciences will live the incomplete life, failing to acquire the understanding of conduct and beauty which 'the student of humane letters' is heir to. 'Letters will call out their being at more points, will make them live more.' Looking to the future, Arnold sees that letters will survive the current clamour for a science curriculum.

On November 27th he wrote home that he was bored with repeating the lecture, though given the interest in education issues, 'There is a perfect craze in New England for hearing it, but I hope the big cities will be more rational.'

Arnold showed himself particularly pleased with Richmond, Virginia, where he spoke at Mozart Hall on December 20th, after lecturing in Washington. There he stayed with former general Joseph Anderson, CSA, who had owned the Tredegar Iron Works which supplied the South with munitions during the Civil War. Part of the appeal lay in the fact that Richmond, former capital of the Confederacy and now a city of 70,000 with 'rather ragged streets', had a strong attachment to England and 'for the better sort of English people'. His hosts, the Andersons, behaved generously and his lecture had been delivered to the 'old families'.

Arnold had one reservation. After he 'insisted' on being taken to some of the 'coloured schools' he observed that 'People like the Andersons are very kind to their negroes, but don't yet like their being educated'. This had brought him to realise that 'The astonishing thing is the line of demarcation between the white and the negro in the South still.' If that concerned him, he remained otherwise admiring of the State and determined to return to the South if he came back to the country, which he did—and to visit California, which he did not.

He returned to Baltimore before going to Washington. There the Arnold family called on President Chester Arthur at the White House. Among other meetings with notables, he saw and wondered at Mark Twain, dined with Henry Adams and William Dean Howells, talked with Oliver Wendell Holmes and the historian George Bancroft, plus a number of Civil War generals as well as Lincoln's secretary, John Hay. He also listened to the controversial clergyman Henry Ward Beecher, once the target of his criticism.

Arnold's third lecture, 'Emerson', had been the one he worked on during the voyage over, when he had managed to read 'half a volume of Emerson's *Essays*, and the two thick volumes of his correspondence with Carlyle'. He told Fan from New York that the Emerson lecture had been 'pretty well formed in my head', though he worried about when he was going to find the time to write it out, given the daily press of visitors from 8.30 a.m. to 10 p.m. But he managed and it begins wonderfully: 'Forty years ago, when I was an undergraduate at Oxford, voices were in the air there which haunt my memory still. Happy the man who in that susceptible season of youth hears such voices! they are a possession to him for ever.' For Arnold, those voices included Cardinal Newman, Carlyle's and Goethe's—and Emerson's. His intention in the lecture is to re-examine this last 'friend of my youth', since 'any veils of illusion which we may have left around an object because we loved it, Time is sure to strip away'.

Reluctantly—in the harsh light of return—Arnold finds Emerson wanting as a poet (merely interesting, not 'impassioned'). He similarly fails to impress as a great writer ('his style has not the requisite wholeness of good tissue') while as a philosopher he fails to 'evolve'. Nonetheless, his reputation is secure, his pre-eminence in prose is the like of Wordsworth's in poetry, because Emerson is 'the friend and aider of those who would live in the spirit'. In his 'conviction that in the life of the spirit is happiness', Arnold assures his audience, lies his greatness.

On December 8th, 1883, writing to Fan again, he reports a letter from Emerson's daughter in response to his Emerson talk, saying 'she found not a word in the lecture on her father to give her pain'. He would not, he says, read that in public, since many do criticise the lecture for not praising the great man 'all round'. In England he reckons he will be accused of being excessive in his praise, but 'I have a very, very deep feeling for him'. He had passed it to his wife and daughter, so that they all visited the family in Concord.

These letters to Fan and his daughter, Nelly, share something of the minutiae of Arnold's days in America and his ambivalence about the landscape. So, after the Emerson lecture and a reception at Andover: 'Scolloped oysters (with iced water and coffee) at eleven, when the people are gone; bed, called at seven, breakfast at eight with a party of professors and their wives—coffee, fruit, fish-balls, potatoes, hashed veal, and mince pies, with rolls and butter.'

Arnold also observed that although the winter weather could be bitter, the country was much better prepared for cold than England. On his way to Buffalo he concluded, after seeing a sledge with horses stopped on a frozen lake, that the scene was picturesque, and yet 'the picturesque is the rarest of things here, and the people have even less of the artist feeling than we have'. Having said that, he declared himself much impressed by a view of Niagara, clipping a little off an arborvitae shrub as a remembrance. Lake Michigan impressed him, too, as a 'glorious sight' and the hills of the Ohio valley were 'really picturesque'. The more he saw the more Arnold grudgingly amended his perspective, though he reacted largely negatively to towns like St Louis—of great interest to him in some ways—for 'in the buildings there is the want of anything beautiful which in all the American towns depresses me'.

By February this note of discontent had entered his correspondence more often. He reported that 'the desire to be back rises sometimes into a passion'. He felt exhausted, touched his milk with a little whisky as a stimulant, though resolutely maintained a public cheerfulness and sense of humour. To Nelly he wrote on January 21st, 'The papers get more and more amusing as we get west. A Detroit newspaper compared me, as I stooped now and then to look at my manuscript on a music stool, to "an elderly bird pecking at grapes on a trellis"—that is the style of thing.'

Arnold did, however, visit Canada with pleasure (and just a little controversy, in angering the Catholics of Montreal by recommending greater liberalism from them) before embarking for home. He declared at the end of his stay in America: 'I feel myself utterly devoid of all disposition to write and publish my intuitions, real or turbid.' Of course he did, by way of the *Discourses* and the essays which appeared posthumously as *Civilization in the United States*.

His *Discourses in America* (1885) is comprised of the three American lectures. In his preface Arnold sought a moment for reconciliation where it might be needed: 'I am glad of every opportunity of thanking my American audiences for the unfailing attention and kindness with which they listened to a speaker who did not flatter them, who would have flattered them ill, but who yet felt, and in fact expressed, more esteem and admiration than his words were sometimes, at a hasty first hearing, supposed to convey.'

Three years after the *Discourses*, in the month of Arnold's death, the 'Nineteenth Century' published his essay 'Civilization in the United States' and that same year a Boston publisher issued *Civilization in the United States: First and Last Impressions of America*. It has four pieces: a two-part essay on 'General Grant: An Estimate'; 'A Word about America'; 'A Word More about America'; and 'Civilization in the United States'.

'General Grant: An Estimate' is a long, leisurely account of the Union Commander's *Memoirs*. It was intended to introduce English readers to 'a man of sterling good-sense as well as of the firmest resolution', who writes in a straightforwardly admirable and modest manner. Although Arnold admired Grant even more than Lincoln, the one 'tic' he finds in the *Memoirs* is Grant's penchant for boasting about his nation. It is a national tic, seen at its most ludicrous—in Arnold's eyes—in the nation's obsession with claiming the existence of an American literature, when everyone must realise, 'We are all contributories to one great literature—English Literature.'

In 'A Word about America', written prior to his first visit, Arnold ruminates on American civilisation. He finds himself sharing Edmund Burke's belief that 'the Americans of the United States are English people on the other side of the Atlantic'. The difference is, 'That which in England we call the middle class is in America virtually the nation.' This does not bode well for, though Americans are industrious and religious, he argues that the 'type of life of which our middle class in England are in possession is one by which neither the claims of intellect and knowledge are satisfied, nor the claim of beauty, nor the claims of social life and manners'. Never the defeatist, Arnold ultimately offers an encouraging proposition for elevating the nation: 'A higher, larger cultivation, a finer lucidity', is to be achieved by the establishment off secondary education for boys between the ages of 12 and 18, with a curriculum 'really suited to the wants and capacities of those who are to be trained'.

The Arnolds proved a little more concerned about 'A Word More about America', since their elder daughter now lived there. He wrote on the eve of publication 'that it would be unpleasant for you if it gave offense over there; but I do not think it will. Mamma, however, is in a thousand agonies.' Nevertheless he published it in James Knowles's British monthly magazine, 'Nineteenth Century'.

It begins with a reference to Arnold's Chicago visit of the year before and offers 'the new and modifying impressions brought by experience'. He will concede that their institutions suit Americans, that they work well (though the tone is lower in American politics than in English politics since it is lacking the distinctions of rank). Arnold will also accept that America is 'not in danger of war from without, nor in danger of revolution from within'. He has realised, he says, that the American 'Philistine' is different from the English one. He grants that 'English aims are confused and our thinking inflexible' and 'how in some important respects', the Americans see and think straight. There is 'the human problem', however, something that has caused an informed, educated person (the diplomat Sir Lepel Griffin) to argue that 'there is no country calling itself civilized where one would not rather live than in America, except Russia'. This Arnold leaves as a cliffhanger.

Written three years later, 'Civilization in the United States' explores the problem: for 'one cannot rest satisfied, when one finds such a judgment passed on the United States as this, with admiring their institutions and their solid social condition, their freedom and equality, their power, energy, and wealth'. Arnold approaches 'the human problem' by first considering what constitutes a 'complete human life'. His answer is a number of elements ('powers'): conduct, intellect and knowledge, beauty; social life and manners.

This raises the question of the 'character and worth of American civilization' (man making progress to his full humanity) and here he concludes that a civilisation must, along with its institutions and culture, be 'interesting'. 'Now, the great sources of the *interesting* are distinction and beauty: that which is elevated, and that which is beautiful.' And here America comes amiss because to Arnold 'There is little to nourish and delight the sense of beauty'. For instance, the country lacks the ancient rural permanence of England (Americans exhausting the land and moving on) and architecturally it is impoverished, its building reflecting only the needs of the middle class.

If beauty is in short supply, Arnold argues, so too is distinction. The best lack it. Hamilton and Washington may have possessed it (the latter without mental distinction) but they were of the 'pre-American age'. Lincoln, a man of many recognised merits, yet fails to have possessed distinction. At the root of this nonsense, of course, is Arnold's patrician sense that what damns American 'elevation' is 'the glorification of "the average man" in a classless society. To Arnold, brash self-praise, 'tall talk and inflated sentiment' are no substitute and the more enlightened (the 'remnant' of the earlier argument) fail to curb this tendency in the national character. Therefore all are doomed to self-deception (witness the pride in the American accent and the notion of American literature, he says). At the end of the article, Americans are left to want 'elevation' and 'beauty' of spirit: hence the 'human problem'.

And so in the end American civilisation did not quite come up to the mark for Matthew Arnold. He could not find it 'interesting'.

Nevertheless, on a personal level things had gone pleasantly well. In fact he would visit again in 1886, to be there with his wife and younger daughter at the birth of Lucy's first 'American' child. Meanwhile, the lecture tour had enlarged his intellectual celebrity and made him some friends, earnt him approximately a year's salary (albeit hardly a triumph of Dickensian proportions), allowed him to indulge in his role as Jeremiah– and changed his perspective very little.

As for America, it had got its response in early. On the 22nd October, 1883—on the day of Arnold's arrival in their city—the New York Tribune had offered the following opinion, 'He is a poet whose fine qualities have never appealed very strongly to the popular sense, and a critic who has addressed himself almost ostentatiously to the refined and cultivated few… he has taken a daring delight in shocking popular prejudices, jeering at popular idols, and showing contempt for the popular intellect.'

FORD MADOX FORD: A FISH IN NOT QUITE THE RIGHT WATER

> He sensed the virgin sucker at once. So we had the stories about Ruskin, and my Uncle Gabriel and my Aunt Christina [Ford claimed to be related to the Rossettis]; the Conrad and James stories; the story of the abbé Liszt's concert and how Queen Alexandra took the beautiful infant Ford on her knees and kissed him; the 'old Browning' stories, and the Swinburne stories; gradually working back through the 19th century. My father was swimming in bliss, although once or twice he looked a little puzzled. And then Ford began telling how he met Byron. I saw my father stiffen.
> – Richard Aldington

Ford Madox Ford (1873–1939), novelist, editor and critic, is one of the great characters of twentieth century literature. Brilliant, generous, tireless in his service to literature and to the work of those he felt talented, he was also widely disliked for an assumed haughtiness, a tendency to self-pity and, especially, an irresistible desire to fabricate, to play fast and loose with facts in the interest of 'impressionism'. Regularly penniless and embattled, Ford lived as a fish in not quite the right water (to appropriate his friend John Galsworthy's self-assessment).

A real sense of Ford comes from his letters, as well as from the novelistic reminiscences written from the last decade of his life: *Return to Yesterday* (1931), *It Was the Nightingale* (1934) and *Portraits from Life* (1937).

One does not have to go as far as to claim, as Ford did in a letter to Herbert Read, 'I learned all I know of Literature from [Joseph] Conrad and England learned all it knows of Literature from me', to accept at least that Ford became a leading influence in Modernism. He produced more than fifty books, including *The Good Soldier* (1915) and *Parade's End* (1924–28). He acted also as the enlightened editor of 'The English Review' (1908) and, in Paris,

'The Transatlantic Review' (1924). Ford's wide circle of acquaintances included most of the most celebrated, late-Victorian and Modernist writers, whom he promoted, including Conrad with whom he collaborated and Ezra Pound, a friend and fellow outsider. An occasional but significant poet, his late free verse with its conversational idiom emerged from archaic Pre-Raphaelite beginnings.

He was born Ford Hermann Hueffer to a German music critic father and an English mother (the daughter of the Pre-Raphaelite painter, Ford Madox Brown, whose influence and connections were formative for the young Ford). After a failed marriage and a long relationship with the Australian artist Stella Bowen—which necessitated he change his name—Ford finally settled in France with another painter, Janice Biala.

An overaged junior officer with the 9th Battalion of the Welch Regiment during the war, Ford endured a breakdown. The fierce shelling had contributed to other health problems. As he explained to the liberal politician C.F.G. Masterman in a letter at the time: 'my lungs were found to be in a devil of a way... partly due to a slight touch of gas I got in the summer & partly to sheer weather'. It little surprise then that the war changed Ford as a man and therefore as a writer. As his biographer Max Saunders says: 'Everything he wrote afterwards is part of a twenty-year attempt to render and to understand the changes wrought by the war in the world and in himself.'

After an attempt at farming in England, Ford turned to Paris and later Provence ('where I have lived for nearly all my spiritual as for a great part of my physical life'). England offered little succour for Ford. America on the other hand offered a more attentive audience and, at the end of his life, a teaching role at Olivet College in Michigan when Ford felt decidedly 'tired of writing for the pot'.

Friendship had always been a difficult business for Ford. Although he *had* friends and was clearly attractive to some women, enemies seemed to proliferate. There were any number of unpleasant descriptions of him, which often conflate appearance with character, including Hemingway's infamous sketch in his

Twenties memoir, *A Moveable Feast* (1964) which begins, 'It was Ford Madox Ford, as he called himself then, and he was breathing heavily through a heavy, stained moustache and holding himself as upright as ambulatory, well clothed, up-ended hogshead.'

More atmospheric is the comment by Iris Barry, the poet, who recalled the wartime Ford as 'Semi-monstrous, bulging out of his uniform, china-blue eyes peering from an expanse of pink face, pendulous lower lip drooping under sandy moustache as he boomed through endless anecdotes of Great Victorians, Great Pre-Raphaelites, Henry James'. To such caricatures, with their insinuation of deceit, grotesqueness, and tiresome self-serving, can be added the charge of egotism. T.S. Eliot's commented to Ezra Pound in an October 1922 letter concerning future issues of 'The Criterion': 'I certainly do not want [Ford] for several numbers yet because there are a great many other people beside myself who do not like him: the difficulty, if I asked him, would be to get some of his really best work but not simply his egotistical meanderings about his own service to English literature.'

'Ford lied like blazes', Malcolm Cowley admitted privately. Others on the writer's side rationalized the habit as a badge of creativity. His companion Janice Biala explained in a 1979 interview that 'he used exaggerations to heighten a truth, as one does in any art', adding, 'So when Ford said that Conrad threw the teacups into the fire, it was not the literal truth—it was a creation of the ambiance, the climate of Conrad's passionate rejection of a criticism of Marie Antoinette. This explains some of those famous "lies" of Ford, I think.'

Ford himself often repeated this view, once in a letter to his daughter, 'I don't really deal in facts. I have for facts a most profound contempt. I try to give you what I see to be the spirit of an age, of a town, of a movement.' *Return to Yesterday* begins with a similar disclaimer: 'So this is a novel... Where it has seemed expedient to me I have altered episodes that I have witnessed but I have been careful never to distort the character of the episode. The accuracies I deal in are the accuracies of my impressions.'

Return to Yesterday describes Ford's experiences between 1894 and 1914, using material from *Thus to Revisit* (1921), for Ford was a great reteller of anecdotes. Here we are treated to glimpses of Conrad, of Stephen Crane (who could kill a fly on a sugar cube with the bead-sight of a revolver) and of Henry James (with his 'astonishingly ornate man-servant'). As Arthur Mizener's reckoned in his Ford biography, *The Saddest Story* (1971), nearly all his anecdotes 'illuminate the character of the man Ford is describing, or at least the character Ford believed the man to have'. What we remember are the private glimpses of the great interacting with him. There is, for example, a quirky image of Henry James: 'Once, after I had sent him one of my volumes of poems, he just mentioned the name of the book, raised both his hands over his head, let them slowly down again, made an extraordinary, quick grimace, and shook with an internal joke..... Shortly afterwards he began to poke fun at Swinburne.'

One has to say that the 'garrulous self-esteem' one critic of the time found in the book does not mar *Return to Yesterday*. There *is* outright confession. He tells us, for example, that 'I am one with the struggling millions who cannot read me' and admits that while James disliked his family circle, thinking them bohemian, 'I, on the other hand, considered myself as belonging, by right of birth, to the governing classes of the artistic and literary worlds. I have said that I was not an agreeable young man.' Generally though, confession is flavoured with self-regard. So Ford confesses to his laziness at school, but adds that 'I was always head of my school classes, and the favourite of my masters.' As far as his adult reputation is concerned he concedes that 'England, I knew, would always regard me as, rather comically and a little suspiciously—too damn in earnest.' The effect is to suggest that it is his commitment that has doomed him whereas, as a matter of fact, he has by now mentioned that 'at one period I must have been one of the most boomed writers in England'.

Ford's self-portrait emerges as that of a patient man who has 'suffered from many injustices and slights'. His dedication to literature is total, as 'it is the only means by which humanity can express at once emotions and ideas'. Yet for all his energies he has been doomed to martyrdom: 'As far as I can remember, except for Ezra, not one of the writers whose first manuscripts I printed or whose second efforts I tried to give lifts to—not one of them did not in the end kick me in the face, as the saying is.'

With his next book of reminiscences, *It Was the Nightingale*, Ford's again offers a disclaimer, 'I have tried then to write a novel drawing my material from my own literary age.' He then discloses the novelistic 'wiles' he will employ—techniques which mark his best prose—'the time-shift, the *progression d'effet*, the adaptation of rhythms to the pace of the action'.

The book begins with Ford's being demobbed in an England depressed by the loss of the war generation. He has dealings with editors and writers there (with George Moore and especially Galsworthy) then the action moves to Paris, appropriately enough since the book's opening sentence reads, 'There was never a day so gay for the Arts as any twenty-four hours of the early 'twenties in Paris.' Ford has realised he is 'not English at all', that Art is his nation ('I used to feel in the company of those who were not artists the same sort of almost physical, slight aversion that one used, during the war, to feel for civilians'). Much is taken up with an interesting account of the establishing, running and demise of his magazine, the initial approach having come from Ford's brother, Oliver ('the sparkling jewel of the family whilst I was its ugly duckling').

The author is in his element in Paris's artistic circles, since he prefers Picasso, Joyce, and Gertrude Stein, to the English or classical traditions, though he remarks ruefully at one point: 'My sympathies are altogether with revolutionary work and with no other… But I cannot see that my own work is the least revolutionary. I go on my way like a nice old gentleman at a tea-party.' He recounts observing Stein driving the chariot of her car ('a vehicle of the original model of my namesake'). He listens to Picasso turn on carping admirers. Hostesses invariably bring him into nervous public conversations with James Joyce. He retells an amusing anecdote about Proust and Joyce meeting in a circle of admirers and, not having read each other's books, discussing instead their shared maladies.

The vital importance of art is again a theme in the book, being in Ford's view the only source for humanity to ameliorate itself.

Free from rivalry, he argues that as long as art is accomplished it does not matter who accomplishes it, yet Ford's worries about his literary-self linger: 'all over the world there are, I am aware, gentlemen and ladies lamenting that I don't write as I wrote when I was eighteen or twenty-seven or thirty-six or forty-five. Or even fifty-four'. The fact is also that while the English press greet his work with 'rapture' the reading public often stay away. He wonders if the problem is in his adopted name. Firstly his publishers hated 'Hueffer', because readers are reluctant to buy a writer whose name they cannot pronounce, and then he considers perhaps that 'Ford' had them thinking that his books 'must be about automobiles, or Detroit—or against bankers'.

Portraits from Life: Memories and Criticisms of Henry James, Joseph Conrad, Thomas Hardy, H.G.Wells, Stephen Crane, D.H.Lawrence, John Galsworthy, Ivan Turgenev, W.H. Hudson, Theodore Dreiser, A.C. Swinburne appeared in 1937. Again the book is a 'novel' of sorts: 'I am, that is to say, a novelist, and I want [the 'circle of strong personalities'] to be seen pretty much as you see characters in a novel'. The next page reaffirms his technique, his deepest article of faith: 'For factual exactitudes I have never had much use. I have, I repeat, been trying to make you see these people whom I very much loved—as I want them seen.' We are similarly treated to a restatement of his belief in the centrality of Literature, the writer further shaping his point: 'The novel is a form—is probably the best, or indeed the only form—of education because the really conscientious novelist, all out to render his day, will come nearer to the truth than either the moralist or pedagogue who have always some *arrière-pensée* with which to stultify their instructions.'

The book has an arresting image with which many readers may relate: Of the great writers he says, 'When you read them you forget the lines and the print. It is as if a remotely smiling face looked up at you out of the age and told you things. And those things become part of your experience.' With a novelist's omniscience we learn of James' 'almost panicked resolve to be dazzlingly clear', which leads to his prose being obscured 'in a sort of cuttlefish cloud of interminable phrases'. We read of Conrad's 'curious, Oriental courtiership', how he would 'greet the humblest of human beings with gestures of servility'. We learn that Lawrence 'had so much need of moral support to take the place of his mother's influence' as to keep everyone 'in a constant state of solicitude'. We are treated to a glimpse of Hardy, 'a kind, small man, with a thin beard, in the background of London tea parties' and Turgenev the 'white-haired, white-bearded, and surely beautiful colossus'. Swinburne is rendered as 'beautiful and shining and kind so that when *he* came on the scene, drunk or sober, all was gas and gingerbread and joybells and jujubes.'

This last reference to the sweets refers to the fact that some of these reminiscences are from Ford's childhood, which explains a preoccupation with size—Turgenev's hugeness and the fact that Swinburne's chin is described as not reaching much above the level of the door handle. The young Ford, apparently an attractive blonde child, seems regularly to have been dandled on the knees of greats like Turgenev. Being of the Pre-Raphaelite circle allows the young Ford an amused perspective. So, 'Mr Hunt had a voice like a creaking door, endlessly complaining' and 'Mr. Ruskin fairly hissed like an adder'.

And always there is Ford Madox Ford, larger than life. His chapter on Wells begins, 'Mr H.G.Wells and I must have been enemies for more years than I care now to think of. And the situation is rendered the more piquant by the fact that one or the other of us must by now be the *doyen* of English novelists—though I prefer not to discover which of us it is.' If, as one critic detected, there is a faint flavour of malice in this work, what makes *Portraits from Life* a success is, as V. S. Pritchett noted, that 'Somehow Mr. Ford escaped the peculiar seriousness of his seniors in the period.'

It is always a pleasure reading Ford. The writing is accomplished, exhibiting the kind of craftsmanship, the stylishness he admired in others. At one point he tells us with characteristic hyperbole that by 1890, 'The literary Language had grown perfectly unfit for the communication of any kind of daily thought, or indeed for any kind of thought at all.' Consequently, while working with Conrad, he succeeded in evolving 'a vernacular of an extreme quietness that would suggest someone of some refinement taking in a low voice near the ear of someone else he liked a good deal'.

Finally, ought we to take Ford at his word when he cautions us against making the same *faux pas* that he once did: 'You should never say to a novelist that you prefer his "serious" writings to his fiction though I find that such few novelist friends as I have always say that to me. But novel writing is a sport infinitely more exciting than the other form so that almost all writers would prefer to be remembered by their imaginations rather than by their records'. It probably would be a mistake, but one I would make cheerfully. Like Dickens or Turgenev, the man rivals his fiction. In fact we might well agree with V.S. Pritchett, who suggested in his essay, 'Fordie', that we could think of Ford Madox Ford himself as 'as an incurable and dedicated work of fiction'. Warts and all he is certainly one of the most entertaining.

REMEMBERING WILSON & TRILLING

What chance of a decent posthumous reputation? Edmund Wilson (1895–1972) and Lionel Trilling (1905–1975) were the dominant American critics of the Age of Criticism (in Randall Jarrell's negative phrase). They were frequently bracketed together and Wilson seems to have been the more sensitive to the fact. He ended a 1955 letter to Trilling with 'Yours fraternally in whatever it is that you and I are always supposed to represent', two years later complaining that an English weekly implied that they were mutually exclusive influences. On his part, Trilling responded airily to such misrepresentations: 'Glad to see we are still hand in hand. Always a pleasure to me. Two *general* critics. Two *American* critics. Two critics not *New*—yet, of course, not *old*. It is pleasant to think that Literary History may be preparing to receive us together.' He made light, too, of the English blunder, addressing Wilson in a late reply to the news, as *Dear semblable, dear frère* (his likeness, his brother) which played on Baudelaire's line, later famously taken up in the English-speaking world, of course, by Eliot in *The Waste Land*.

The English critic had got one thing right: they both *had* read Matthew Arnold. In fact Trilling had written an excellent intellectual biography of Arnold and Wilson had encouraged him at a time when the vision of the English poet-critic was considered by many passé. But not to them, as Castronovo and Groth point out in a note to *Edmund Wilson, The Man in Letters* (2001): 'Arnold's *Culture and Anarchy* typifies his method of interpreting the practice of criticism as embracing broadly humanist as well as strictly literary concerns—an interpretation emulated by both Wilson and Trilling.' Literary critics cum moralists, they wrote of novels and even attempted them, but avoided the narrow explication of texts that the *New* Critics thrived on (and consequently spent relatively little time with poetry).

They were, of course, very different critics, from different generations, with different agendas. Wilson was the more catholic in his interests, an independent journalist, critic and editor, Trilling a professor and literary-cultural critic. Wilson had been a facilitator both of modernism and of an understanding of Marxist theory, while Trilling took up Freud and then his place 'at the dark and bloody crossroads where literature and politics meet'—or met during the Cold War. To Wilson criticism was something of an art, to Trilling as much a philosophy. Wilson wrote *of* literature, Trilling, as it were, *through* it. William M. Chace expressed their difference in a lively way: 'Wilson surveyed more from his vantage point of dispossessed old-fashioned American cantankerousness and probity than did Trilling from his position as deracinated, aloof, and inquiring university teacher. But Trilling pursued more energetically than did Wilson the ways in which he could employ the terms of literary criticism to understand the struggle for self-knowledge his reading evoked in him' (*Lionel Trilling*, 1980).

If the British press had in some way confused the pair, worse was to follow in subsequent decades, with both critics being marginalised by changing fashion (and the arrival of 'theory'). In *Lionel Trilling and the Fate of Cultural Criticism* (1986), Mark Krupnick pondered, 'It would require a book by itself to explain how American graduate schools have produced a generation of students so knowledgeable about Georg Lukács, Antonio Gramsci, and Walter Benjamin and yet so ignorant of Van Wyck Brooks, Edmund Wilson, and Lionel Trilling.'

Twenty-five years on Noah Kumin would write, 'The works of Edmund Wilson aren't much in vogue today…. in every college library I've ever haunted, his fat, re-bound volumes of criticism and journals invariably huddle together on a shelf of their own, collecting dust and looking slightly ridiculous.' And Cynthia Ozick—three years earlier—offered the opinion, 'Trilling's stature, once prodigious, is so reduced as to have become a joke to certain young critics who favor flippancy and lightness and who, if they are aware of Trilling at all, have learned to despise what he called "moral realism."'

If we take Trilling's, 'It is pleasant to think that Literary History may be preparing to receive us together' without a shade of irony, then he at least might enjoy finding the two of them in its maw. Once their provocative work avoided or transcended the campus, now it is generally confined there—though like all artists they receive the ongoing prying flattery of biography, letters and publishers' reissues. Such works as Wilson's *Axel's Castle: A Study in the Imaginative Literature of 1870–1930* (1931) and Trilling's *The Liberal Imagination: Essays on Literature and Society* (1950) are still recognised as key texts *of the period.*

Edmund Wilson was born in New Jersey, the son of a lawyer who served as Attorney General for the state, and educated at Princeton, where he knew F. Scott Fitzgerald. He began his career as a reporter and, during the First World War, served in France. He was the editor of 'Vanity Fair', an associate editor for 'New Republic' and a book reviewer for the 'New Yorker'. His services to literature were frequently honoured throughout a long writing life (including the National Medal for Literature in 1966). He helped promote the reputations of Hemingway and Fitzgerald, explained Eliot, Joyce and company relatively early, traced the history of socialism through to the Russian Revolution and, in old age, turned to the Dead Sea Scrolls. His many publications included *To the Finland Station* (1940) and *The Shores of Light* (1952). *Patriotic Gore: Studies in the Literature of the American Civil War* (1962) earned him Alfred Kazin's accolade as 'our American Plutarch'. Collections of his sometimes racy notebooks and letters appeared after his death in 1972.

Wilson once waxed modestly about his achievement, in 'A Modest Self-Tribute' (1952): 'I have tried to contribute a little to the general cross-fertilization, to make it possible for our literate public to appreciate and understand both our own Anglo-American culture and those of the European countries in relation to one another'. His style was open, opinionated, omnivorous, authoritative and sometimes chiding. His voice inspired trust, being independent of fashionable jargon and resolutely out of sympathy with contemporary practice for half a lifetime:

'The old nineteenth-century criticism of Ruskin, Renan, Taine, Sainte-Beuve, was closely allied to history and novel writing, and was also the vehicle for all sorts of ideas about the purpose and destiny of human life in general. The criticism of our own day examines literature, art, ideas and specimens of human society in the past, with a detached scientific interest or a detached aesthetic appreciation which seems in either case to lead nowhere." (*Axel's Castle*)

Later he would return to the theme of a personal detachment. In 'Thoughts on Being Bibliographed' (1944) he acknowledged that for the academic 'the literary man of the twenties [e.g. Wilson] presents himself as the distant inhabitant of another intellectual world'. And then 'The Author at Sixty' begins with his day-to-day frustration: 'I have lately been coming to feel that, as an American, I am more or less in the eighteenth century-or, at any rate, not much later than the early nineteenth.' Actually, Louis Menand, in his essay 'Edmund Wilson in His Times', noted that being no longer bound by his generation (with such luminaries as Van Wyck Brooks and H.L. Mencken) 'gave Wilson much more intellectual freedom than he had enjoyed in his first life, since it allowed him to write on only what he chose. His stature had been established.'

To Michael Dirda, writing in 'The Washington Post' in 2002, 'one doesn't turn to Edmund Wilson for humor or charm' but for what Wilson himself described as "cleanness, precision, ease and force"'. Yet if to Dirda, Wilson was 'the grandmaster of interpretive summary and paraphrase', to James Wood he exhibited 'a rather synoptic voraciousness, as if texts exist to be paraphrased and summarised, to be crushed into clarifying prose'. All critics agree, however, on Wilson's confidence, a confidence we might call patrician, according to John Updike. It allowed for what Norman Podhoretz described in *Making It* (1967) as his 'matter-of-fact professionalism'. Wilson's formidable range of interests was also always acknowledged. According to Colm Tóibín, in 2005, he would write 'about new work, fresh from the printers, while deepening his engagement with iconic figures like James and Flaubert, Ben Jonson and Pushkin'.

However elitist he may sound to some ears, the relaxed Wilson remains infinitely quotable: 'Mr. Hemingway's poems are not particularly important, but his prose is of the first distinction' (1924); 'though I have read only two of [André Malraux's] half-dozen books and am unable to deal with his work in any thoroughgoing fashion, I want to bring this fascinating and profitable writer to the attention of American readers'; of *Finnegans Wake*: 'the book has now been out five years, and it is time that these doubts and inhibitions were dispelled' (1944); and of the Justice Holmes-Harold Laski correspondence: 'This reviewer has read the whole correspondence with never-flagging fascination and has found it the perfect resource for railroad trips and bedtime entertainment' (1953).

Lionel Trilling was born in New York and educated at Columbia University there. He returned to it as a teacher in 1932 and remained throughout his career. His fame came later than Wilson's, being a product of the 1940s through the 1960s. He was also one of the first Jewish intellectuals to be accepted into a teaching faculty at a time when anti-Semitism prevailed even in education. Trilling wrote for a number of magazines including the leftist 'Partisan Review' and was able, therefore, to mediate between the academic and the independent cultural worlds. He was the author of several books of essays, including the influential *The Liberal Imagination* (1950) and *Sincerity and Authenticity* (1972), as well as a critical study of E.M. Forster and the Arnold. In these he recognised that the worlds of literature and politics were contiguous and that the critic's responsibility was to explore the implications of literature in contemporary culture. Trilling's essay titles have a sturdy Freudian/philosophical flavour belying their subjectivity: 'The Mind in the Modern World', 'The Fate of Pleasure', 'Art, Will and Necessity'. Typically they are delivered in polished paragraphs rife with periodic sentences, bearing his inclusive 'we', and 'our' and the graceful deployment of the 'I'.

Trilling's concern with the 'moral nature' of man and the times (the Cold War) was reflected in a number of essays: 'Manners, Morals, and the Novel' and 'Huckleberry Finn' (from *The Liberal Imagination* (1950); 'The Morality of Inertia' and 'Dr. Leavis and the Moral Tradition' (from *A Gathering of Fugitives* (1956)). The word 'moral' provided a key to his lexicon. According to Krupnick, 'One of Trilling's critics wondered why, given his Freudian orientation, he spoke of the "moral imagination" instead of "psychological insight." Trilling's response was that "in literature as well as in life, the psychological is subsumed in the moral…

But in stressing the moral rather than the clinical dimension of Freud's work, Trilling was masking the *political* implications of his particular use of Freud... he was addressing a political-cultural situation, the corruption of America's liberal intellectuals by Stalinism.'

The moral concern is central to 'On the Teaching of Modern Literature' (1961) which illuminated Trilling's approach to teaching students at Columbia in the 1950s, one that involved putting the subject first, but 'since my own interests lead me to see literary situations as cultural situations, and cultural situations as great elaborate fights about moral issues, and moral issues as having something to do with gratuitously chosen images of personal being, and images of personal being as having something to do with literary style, I felt free to begin with what for me was a first concern, the animus of the author, the objects of his will, the things he wants or wants to have happen'.

This approach of Trilling's became highly influential. In conversation with Philip French, the cultural critic Morris Dickstein remembered reading and rereading *The Liberal Imagination* until his copy disintegrated. Traditional literary critics were not perhaps as impressed. Leon Wieseltier, introducing *The Moral Obligation to be Intelligent: Selected Essays of Lionel Trilling* (2000), made the point that Trilling was 'an extremist for thought. This marked his limitation as a critic of literature. He was singularly unstimulated by form and by the machinery of beauty... He did not read to be ravished. He was exercised more by "the moral imagination" than by the imagination. And he grew increasingly suspicious of art.' (We might contrast this position with that of Wilson's: 'writing about literature, for me, has always meant narrative and drama as well as the discussion of comparative values').

In fact, Trilling can border on the literary-apocalyptic at times. So in his 1951 essay defending the 'indomitable' William Dean Howells, Trilling argues that our delight in Joyce, Eliot, Kafka, even Yeats, masters of 'the commonplace as it verges upon and becomes the rare and strange' militates against recognition of Howells. And then this essay, which also invokes Nietzsche,

Hannah Arendt, Mary McCarthy and the Cubists, ends: 'The extreme has become the commonplace of our day... while it endures we are not in a position to make a proper judgment of Howells, a man of moderate sentiments. It is a disqualification that we cannot regard with complacency, for if Gide is right, it implies that we are in a fair way of being disqualified from making any literary judgments at all.'

In another mood, Trilling returns to the inspiring power of literature, as in his famous 1947 essay, 'Manners, Morals, and the Novel': 'For our time the most effective agent of the moral imagination has been the novel of the last two hundred years. It was never, either artistically or morally, a perfect form... but its greatness and its practical usefulness lay in its unremitting work of involving the reader himself in the moral life, inviting him to put his own motives under examination, suggesting that reality is not as his conventional education has led him to see it.'

The relationship between Wilson and Trilling was polite and intermittently interesting to them both, but never close. In 'Edmund Wilson: A Backward Glance' (1952) Trilling wrote of his move to Greenwich Village in 1929 and how he had become an anonymous neighbour of Wilson's: 'Someone had pointed out his apartment to me and I used to take note of his evening hours at his desk.' It provided early encouragement to Trilling as the older critic 'seemed to represent the life of letters in an especially cogent way...One got from him a whiff of Lessing at Hamburg, of Sainte-Beuve in Paris'.

Wilson at the time was editing 'The New Republic' and the two met later in the year when Trilling called to request work as a reviewer. Wilson—lean at the time—gave 'no hint of the engaging appearance of a British ship captain closely related to Henry James which he was to have a few years later'. The quip aside, it could hardly be called an eventful meeting: 'Nor, indeed, did we ever become at all well acquainted after other meetings during the years, but I speak of Wilson in a personal way because he had so personal an effect upon me.'

A dramatic effect, also, in terms of Trilling's *Matthew Arnold* (1939). Their second meeting came at a time when Trilling was most concerned about his choice of Arnold as a doctoral subject and a possible book. Meeting in the men's-room of the New School for Social Research, Wilson had enquired about his progress in such a way as to assure Trilling that he would like to read it. 'It is impossible to overestimate the liberating effect which this had upon me', remembered Trilling.

Encouragement turned to promotion when Wilson reviewed the published book in glowing terms in 'The New Republic' (March 21st, 1939) under the title 'Uncle Matthew': 'Mr. Trilling has thus, if I am not mistaken, written one of the first critical studies of any solidity and scope by an American of his generation. And he has escaped the great vice of that generation: the addiction to obfuscatory terminology.' His review ends generously, 'Mr. Trilling's book is a credit both to his generation and to American criticism in general.'

They were naturally to carp at each other from time to time. In an essay, 'Art and Neurosis', Trilling took to task Wilson's thesis in *The Wound and the Bow* (1941) that art is a product of neurosis and—in the essay mentioned earlier—he corrected Wilson in noting that Stephen Crane was in Howell's debt. On his part, Wilson wrote little about Trilling after his substantial encouragement with the Arnold book. He did not review him again. Only in *The Bit Between My Teeth*, the 1965 collection of pieces, is there a swipe at Trilling repeated use of the word 'massive' in some 'Partisan' piece.

There were, though, brief letters of literary business over the years: on Arnold, on Edward Lear (and the word 'runcible), on Robert Frost, Marx's Palmerston pamphlet, *Mansfield Park*. Wilson once enquired about a teaching job and, on another occasion, requested a review of a Shelley biography. He wrote in appreciation of Trilling's review of Fitzgerald's, *The Crack-Up* (1945), which Wilson had edited. He also wrote to thank Trilling—a tad remotely—for defending in court Wilson's *Memoirs of Hecate County* against obscenity charges ('The Doubleday lawyer has just written me that you appeared at the trial of my book and testified in our behalf.' Trilling modestly protested that he could hardly 'take credit for having gone through anything unpleasant', either then or at the hands of the press).

In later life Trilling wrote and talked of Wilson upon request. Correcting the critic Jeffrey Hart in a letter of 1963 he described Wilson's 'old-fashioned (anti-centralizing) liberalism, conditioned by patrician rearing and a strong infusion of the artist's and the gentleman's anarchism'. It might seem an ingratiating view of the world, he suggested, though he was critical of it, 'for I find it lacking in depth and breadth, and energy'. Wilson, he supposed, 'rather dislikes the very idea of society and is "for" only certain of its occasional fruits—amenity, art, and idealistic and honorable people'.

In the early seventies—in a radio interview with Philip French (transcribed in *Three Honest Men*)—Trilling expressed the view that academic critics had found nothing of 'special importance' in Wilson or been influenced by his example. This was contested by Jason Epstein, Wilson's publisher, who pointed to Alfred Kazin as a self-confessed disciple. Epstein saw the problem really as the difficulty in pigeonholing such a brilliant, wide-ranging writer as Wilson. Trilling did at least assure his listeners in that interview of his own respect for the man. He saw Wilson, he said, as a Sainte-Beuve rather than a Matthew Arnold, 'as a disinterested, detached commentator on literature in all its aspects'. (This was an idea Wilson had attempted to pre-empt in 'A Modest Self-Tribute', though he had to concede that his influences—Arnold, Henry James and Leslie Stephen—may have in turn been influenced by Sainte-Beuve).

In *The War Against Cliché: Essays and Reviews 1971–2000* Martin Amis wrote of the centrality of literary criticism to his group in the early seventies: 'I read it all the time, in the tub, on the tube; I always had about me my Edmund Wilson—or my William Empson. I took it seriously. We all did.' The days of the greatly influential critics, like Wilson, Trilling and F. R. Leavis, may have gone forever. As we all know, the critical impulse not only survives but is exercised ceaselessly, thanks to social media. These days the professionals (i.e. the paid) go largely unheeded, except by a small coterie. Perhaps it was ever thus—or worse. Trilling observed in 1952: 'The image…of the man of letters…no longer pleases and commands us.' And Wilson himself wrote—as long ago as

1928—in 'The Critic Who Does Not Exist', 'It is astonishing to observe, in America, in spite of our floods of literary journalism, to what extent the literary atmosphere is a non-conductor of criticism.'

PETTED AND FUSSED OVER: WILLIAM EMPSON & AMERICA

William Empson had just the right level of English eccentricity to be the delight of friends and biographers. His neck beard, bohemian habits and unconventional marriage were worth a thousand anecdotes, although what gives the man his posthumous staying power, of course, is his brilliance as a critic and poet. Frank Kermode once wrote of those who 'experienced the exhilaration and daring of Empson's early books'—*Seven Types of Ambiguity* (1930), *Some Versions of Pastoral* (1935) and *The Structure of Complex Words* (1951). For thirty-five years Empson (1906–1984) made frequent visits to America. It was there he made his reputation as a teacher, after early fame and notoriety in England. America also enabled him to refine his ideas, promoted his poetry and played a recurring financial role in Empson's life from the end of the war onwards.

After an initial 1938 visit, Empson held seven lucrative appointments in the United States between 1948 and 1982, mostly teaching summer schools at universities there. He also contributed articles to prestigious American publications. What appealed to Empson's hosts were his immense talent, his profound seriousness about art, his good humour and his thoroughly British eccentricity (with its East Asian flourishes). What appealed to Empson about America—salary aside—was the readiness with which academics and students embraced him and his ideas. Empson's crusading study of the ambiguities in language had helped create the critical spirit of the time, for the close reading of a text (called New Criticism) had begun to sweep campuses.

The legend came earlier and at Cambridge, where Empson switched from mathematics to study with I. A. Richards, who had brought rigour to the pursuit of principles of literary criticism. This gave a scientific sheen to a subject many felt had hitherto lolled in subjectivity and was to influence all that followed in the literary criticism of England and America. As Richards's student, Empson had been encouraged to follow his instinct in pursuing alternative interpretations of lines in a text. He saw everywhere what he called 'ambiguity' ('any verbal nuance, however slight, which gives room for alternative reactions to the same piece of language'). He explored it—along with puns and paradox—in canonical texts arriving at (loosely) seven types. His published result made his name at twenty-four years of age.

When condoms were discovered in his rooms at Cambridge in July 1929 the news played to his notoriety. The incident led to rumours, including one that Empson had capped his candles with condoms. More seriously, it deprived him of his fellowship. Briefly setting up in London as a freelance writer, he met notable literary figures like T. S. Eliot and Virginia Woolf, before taking up teaching posts in Tokyo the following year and—after a return home to journalism—in China later in the 1930s, where he entered into the university's exile brought on by the Japanese invasion. January 1939 saw Empson back in England, then war service (with George Orwell at the BBC). He married the South African artist Hetta Crouse in 1941. They returned to teaching in Peking from 1947–52, witnessing the Communist takeover, of which Empson approved. In autumn 1953 Empson took up the Chair of English Literature at Sheffield University, which he would hold until his retirement eighteen years later and from which he would emerge for North American sabbaticals. His publications and awards were many, including a knighthood in 1979, five years before his death.

Empson's eccentricity was no doubt one aspect of his success as a teacher, particularly in the U.S.A where he conformed to a British stereotype, being by birth a member of the Yorkshire gentry. Al Alvarez remembered, in his highly entertaining autobiography, *Where Did it All Go Right?* (1999), a disillusioning meeting with his idol in 1950 Oxford: 'He may have hated being back in England, yet he was a peculiarly English figure, bony and bleak and abrupt, more like a country squire than a poet and intellectual. What set him apart was the strange, Chinese-style beard... He spoke hardly at all [to the student society] and when he did his voice was so squeezed and plunging that it was almost impossible to understand.' To his friend, the poet Kathleen Raine, the infamous neck beard revealed 'the instinct for [a] mandarin form of barbarity'.

Another aspect of Empson's eccentricity was a lifelong tolerance for domestic chaos. Raine confessed to Edmund Wilson that on one visit 'she had picked up a book that had the spine of a kipper for a bookmark'. The American professor/publisher, Steven L. Isenberg found himself treated to a Bloody Mary: 'Empson picked out of the kitchen sink three large glasses that may have been washed within the week. On the counter was a large open can of tomato juice with a rusted top. He poured juice into each glass and, after that, generous amounts of something that could have been either gin or vodka—I couldn't see. Then he sprinkled on something that might have been Worcestershire sauce and from a bin dredged up browned celery stalks. And then he stood back to admire his work and repeatedly stretched and fanned his pants.'

Empson's letters testify also to his renowned wit and bluntness. A furious T.S. Eliot responded to one concerning American publication rights, describing it as 'the most insulting letter which I have ever received'. Another, to his friend and former student Christopher Ricks begins, 'It is extremely kind of you to send me this horrible book'. He thanked poet and critic George Fraser in the following terms: 'Your little book on Pound is very much better than your usual work, George... a good little book, in fact...not that it actually makes me want to *read* the old boy, again!' Empson preferred to be equally frank about colleagues ('What a puzzling case [A.L.] Rowse is; one might think he was going off his head.') and readily argumentative. In an exchange with Stephen Spender about 'Encounter' and CIA funding, he wrote to the poet: 'I thought "Poor old Spender; though never a sensible man I could like at all, he never deserved such a grisly end as having to get his bread from such nastiness as all that amounts to."'

Empson described his own professional territory in an article in the 'Kenyon Review' in Autumn, 1950: 'The kind of criticism that most interests me, verbal analysis or whatever one calls it, is concerned to examine what goes on already in the mind of a fit reader; sometimes bringing it up from levels of unconsciousness deep enough to make it look surprising, but even so not expected to make much difference to the feelings of the fit reader after he has got over this surprise.'

He liked to go about his business as a critic, trusting 'his nose, like the hunting dog', though increasingly he felt the need to engage with what others were doing, those he deemed bound by Christian ideology. After his return from China, he felt he was teaching in a critical atmosphere favouring this 'neo Christian movement', a position heavily influenced by eminent critics like T.S. Eliot and young acolytes like the New Critics (American professor-editors like Allen Tate, Robert Penn Warren and Cleanth Brooks). Eliot had been a wonderful influence up to a point ('like most other verse writers of my generation, I do not know for certain how much of my own mind [Eliot] invented' he wrote for a 1948 symposium). However, he felt in Eliot's case that poets such as Donne and Milton were misrepresented that, as his biographer John Haffenden explained, 'Christian literary critics...insultingly reduce to pious paradox all too many productions of complex mental struggles; they offend authorial integrity by bleeding works of literature of their rational conflicts and moral resistances.'

In a recent TLS review David Hawkes argued–pushing a case rather hard—that since Empson's academic career in England had been blighted for many years by the condom debacle at Cambridge, 'he retaliated against his persecutors by developing a brilliantly subversive and proudly anti-Christian approach to life and literature, whose extensive influence would eventually help to weaken the ideological power of natural teleology, thus hastening the obsolescence of the petty moralism that had destroyed his early career'.

That Christian influence in criticism faded, but Empson found an equally pernicious tendency in New Criticism's fondness for the bare text. This American movement, which took its name from John Crowe Ransom's, *The New Criticism* (1941), replaced the traditional approach to literary criticism, which had been aesthetic, historical and philological. According to Morris Dickstein, 'Starting with *Understanding Poetry* in 1938, Cleanth Brooks and

Robert Penn Warren were turning the experimental methods of Eliot's *Sacred Wood*, I.A. Richards's *Practical Criticism*, and William Empson's *Seven Types of Ambiguity* into pedagogy.'

New Criticism came to dominate the teaching of literature from mid-century until the early seventies when literature became increasingly politicised, theorized and French influenced. In its day it focused purely on text: the poem itself. To Empson, marginalising authorial intention and historical context ran counter to common sense. He harried for many years the rationale of the Intentional Fallacy, as expressed in W. K. Wimsatt Jr.'s *The Verbal Icon* (1954). 'It seems clear that a critic needs to wonder what his author wanted to mean… To say that you won't be bothered with anything but the words on the page (and that you are within your rights, because the author didn't *intend* you to have any more) strikes me as petulant, like saying "of course I won't visit him unless he has first-class plumbing." If you cared enough you would. For one thing, you might want to know whether the author has really had the experience he describes, or is writing "conventionally"'.

In a letter to Cleanth Brooks he complained of the absurd attempt 'to put literary criticism in a pseudo-scientific strait-jacket'. Even as late as 1984—the year of his death—in *Using Biography* Empson is still worrying the bone of what he refers to as the 'Wimsatt Law': 'A student of literature ought to be trying all the time to empathize with the author (and of course the assumptions and conventions by which the author felt himself bound); to tell him that he cannot even partially succeed is about the most harmful thing you could do.'

Empson showed equal élan in his pronouncements on contemporary American literature as well as criticism, both publicly and privately. He criticised Faulkner's trickery with Fate, Hemingway's boorish, wealthy characters and Fitzgerald's novels for their (charming) simplicity. Poets did not always fare well, either. He criticised Wallace Stevens in print for supposing 'that it is enough entertainment for a reader to see the poet trying on a new fancy dress'. Allen Tate he savaged in a letter as 'merely a follower of T.S. Eliot, content to say anything he believed to be in the current fashion' and able to 'whine and moan with particular resonance because he comes from the Southern States'.

Indeed America itself offered a congenial home to Empson. As he wrote to Hetta in Peking (Beijing) during the summer of 1948, 'there is no doubt that I am somebody in the academic world here and not in England'. He made his first visit in 1938 after leaving China at war, crossing the country to visit I.A. Richards in Cambridge Massachusetts, where the professor taught at Harvard. Empson had a taste of lecturing on 'Basic English in Criticism' at Princeton University, then took a temporary job writing radio scripts for a Boston station.

A decade passed before he returned, the year his *Collected Poems* was published there. This time Kenyon College, in Ohio, employed him to teach summer school with a faculty that included the New Critics Ransom, Tate and Brooks. The Rockefeller Foundation funded the eight week summer school, paying him the handsome sum of $1,250. Empson met with his class of thirty for three, two hour sessions a week, finding them 'clearheaded and energetic and willing'. They afforded the opportunity to polish *The Structure of Complex Words* before its publication three years later.

As he confessed in a July letter to his friend and publisher, Ian Parsons: 'I get here what is probably a misleading impression of my fame in America, as we all seem to be on the same side in a literary war, with the enemy in the majority. I have a vague suspicion that the side I am supposed to be a leader of is rather a reactionary one.' The left-wing Empson's found his New Critic colleagues initially worrying: 'Most of the other lecturers are Southerners... pro-ambiguity-stuff, but have mixed it up with being pro-South, anti-Machine Age, and anti-Negro. I have not yet cared to plumb this rather disagreeable complex.' Although clearly against their reactionary values, later in the summer he wrote wryly that they were 'anti-negro in a very charitable style and concerned to keep up the "values" of the country gentleman, who is a humanist'.

He skirted controversy not by such views, or his popular eccentricities, but by his passionate defence of China and criticism of American foreign policy. Nevertheless, Empson felt he 'really couldn't have been more petted and fussed over' on this visit. With typical candour he reckoned he must finish *Structure* in America, 'where I think it would sell (I seem to be on the crest of a wave here, perhaps because they tend to be a bit behind the times, but never mind)'.

He returned for a second lucrative summer to the Kenyon in 1950, when the Korean War had broken out. His colleagues included Kenneth Burke, the literary theorist with whom Empson liked to argue and admired; Fitzgerald and Ford biographer Arthur Mizener, Empson's favourite party host that summer; Robert Lowell and Delmore Schwarz. Lowell and Empson each admired the other's poetry. The thirty-seven year old Schwarz, a more prickly case, argued while drunk with Allen Tate and then Empson over Ezra Pound's right to the Bollingen Prize.

As on the previous visit, Empson made a colourful figure. In the classroom his tendency to talk to the blackboard while he wrote down his lectures amused his twenty-five students, who were taken with the flow of insights and the unpretentiousness of the man. The then student George Lanning characterised them all as engaged in the wilderness of literary criticism, locking horns with the Victorian sensibility of their predecessors, 'the wooly headed Beast of primitive criticism'. Partying, Empson indulged his fondness for argument and silly behaviour.

After his appointment at Sheffield University in 1953 he returned a number of times to other North American universities. In June 1954 he taught at Indiana, lecturing to graduate students on 'Studies in Shakespeare'. The faculty included Leslie A. Fiedler, whose *Love and Death in the American Novel* (1960) was to scandalise/amuse with its view of the immaturity of American literature. Empson in turn shocked Fiedler by his slovenly ways, as well as his readiness to quarrel over American versus British policy on communist China, about which he had written and lectured controversially. The students were again receptive to the peculiar Englishman, though a little given to Christianity and to philosophy for Empson's taste.

His reputation continued to grow. The collected poems appeared as an American paperback in 1961. In that same year he published the controversial *Milton's God* ('the moral character of God had become very hard to defend', as he acknowledged in response to a NYRB review of his book). In 1968 he was Visiting Professor at the State University of New York, having just been awarded the Ingram Merrill Foundation Award in Literature for 1967 (worth $5000). On this occasion Empson's flamboyant wife accompanied him, which stabilised the professor *and* fuelled the legends. Lecturing on the Metaphysical Poets he joined a faculty that included Fiedler and John Barth (author of the postmodern *The Sot-Weed Factor* (1960)). Things went well, aside from an embarrassing panel argument with the Canadian scholar Hugh Kenner, the source of which lay in Empson's disapproval of the Catholicism of Kenner's reading of Joyce.

He recognised that America would continue to be his land of opportunity. Considering the future Empson indicated in a letter to Christopher Ricks: 'In six years' time I have to retire (becoming 65 in 1971) and after so much fun abroad I only get £500 a year pension. I shall thus badly want congenial paid employment, and the money won't largely go in tax, as it would at present.' As a visiting professor at York University, Toronto in 1973, he undertook speaking engagements, lectures or readings in New York, Vermont, Seattle and San Francisco, though now his delivery could not always be relied upon.

1974 brought him honorary membership of the American Academy of Arts and Letters. In September of the same year he took up a year's teaching at Pennsylvania State University at a salary of $20,000. Unfortunately Empson felt uncomfortable with the noise and isolation of campus living, which was exacerbated by dental problems. He relied a little too much on alcohol when dependent on his own disorganised company. Although he had the pleasure of meeting with C.P. Snow and his wife, he found difficulty in being understood in the classroom. As he wrote to Hetta, 'I do feel outside the place; and if the economic situation or perhaps some family need does not drive the old horse over the jump I do not want to take this type of assignment again. In the long run, and if there is a long run, I will earn more by writing my books, and I have only just time to do that before old age.' He found 'America very numbing this trip', being disappointed also by the fact that his other course, on the 'Spirits of Nature' (on sixteenth century texts, especially *Doctor Faustus*) attracted only two students. 'We had bought, briefly, a literary reputation of little or no practical value', was the university's verdict.

However, Empson's last two teaching visits to America proved happier experiences. In September 1976—now an Honorary Fellow of the Modern Language Association of America—he taught at the University of Delaware. He and Hetta stayed in a spacious apartment ten minutes from campus where, with the aid of a microphone, Empson connected with large audiences. Two years before his death he taught a semester at the University of Miami. They rented an apartment with pool access and a car, which gave them the opportunity to visit the Everglades. Empson enjoyed teaching his Modern English Poetry course. Unfortunately he also experienced the ominous onset of illness that curtailed his drinking, manifesting itself firstly in backache. It was the end of America.

Michael Wood, in *On Empson* (2017), rightly observes that, despite his public disavowals, Empson is connected with 'all the major modern movements of criticism and theory' because 'his preoccupations are central to any sort of ongoing thought about literature'. America, which constantly indulged him and had been well rewarded for it, had recognised this early.

REGARDING WILLIAM STYRON

> I have absolutely no doubt—I will say this without modesty because I don't think modesty is involved—that in 40 years my work will be read with at least the same interest as anyone who is living contemporaneously with me. I simply have no doubt. (1980)

The American novelist William Styron had been overly optimistic when he made the claim quoted above. According to a 2015 review in 'The New York Times', his 'literary reputation was in limbo, if not apocalyptic decline, well before his death in 2006'. In his defence it has to be acknowledged that his contemporaries (Mailer, Heller, Capote, James Jones) are largely under-read, also. Yet the pity of it, in Styron's case, comes from the fact that his novels explore abuses of power and states of moral disengagement— from indifference to pure evil—which are always relevant and poignantly so in contemporary Europe and Trump's America.

Styron saw his task in Malraux's 'I seek that essential region of the soul where absolute evil confronts brotherhood.' He dealt with resurgent, uncomfortable truths in big novels: *Lie Down in Darkness* (1951), *Set This House on Fire* (1960), *The Confessions of Nat Turner* (1967) and *Sophie's Choice* (1979). He also wrote a fine novella (*The Long March*, 1956) and a courageous autobiographical classic, *Darkness Visible: A Memoir of Madness* (1990). A constant in his fiction is a commitment to the architecture of the novel. As Willie Morris observed of his friend's work in his brilliant memoir, *North Toward Home* (1967), 'His poet's sense of ruin, guilt and tragedy, his extraordinary structural genius for the progression of time in a work of fiction, gave Styron his own particular vision as an artist.' His narratives are long and manoeuvres with time are handled dexterously, while the settings are carefully evoked. Styron found early the animating theme of his fiction: the complex relationship between authority and victimhood. His world is peopled with the destructive, who intimidate through love, authority, charisma or madness, and the ineffectual, victims and conflicted observers. At its darkest, his vision centres on the barbarism of slavery and The Holocaust.

Styron was born in the once-slaveholding South (in Newport News, Virginia) in 1925, to an engineer father and Pennsylvania mother who died when he was thirteen. As fellow Southerner Robert Penn Warren noted, Styron 'was born at almost the last moment when it was possible to get, firsthand, a sense of what old-fashioned Southern life had been, or to hear, actually, the word-of-mouth legends about it.' He was therefore one of the last of authors born under the influence of William Faulkner, who dominated a literature often characterised as elaborate and poetic in style, singular in idioms and mythic in its imagination. It represents a culture marked by guilt through its troubled race relations and its tendency to religious fever, one scarred deeply by defeat in the Civil War.

Throughout Styron's career the question of his Southernness frequently arose, unsurprisingly given the number of his Southern characters. He readily acknowledged a debt, while being careful to maintain some distance from its literary tradition. In a 1980 interview he stated his position clearly: 'I would not call myself a Southern novelist. I would call myself a committed American novelist who happens to write out of an awareness of his Southern roots and Southern heritage, but I do not wish to consider myself a "capital S" Southern writer.' He recognised, he said, the degree to which the South was changing; he himself no longer lived there, nor set his novels there; and he had a natural antipathy to being pigeonholed by critics. Besides, he said on another occasion, 'I didn't want to exploit the old idea of wreckage and defeat as a peculiarly Southern phenomenon'. Styron's commitment to wreckage is on a more cosmopolitan stage.

Educated at Duke University, North Carolina, he enlisted in the marines in 1944, remaining stateside during the war. In 1947, upon graduation, he began working for the publisher McGraw-Hill in New York City, before being dismissed for lack of commitment. He then focused solely on writing, completing his novel, *Lie Down in Darkness*, just as he was recalled to the marines in 1951 during the Korean War. He gained a medical discharge that same year.

Lie Down in Darkness, with its Faulknerian echoes, remains in my opinion his most realized, rawest novel, examining as it does the corrosive way in which parental irresponsibility can ruin lives. It is his only novel to take place almost wholly in the South (in the fictional Port Warwick, Virginia). Set in 1945, it opens with the arrival from New York of the body of the Loftis's daughter and describes in a series of painful flashbacks the disintegration of the family leading to her suicide.

Milton Loftis, the father, is a barely successful lawyer, an adulterous alcoholic, alienated from his wealthy and emotionally withdrawn wife, Helen. She has devoted herself to their crippled elder daughter, Maudie, while shunning the lovely Peyton who has been her father's obsession. Peyton has found it hard to take her mother's embittered rejection and fled to New York City. To Helen, Peyton is 'a shameless little seducer who's used her father's love to get everything she wants in life, who half-killed her own sister through negligence' and then rejected Loftis with the words, 'Don't smother me!' We share Peyton's consciousness only toward the novel's end, with her long Joycean monologue. She is a girl fated by her life, who acknowledges at its end, 'not out of vengeance have I accomplished all my sins but because something has always been close to dying in my soul, and I've sinned only in order to lie down in darkness and find, somewhere in the net of dreams, a new father, a new home'.

Styron's highly successful debut is evocative of the manners of the time and place (including some sense of race relationships). He reported to friends and relatives the following year that 30,000 copies had been sold and that the print run for the Signet pocket edition would be 200,000 initially. He would also to be awarded the 'Prix de Rome' with a $3500 grant and the chance to live a year in Rome. When Styron embarked on his European travels, he wrote *The Long March* in Paris and helped to launch 'The Paris Review'.

The Long March is an outstanding novella set during the Korean War. It details the confrontation between a Marine captain and his commanding officer during a thirty-six mile forced march on manoeuvres in South Carolina. The episode is witnessed by the narrator, a reluctant reservist, Lieutenant Culver. The intention of the cordial but implacable Colonel Templeton is to soften his reserve troops, who have been recalled from WWII service. To Culver and the huge, Jewish New Yorker, Captain Mannix, a man whose 'disgruntled sense of humour' is obliterated, it is an act of madness, even sadism. Yet Mannix's protestations are meaningless and result only in his own undoing for, as Culver ultimately realises, 'the hike had had nothing to do with courage or sacrifice or suffering, but was only a task to be performed'. Tragedy is here a consequence of indifference rather than intention and the narrator powerless to intervene.

In Rome in 1953 Styron married Rose Burgunder, whom he had first met in America. The couple settled in Roxbury, Connecticut, where he began work on his next novel, completed in late 1959, by which time the Styrons had three children. *Set This House on Fire* is probably Styron's most ambitious yet flawed novel. Its title comes from a sermon of John Donne's, which witnesses the torment of an absence of God. The novel is riddled with torment resulting from the irresponsible exercise of power, the abuse of alcohol and from carnal appetites.

It tells firstly of the relationship between a New York lawyer, Peter Leverett, and his school friend, the charismatic Mason Flagg, scion of a wealthy Northern family connected with the film industry. Flagg is representative of the worst of American materialism. Everything in the novel takes place in reaction to his destructive energies. He is also a charming, inveterate liar: 'I mean, to think that you—you of all people—can't make the subtle distinction between a lie—between an out-and-out third-rate lie meant maliciously—between that, and a jazzy kind of bullshit extravaganza like the one I was telling you, meant with no malice at all, but only with the intent to edify and entertain.' Leverett, a Southerner and the first-person narrator, is endlessly forgiving. Drawn to Sambuco, Italy, by the promise of one of their eventful meetings, he finds his friend in monstrous form. A death, a rape and suspected suicide follow.

Sometime later Leverett turns his attention to Cass Kinsolving, a cruelly poor and alcoholic artist and family man, originally from

South Carolina. Kinsolving had been implicated in the events in Sambuco, where the two met at the time. Styron shifts the narrative to him, in the form of conversations, flashbacks and comments from Cass's notebooks. When the two meet again in Charleston the mysterious events surrounding the deaths are there explained and we are to imagine some form of redemption.

In America *Set This House on Fire* was the most coolly received of Styron's novels (though it was critically admired in France) partly because, in attempting to switch naturally from a first person to a third person narrative, we seem to have two novels in one. Also, the characters are given long monologues by way of exposition, most unconvincingly in the case of Kinsolving, who remembers events in inordinate detail despite the fact that with his chronic alcoholic bouts he might have been expected to have blotted out much of his memory. Then there are characters like Luigi, the pragmatic Fascist intellectual police corporal, who do not entirely convince.

In 1964 the Styrons bought a house on Martha's Vineyard, and a fourth child followed the year before *The Confessions of Nat Turner* was published. There are two narratives to this novel: one Styron had contemplated for many years; the other concerns its reception. Styron intended his novel to deal with the problem of responsibility, of moral choice, of the use of violence. It also pointed to contemporary race relations.

In his hands, Nat Turner—the leader of a slave rebellion that cost seventy lives—is given more depth than the scant historical records allow. At the opening of the novel we meet the 30 year old Turner in his Virginia jail cell, the day of his trial in November, 1831. The story flows from him in flashbacks, a device Styron borrowed from Camus's *The Stranger* ('For me there was a spiritual connection between Meursault's frigid solitude and the plight of Nat Turner'). Both men are abandoned by God and both react violently. Turner is prompted to his 'confessions' by the prosecuting attorney, though it is the reader who hears the truth.

Turner, a house slave taught to read and write, learnt also to aspire. With the collapse of his owner's expectations comes the failure of his own dreams. As Styron said 'The seeds of revolt are in the promise.' The victim of moral and sexual humiliation, he turns to the apocalyptic violence of the Old Testament ('Of all the Prophets it was Ezekiel with his divine fury to whom I felt closest by kinship') when sold to a deviant preacher and then hardscrabble farmers. A 'vision' leads him to attempt to seize the armoury of the county seat, Jerusalem, by killing all in his way. His intention is to establish an empire in the neighbouring Dismal Swamp. The result: a macabre failure.

Initially the novel received acclaim, winning the Pulitzer Prize for fiction in 1968 and selling in great numbers. While to Styron the novel offered a way to understand the African-American experience by adopting the consciousness of a slave, to others this merely constituted dressing up. The adoption of a first person narrator, plus what were seen as racist stereotypes in the novel— the lust for a white girl, the idea of virtuous slave-owners and the issue of the urge to violent rebellion—alienated many readers, who also balked at the nature of the presentation of slavery, particularly the way Styron 'voiced' the slave.

Many defended Styron. A 'Yale Lit' interview from 1968 described him as 'a liberal caught in an intensified, perhaps paradigmatic version of the dilemmas which beset the contemporary white intellectual: how to help the black man without condescension; how to balance the demands of black power with an intellectual and visceral commitment to integration'. However the novel appeared at a time—as now—of heightened racial tension, with the assassinations of Dr. Martin Luther King and Senator Robert Kennedy, the rise of the Black Panther movement, the rioting in cities. A collection of essays, *William Styron's Nat Turner: Ten Black Writers Respond* further polarised opinion on the novel's value.

While the furore passed, the novel's impact upon literary issues continued. According to Jess Row, in a 2008 piece for 'The New York Times', 'Almost overnight, "The Confessions" became the center of a debate that has helped shape American literature ever since.' At issue was the way the past might to be adapted for the purposes of fiction: 'to take a term from the Russian literary theorist Viktor Shklovsky, novelists have [since] wished to "defamiliarize" history by making it unrecognizable, unknowable, fantastic, brutal. "Beloved," with its harsh, fragmented narration of infanticide, is the most obvious example'. The novelist John A. Williams did have this to say in *Ten Black Writers Respond*: 'I do not believe that the right to describe . . . black people in American society is the private domain of Negro writers.'

Mortified by the reception if not the sales of *The Confessions of Nat Turner*, William Styron moved on to his next project, a play entitled *In the Clap Shack*, performed at Yale before being published in 1973. It is described as 'a darkly humorous play' set in a military hospital, but it did not prosper critically. Consequently Styron turned back to the novel which would bring him his greatest success: the National Book Award winning, *Sophie's Choice*. By 1981 nearly two million copies had been sold. Five years' work had earned its author $700,000.

Set in New York City in the summer of 1947, *Sophie's Choice* concerns an aspiring writer who moves into a cheap boarding house in Brooklyn where he becomes enmeshed in the lives of two unstable lovers, Sophie Zawistowska, a beautiful Polish Holocaust victim, and the brilliant but volatile Nathan Landau. It is another tragedy of the enslaved, though a complex one, since its characters are no mere ciphers. Behind the wildly dysfunctional love relationship, Styron's intention had been to deal with the subject of Auschwitz and, by extension, human evil generally, thereby extending his preoccupation with the 'brutalized spiritually' of Nat Turner's time. As with the earlier novel, *Sophie's Choice* was plunged into controversy, on this occasion through the author's perspective on the Holocaust.

His Sophie Zawistowska is a Catholic, sent to the concentration camp for smuggling food to a dying parent. Styron presents Auschwitz, therefore, not as an exclusively Jewish suffering, but as a nightmare for all mankind. His aim in exploring human evil here is to avoid the notion of purely Christian sin and guilt, as well as to tie the demented capitalist slave society of the camps to other historical experiences of slavery.

The novel does not flinch from the horrors of the events or the conditions of the camp, which are powerfully presented ('the

Russian voice—a bass baritone but harsh, corrosive as lye—pierced her delirium, penetrated the sweat and the fever and the kennel filth of the hard straw-strewn wooden shelf where she lay, to mutter over her in an impassive tone, "I think this one is finished too"'). Styron also seeks to bring home the horror by domesticating it in New York City: by telling much of the tale there, by implicating its citizens for their innocence of those events taking place while they lived cushioned lives ('the enormity of [the camps existence] had been for Nathan, as for so many Americans, part of a drama too far away, too abstract, too *foreign* (and thus too hard to comprehend) to register fully on the mind'). New York has its own horrors notwithstanding. Sophie Zawistowska is violated in the New York subway as well as being the victim of violent arguments with her lover. Yet the tale is otherwise told with vigour and often humour, especially in the sexual obsessions, activities and obscenities of its characters. (Styron's narrator is a younger version of the author with some of his own experiences). All this guaranteed contention.

Despite the success of the novel and the Oscars showered on the movie version with Meryl Streep, the following years proved difficult for the author. Styron seems to have been something of a tortured man and artist. According to his daughter, Alexandra Styron (in *Reading My Father: A Memoir* (2011), he could be 'at times querulous and taciturn, cutting and remote, melancholy when he was sober and rageful when in his cups'. In the 1980s he suffered depression. The buried origins of this, he concluded, lay possibly in the death of his mother when he was thirteen, although there were other factors, including his father's bouts of 'the morbid condition', and his own dependence on alcohol, which he had recently stopped. When the depression became clinical, he was hospitalised. These experiences led to *Darkness Visible: A Memoir of Madness,* a book enormously helpful to some readers.

This short book began with readers' responses to a piece Styron wrote for 'The New York Times' when angered by negative reactions to Primo Levi's suicide. He had, he said, 'apparently underestimated the number of people for whom the subject [of depression] had been taboo, a matter of secrecy and shame'. His unflinching personal account of his descent into life-threatening depression over several months became in turn a conference paper and then, enlarged, published as a memoir. The book was pioneering in its aim: to illustrate the crippling effects of, and to try to help to remove the stigma from, the illness, the 'disease'. While the book became something of a classic in the field, Styron continued to be subject to bouts of depression which hampered his later life and work.

In 1992 a collection of non-fictional writings appeared, *This Quiet Dust and Other Writings*. Styron published only one more work of fiction: *A Tidewater Morning: Three Tales from Youth*, which recounts key experiences in the earlier life of his alter ego, Paul Whitehurst. In the first he is a young marine lieutenant waiting to land on the island of Okinawa; in the second a child witnessing the end of an ex-slave's odyssey. 'Death ain't nothin' to be afraid about', one frustrated character pronounces. 'It's life that's fearsome!' In the title story we witness a crisis in Paul's early adolescence with the death of his mother. By the end he understands how 'fearsome' life is, how 'we all devise our means of escape from the intolerable'.

William Styron became an author ready to court controversy in order to articulate a vision of human suffering, universalised from his experience of Southern history. He once acknowledged, 'I suppose the pathos of the victim has always been a central consideration in what I've written—the victimization of people by life or by other human beings'. But a corollary of that thematic preoccupation is, as the poet Dave Smith (also born in Tidewater, Virginia), points out: 'The self-conflict that permits or enables terrible things to happen—because you did not or could not stop them—is the heart of his vision.' And there could be no more relevant issue today.

AL ALVAREZ AT RISK

> 'If you ask me what I came to do in this world, I, an artist, will answer you: "I am here to live out loud."'
> – (Zola)

Al Alvarez is in high profile once again, as others evaluate his contribution to poetry criticism from the late nineteen fifties on. In a long life he has been highly influential, but particularly for his stint as poetry editor and critic for 'The Observer' and through his anthology *The New Poetry* (1962), the *Penguin Modern European Poets* series (from 1967) and *The Savage God: A Study in Suicide* (1971). Essentially Alvarez promoted American poets like Robert Lowell, John Berryman and, perhaps most importantly, Sylvia Plath. He also introduced many British readers to what were called—in Churchill's popular metaphor—'Iron Curtain' poets. Despite other contending perspectives, Alvarez's own tastes dominated. He offered a view of poetry as disciplined, exciting, risky—and risk was very much to the taste of the time.

It is hardly surprising, then, that he should title his selected essays in 2007 *Risky Business*—albeit that the title firstly addresses the perils of freelancing—since risk has been a great stimulus to his own writing, as well as to his other pursuits. Influenced by Freud's contentions about conflict in the psyche, Alvarez has been remarkably consistent in the view that 'Risk concentrates the mind, sharpens the senses and, in every way, makes life sweeter by putting it, however briefly, in doubt.' To him, 'risk' in poetry is a central feature of Modernism. It is about letting air into what he refers to ironically as 'the hallowed tradition'. In an essay on Derek Walcott for the 'The New York Review of Books' in 2000, Alvarez referred to the Nobel Prize winner as being in the Victorian tradition: 'He is not an experimental poet and has never been easy with the fast-talking, hard-edged high anxiety that gives the Modernist writers their peculiar sense of strain.' Again, in *The Writer's Voice* (2005), he defined Extremism (aka risk) as 'an art that goes out along that friable edge between the tolerable and intolerable, yet does so with all the discipline and clarity and attention to detail Eliot implied when he talked of Classicism'.

The roots of risk lay in Alvarez's personality and personal circumstances. In a 1992 essay titled 'Risk' he wrote: 'In my early thirties, after my first marriage broke up, I acquired a brief reputation as a wild man: I drove fast cars, played high stakes poker, and spent more time than I decently could afford off in the hills, climbing rocks with the boys.' The obverse of this is his irritation with the staid. It reflected in Alvarez's disenchantment with English as a student at Oxford, where he found the lit. crit. old fashioned (unlike Cambridge where F. R. Leavis, I. A. Richards and William Empson were active in the same way as the New Critics in America, influenced by Richards and T. S. Eliot in liberating the text from its author's ownership).

With honourable exceptions (such as D. H. Lawrence) British poetry had shied away from Modernism, Alvarez began to feel, and with it recognition of vital twentieth century preoccupations (the influence of Freud, the concentration camps, Existentialism). In *The Shaping Spirit* (1958) he wrote 'in the very broadest terms... modernism has been predominantly an American concern, a matter of creating, almost from scratch, their own poetic tradition. It has affected English poetry peculiarly little'. His 1980 piece on Seamus Heaney in the 'New York Review of Books' ('beautiful minor poetry') echoed the same disenchantment:

> Apart from Joyce and Beckett, the great experimental movement in literature was largely an American concern... In contrast, the British adjusted to the times by a process of seepage, gradually adapting the old forms to the rhythms of twentieth century speech: Yeats, Auden, Graves, and so on, down to Larkin. So they are comfortable with Heaney because he himself is comfortably in a recognizable tradition.

In an essay on T.E. Hulme and Wilfred Owen in the same magazine he suggests that the fact that a generation had been slaughtered in the trenches might have a bearing on this, adding that 'The line of English verse in the 20th century runs directly from the Victorians, via Hardy and Housman, to Larkin and Hughes, almost as if Modernism had never happened.'

With a sense that contemporary British poetry and criticism having failed him, Alvarez turned to America as early as 1953. 'It was love at first sight', he wrote in his autobiography, *Where Did It All Go Right?* (1999): 'I loved the energy of the place, the busyness and cynicism of New York and the intellectual openness, even in staid Princeton' (where he experienced what the theoretical physicist Freeman Dyson had described as a post-war world for the young 'without shadows'). There he delivered the Christian Gauss lectures at the age of 28. He also fell under the spell of Richard Blackmur ('one of the first and most original of the New Critics'), Kenneth Burke and others. Later he established a friendship with Robert Lowell.

Alvarez's highly influential 'Observer' years had begun in 1956. The reviews helped establish him and—beginning in 1959 with R.S. Thomas—the paper published poems by well-established poets, followed by Hughes, Thom Gunn and Americans like Lowell, Berryman and Roethke. What he did not want, he made clear in one of his 'Observer' columns:

> The style of the fifties is now achieved and accepted: that is, a large number of poets write in much the same way and share much the same emotional stance: a no-nonsense, let's-get-down-to-it, common-chappery, determinedly competent and determinedly restrained. Where Modernist posts used to rally to Ezra Pound's war cry, "Poetry should be at least as well written as prose," they now settle for more Somerset Maughamish principles, as who should say, "A poem should have a beginning, a middle and an end." (June 19, 1960)

As William Wootten notes, in *The Alvarez Generation: Thom Gunn, Geoffrey Hill, Ted Hughes, Sylvia Plath and Peter Porter* (2015), Alvarez became the critic 'as commentator, populariser or provocateur'. His anthology, *The New Poetry*, helped secure the British reputations of two (and, in the revised edition of 1968, four) American poets, while many contemporary British poets, like those involved in 'The Movement', were in effect damned with faint praise.

Alvarez introductory essay 'Beyond the Gentility Principle' (with its Freudian homage) lit the fuse of *The New Poetry*. As he explained in *Risky Business*, 'I wrote it in 1961, a particularly dreary moment in British poetry, in the hope of stirring things up.' Our poets, he felt, offered 'a tetchy vision of post-war provincial England populated, like a Lowry painting, by stick figures united, above all, by boredom'. The essay calls for an Arnoldian 'new seriousness' to take modern poetry forward: 'I would define this seriousness simply as the poet's ability and willingness to face the full range of his experience with his full intelligence' (Behind this argument, according to Wootten, lay the influence of Harold Rosenberg's seminal comments on American painting and culture in *The Tradition of the New* (1959)).

Alvarez recognised a negativity in the '50s 'Movement': 'academic-administrative verse, polite, knowledgeable, efficient, polished, and, in its quiet way, even intelligent.' Bloodless, in other words. Circumstances might change, he believed, the class system might disturb the surface calm, but Britain remained impervious to events and ideas. In short, 'the concept of gentility still reigns supreme'. Gentility, as he later explained, 'didn't seem an adequate response to a century that had spawned two world wars, totalitarianism, genocide, concentration camps and nuclear warfare'.

'The Movement' poets had been so dubbed by 'The Spectator' in 1954 and initially including Kingsley Amis, Donald Davie, Philip Larkin, Elizabeth Jennings, John Wain and Robert Conquest. Although he featured some of them in *The New Poetry*, to Alvarez 'The Movement' poets represented all that was unadventurous and xenophobic about contemporary British verse:

> For Amis & Co., Modernism was a plot by foreigners— Americans, Irishmen and Continentals, people with funny accents they could mimic—to divert literature from its

true purpose; and their business was to get it back on its traditional track, back to Arnold Bennett and Galsworthy, back to Chesterton, Hardy and Housman.
— (*Where Did It All Go Right?*)

The two best Movement-associated poets were, for him, Philip Larkin and Thom Gunn. Wootten quotes an Alvarez comment from 1958 on Larkin's under-achievement in not having 'mapped out any great new continent of poetry' but simply having 'created a tone of voice for the time'. Again in Alvarez's judgment this is a shying away from the demands of literary Modernism, of risk. This was the case also in *The New Poetry* essay, where he favoured Hughes's energy ('a nexus of fear and sensation') over Larkin's accomplished restraint. Although Alvarez recognised Larkin's eminence among his British peers, he also felt that the poet had 'a beady understanding' of his own limitations. The fact that he had not been represented by more poems in *The New Poetry* had to do with permission fees, however, not craft.

Alvarez had admired Thom Gunn's early poetry for its technical control and subject matter. In exploring 'psychic pain' Gunn belonged with Alvarez's risk takers, but when the poet moved to California, coming under the influence of Ivor Winters, whose antipathy to the New Critics was well-known, Alvarez began to feel that 'The unease and energy that had made the early poems tick so ominously gave way to decorum, strict reasonableness and formal grace—to smoothly flowing rhythms and bland rhymes.' Gunn's technique finally redeemed itself, for the critic, in the fine elegies of his late book, *The Man With Night Sweats* (1992), written to friends who died of AIDS.

Although some of Alvarez's judgments seem harsh, unfair, there were those who agreed with him about 'The Movement'. As David Perkins wrote in *A History of Modern Poetry* (1987): 'Even poets who had been featured in the Movement anthologies were snipping at the "tame," "academic," "arid," "mean spirited" style and ethos the anthologies had promoted.' Perkins sees poets such as David Jones, Basil Bunting and Charles Tomlinson as otherwise being outside their 1950s orthodoxy.

Now Alvarez turned in his introductory essay in *The New Poetry* to the example of American poets Robert Lowell and John Berryman who, while learning from Eliot, nevertheless rejected his idea of 'impersonality', turning the focus frankly on themselves. So, he later recounted, 'I put the two Americans at the beginning [of the anthology] in order to set a standard, as an antidote to the complacency of the Movement, as a deliberate provocation.'

Alvarez had taken to Robert Lowell's work early, seeing the 'dis-ease' beneath its carapace of Catholic symbolism. In *The Shaping Spirit* (1958) he wrote of Lowell and Lowell's one-time teacher, Richard Eberhart: 'Both Eberhart and Lowell have worked with considerable power to make of their obscure emotional disturbances a matter of more general and deliberate truth.' When Lowell's brilliant *Life Studies* (1959) appeared in England, Alvarez recognised its worth immediately. As he remembers in his autobiography: 'Instead of rounding up the usual suspects in 800 words, I wrote a much longer article on Lowell's book alone.' He would maintain his commitment to Lowell's verse for its technical accomplishments as well as for its courage *in extremis*. He felt that the 'inwardness' of poets like him (and later Plath) when confronting their demons should not be read as a turning from the world but as a way of reflecting the 'bewildering nihilism' consequent upon the Second World War.

In *The Savage God* Alvarez even compared *Life Studies* to *The Waste Land* for its courage and revolutionary innovation. Behind it burnt his frustration at British criticism of the time, as well as the poetry. He wrote in 1977 of having been irked that 'In Britain [Lowell's] originality was acknowledged, but grudgingly, as though it were not quite the done thing for a serious poet to lay himself on the line so nakedly.'

Alvarez also praised John Berryman's best poetry very highly, again for the inventive risks it took in exploring its author's angst. Berryman speaks through his alcoholic, picaresque hero, Henry, a man with 'badly frayed nerves and an unremitting case of morning-after guilt'. Berryman's suicide in 1972 (after Plath's of nine years before) gave Alvarez pause for thought. In the 'New York Times' he wrote:

> For years I have been extolling the virtues of what I have called extremist poetry, in which artists deliberately push their perceptions to the very edge of the tolerable. Both Berryman and Sylvia Plath were masters of the style. But knowing now how they both died I no longer believe that any art—even that as fine as they produced at their best—is worth the terrible cost.

Yet Alvarez's partiality for risk had influenced him against other poets, whatever their status (as we saw with Heaney). For instance, he concluded a less than impressed Observer review of Wallace Stevens in February 1960 with the words: 'The idea that art could come from immersing in the destructive element never seems to have occurred to him. It is as though he had never really *read* Shakespeare.'

Eventually Alvarez turned from his favoured American 'extremist' poets to what he considered the even higher seriousness of Central European practice. During his time at 'The Observer', he would feature groups of poems in translation. Through his connection to the BBC Third Programme he journeyed to Warsaw to write a feature on intellectual life, meeting Zbigniew Herbert, who became a good friend. He followed up with features on Czechoslovakia, Hungary and Yugoslavia. This led in turn to Penguin initiating the 'Penguin Modern European Poets' series, with which Alvarez was connected for 12 years and 22 volumes. He wrote introductions for two of the collections, those by Miroslav Holub (1967) and Herbert (1968). Given the political conditions in Czechoslovakia and Poland at the time, risk characterised the métier of these poets. Alvarez wrote of the first:

> In its way, Holub's poetry is no less exploratory than that of the Extremist poets of the West, but it takes the opposite direction. His business is with the way in which private responses, private anxieties, connect up with the public world of science, technology and machines.

In a recent 'Commentary' essay for the 'The Times Literary Supplement', Justin Quinn has criticised Alvarez's failure to recognise in Holub's poetry the influence of the Beats, despite Holub's insistence on that influence. The significance of the criticism is for Quinn that Alvarez 'rescues a public voice for poetry, but only writers from communist regimes are allowed to write it'.

Alvarez had the highest opinion of Zbigniew Herbert's poetry recognising (in 1985) its superiority, even in translation, over that of anyone writing in England or America. He had been deeply influenced by Herbert's classicism and dangerous anti-establishment perspective: 'He had been inventing and overthrowing gods ever since, a party of one, permanently and warily in opposition.' For Alvarez, Herbert had 'a moral authority which poets in the West lacked'. In fact it had made him feel 'shabby' and 'pompous' for ever having called for a 'new seriousness' when he read Herbert. 'Now I was faced with a poet with a different scale of values', he wrote. Whether or not the needs of post-war poetry were the same in Poland and England, as Wootten queries, it does not alter the fact that Alvarez brought these poets to a large audience in Britain. He also wrote persuasively on other European poets in translation, like Vladimir Mayakovsky ('a genius for exhibitionism') and Czesław Miłosz (suffering 'the vacuum of exile').

Arguably, the two poets who gained most from Alvarez's support—and most controversially—were Sylvia Plath and Ted Hughes. According to his account in *Where Did It All Go Right?* after ten years he had had a 'bellyful of poets'. He turned instead to other books, novels and magazine pieces, but first came *The Savage God: A Study of Suicide*, which contributed to the legend around Sylvia Plath.

Alvarez had met Plath through her husband, Ted Hughes, being initially more impressed with the excellent early poetry of Hughes. In *The Savage God* he wrote of these poems, 'They seemed to emerge from an absorbed, physical world that was wholly his own.' With his first two books, *The Hawk in the Rain* and *Lupercal*, 'A figure had emerged on the drab scene of British poetry, powerful and undeniable.' Alvarez saw the connection in Hughes between 'the violence both of animal life and of the self… It was almost as though, despite all the reading and polish and craftsmanship, he had never properly been civilized'.

Gradually, as the friendships developed, Alvarez came to recognise and respect Sylvia Plath's poetry. In *The Savage God* he recounts how he warmed to *The Colossus*, to 'the precision and concentration with which she handled language, the unemphatic range of vocabulary, her ear for subtle rhythms, and her... rhymes'. Both Plath and Hughes were 'intent on finding voices for their unquiet, buried selves'. In an article on Ted Hughes's *Birthday Letters* in 1998, Alvarez explained:

> Hughes calls her father 'The Minotaur' and a large number of the *Birthday Letters* chart Plath's gradual, fatal descent into his lair. As he describes it, it was Hughes who showed her how to get there and he did it in the name of poetry.

She, of course, transcended her influences, becoming a brilliant, original poet who wrote poems with courage and insight that were 'proved on her pulses'. Hughes and Alvarez were there at a crucial period. They contributed to her reputation by their encouragement and promotion.

Although Alvarez did not know this at the time, Plath was in the last days of her life when she came to him for help as friend and editor. As a guest on radio's 'Desert Island Discs', he put his inability to recognise her clinical depression down as 'stupidity' and, characteristically, added:

> And the more subtle reason is that her poems were so good and there was such liveliness. I mean, there was more life and liveliness and appetite in Plath writing about death than there is in the collected works of Philip Larkin writing about what a bitch it is to be alive.

The Savage God offers a long, disturbing late portrait of Plath. It is a portrayal which did not go unchallenged. Ted Hughes wrote to Alvarez, in November 1971, deploring the appearance of extracts from it in 'The Observer', with some justification because of the revelation of intimate details of Plath's suicide. He blamed Alvarez for turning the children's 'guardian angel' into a 'public statue' for others to gawk at. Alvarez could only point out, as he did, that it had been 'written with great care and as a tribute to Sylvia'. In fact he had gone as far as to compare her prolific last months to Keats' 'marvellous year'. He had neither sensationalised nor criticised, but the account remained, inevitably, intrusive.

Alvarez has had several opportunities to express his insights into Plath's work and personality. In his autobiography, for example, he returned to the irony he noted in his radio interview: 'the poems she wrote in her suicidal depression are sardonic, angry, unforgiving, tender, yet disciplined and always curiously detached; they are full of life, not death.' Above all he has remained alert to the injustice to Plath that a misreading of her life has meant to her and her poetry. In the pages of 'The New York Review of Books' in 1989 he deplored Anne Stevenson's biography *Bitter Fame* for turning Plath into a suicidal 'monster'. He rejected the 'cult' of Plath as being 'based on the suicide rather than on the pure, disciplined, hard-edged poems' and became disgusted at her misuse as a feminist cause, which he felt involved 'the crudest sentimentality'.

Al Alvarez has always been a controversial figure, which he doubtless relishes. His critics challenge the idea that poetry needs to be wedded to anxiety, risk and extremism. With the passage of time other anthologies have had their say (including Bloodaxe's 2002 bestseller, the appropriately titled *Staying Alive*). Also, Alvarez's favourite poets are increasingly becoming their biographies, especially given the near-inseparability of their lives and work. And, most obviously, other poets are in the spotlight: John Ashbery, Seamus Heaney and Paul Muldoon among them. Philip Larkin, Ted Hughes and, most recently, Geoffrey Hill have been canonised, and Britain's most popular living poets—Carol Ann Duffy and Simon Armitage—hold centre stage.

If poetry lives the second time as biography, this is true too for a handful of critics. Today we are as apt to read *about* T.S. Eliot, F. R. Leavis, William Empson, Lionel Trilling and Edmund Wilson as read their work. Harold Bloom will soon face the treatment. Al Alvarez too is beginning to draw attention for his active participation in the events of the time. After all, Wootten's book is not named *The Alvarez Generation* for nothing. Justin Quinn, reviewing it in the 'TLS', observed, 'Like his favoured and favourite poets, Alvarez has had the gift of making his own preoccupations those of the age.' But to give the last quote to the infinitely quotable man himself (who until very recently swam in the cold ponds of Hampstead Heath each morning): 'Freud has written, "Life loses in interest, when the highest stake in the game of living, life itself, may not be risked."'

JIM BURNS, JONATHAN ELLIS

> Jim Burns, *Paris, Painters, Poets*, Penniless Press Publications, 2017
> Jonathan Ellis (ed.), *Letter Writing Among Poets*, Edinburgh University Press, 2016

Reading Jim Burns—poet, essayist, reviewer and former editor—one is in excellent company. He is enthusiastic, affable and entertaining. *Paris, Painters, Poets* is the latest—the eighth—collection of reviews and essays that celebrate often little-known artists, writers and radicals. It is little wonder that his knowledge of the neglected has been described as encyclopaedic and his work as 'an entertaining homage to bohemia' ('The Times Literary Supplement').

Paris, Painters, Poets deals thematically with a number of issues, as the title implies: Paris (in history and art), Jewish and British painters, American and English poets, little magazines and American pulp fiction, the Comintern and American labour history, Jazz and McCarthy's Hollywood exiles. Behind them is Burns' habitual sympathy for left wing causes, his wariness of authority and a lifelong fascination with outsiders. While observing that 'The English just don't have a taste for bohemianism, flamboyancy, and versatility', he nevertheless follows the trail because, as he writes of the Soho art crowd, for instance, 'it will be a pity if [the secondary figures] are overlooked or dismissed as of no interest'.

There are many richly informative pieces here, including an essay-review of immigrant artists in *Shocking Paris*; a fascinating article on a biography of Lola Ridge, the adventurous, radical poet; a history of the bloody strike of North Carolina mill workers (1929); a study of the detective figure; and 'Invisible Jewish Budapest'.

What interests me about Burns' work is his knowledgeable enthusiasm for the subjects he chooses to write on, whatever the merit of the book he is reviewing. Lines like, 'It would be fascinating to track down details of what happened to…' typify his curiosity. He is never dogmatic ('I'm not going to claim that I've ever read McGrath in what might be called a systematic way.') and is quick to do justice to his sources ('I've jumped around a little… and I'm conscious of not having referred to…). He is also keen to concede a personal perspective ('Perhaps it is my own prejudices coming out that incline me to think this…'). Yet his wide reading is reassuring. He names, for example, four books in which he had earlier glimpses of Lola Ridge, before the biography under review, and a similar number on the influence of American pulp novels and on Parisian intellectuals. For Americans serving in the Lincoln Battalion during the Spanish Civil War, he gives a personally recommended booklist.

Like many veteran reviewers, Burns tends to explore his own experience of a subject as well as involving the book concerned. In fact the autobiographical touches, along with the conversational tone, lead the reader to forget sometimes that someone else's book might have prompted the essay. It is a technique that relies on being knowledgeable, experienced, fair—and honest ('I've got to admit that I bristled a bit at what I take to be an unnecessary slight on John O' Hara').

Those autobiographical moments are certainly supportive of Burns' opinions. For instance, in reviewing Sarah Bakewell's entertaining *At the Existentialist Café*, he writes 'I never found Ginsberg, but I did track down Burroughs to a shabby little club on the Left Bank and listened to him read excerpts from *Naked Lunch*'. As a poet and editor, he has been a friend of many practising poets from the 1950s onwards. And his labour sympathies are evident, also, since he worked in the mills before entering the army in the mid-1950s ('my university'), where he was posted to Germany (and was subsequently influenced by the imported American music and books not then available in Britain).

Burns writes well on art, for which he is a tireless enthusiast (and traveller). Again he is self-taught. He writes of Daubigny, 'I'm not about to claim that before the Edinburgh exhibition I knew a great deal about his life and work.' On another occasion, 'I recall an exhibition at the now sadly-closed Montparnasse Museum, which focused on Jewish painters active in Paris before the Second

World War.' He writes of attending an exhibition of bohemia at the Grand Palais in Paris in 2013, of a Picasso exhibition in Malaga and another in London in 2013.

There are interesting ideas and sound common sense throughout *Paris, Painters, Poets*. Of the eccentric Stanley Spencer he writes, 'Personally, I don't think it's always possible to separate the life from the art in any meaningful way'. On the work of the English painter John Bratby he concludes, 'It seems to me that much of his work is so autobiographical that responding to it personally is a perfectly valid way to look at it.' This resonates with Burns' antipathy to dry academics. In another review Burns finds himself wondering at the appeal of the detective story and observes, 'It's perhaps that friction with the world in general, and often with authority, in particular, that appeals to the anarchist in us.' He takes us back to the England of the 1950s and '60s—in scenes from his northern working class youth—which illustrate that 'opportunism and disillusionment were as much a part of the 1960s as the enthusiasm and idealism'.

Jim Burns is in the enviable position of writing on what interests him and perhaps the best tribute one can pay to *Paris, Painters, Poets* is to his choice and treatment of the subjects here. The one theme that seems to connect all his work is his belief in the resilience of the creative human spirit in adversity.

Letter Writing Among Poets is a largely excellent collection of essays on epistolary writing from Wordsworth to Elizabeth Bishop. It takes its subjects from deep in the age of great letter writing (c.1700–1918) to its supposedly mortal hurt at the hands of the internet and the mobile phone. The book grew out of a series of 2010/11 lectures in Sheffield and the contributors share the sensible opinion 'that every letter, however authentic-seeming, is a mix of fact and fiction, self and other, storytelling and wish-fulfilment'.

The question of the reliability of letters is fundamental and not only because they might have any number of motivations: to share autobiographical impressions or construct a self; as drafts or glimpses into the creative process; as self-justification or confession; as business or networking; as self-conscious conversations with the ages—or simply just to keep in touch. That they are a minefield is unwittingly illustrated in the introduction, where Jonathan Ellis suggests a 'personal reason' for Elizabeth Bishop's dislike of Sylvia Plath's *Letters Home:* that she herself never had a home. He also sees Sylvia's mother's parenthetical interruption in one of the letters she edited, as seeming 'petty and unsupportive', even 'gaining revenge' for her not having been shown the letter by Sylvia. Now these may well be the cases, but they may well not. Letters have to lie there and take any third party judgements.

Why *poets'* letters, we may ask? In the book, Hugh Haughton makes the point that we speak of 'hearing' from someone and that 'the notion of a poet's "voice" is uniquely intertwined with the history of poetry, and reading poets' letters offers us a unique opportunity of hearing the writers' voices outside their poetic texts'. Shelley may provide the exception since—according to Madeleine Callaghan—his letters were subject to the same 'self-fashioning' as the poetry. In contrast, Byron apparently found early the authentic voice in his letters which it took his poetry a considerable time to achieve. On the other hand, Wordsworth reckoned he made his letters 'as bad & dull as possible' to avoid the 'horror' of their being '*preserved*'.

Tricky things, then, poets' letters. For Elizabeth Barrett—a perfect subject for a study given her illness-enforced 'idleness'—they were a substitute work ethic. Edna Longley also explores their psychotherapic benefits—to Edward Thomas and Larkin—reminding us that it's the work that counts and that 'the periphery can sometimes blur rather than clarify the core'. Needless to say, the opposite happens also. Wordsworth and Gerard Manley Hopkins are both focused by their letters (*pace* Wordsworth's earlier comment). Frances Wilson dismisses 'the sexlessness of Wordsworth's persona' evident in the poems, his marriage being conducted 'as though it were an illicit affair: stealing kisses, whispering in the dark, hiding billets-doux'. Michael D. Hurley reveals that Hopkins' letters show a 'richly silly sense of humour' that 'expose the inadequacy of his popular reputation for austerity'.

The best essays in *Writing Among Poets* are, appropriately, conversational in tone. Anne Fadiman writes a wonderful study of the fated Hartley Coleridge, releasing the ankle-weight epithet he dragged through life as 'Poor Hartley'. Thomas Travisano treats us to an autobiographical take on editorial self-education with his preparation of the wonderful *Words in Air: The Complete Correspondence Between Elizabeth Bishop and Robert Lowell* (2008). However, this endlessly supportive and generous correspondence of thirty years is misused in *Letter Writing Among Poets* by Paul Muldoon in an investigative piece ('I know that some readers will think I'm exaggerating the nasty subtext here, but…'). And Lorine Niedecker's plain style ('I carry / my clarity /with me') is obstructed by the scholarly discourse of Siobhan Phillips, which leaches away some of their pleasure ('Lyric was the exemplum, since a poem was defined precisely in its detachment from contextual specificities.')

The most obvious problem with letters is that, by and large, they were meant to be private. Poets like Auden did not always practice what they preached, but one is drawn to his remark: 'When we were young, most of us were taught that it is dishonourable to read other people's letters without their consent, and I do not think we should ever, even if we grow up to be literary scholars, forget this early lesson.' We rationalise instead. Hermione Lee is looking forward to T.S. Eliot's biography 'even though he forbade it' on the grounds that 'Writers deserve all the after-lives they can get, if it means they continue to have readers.' It wouldn't necessarily make them happy though, would it? It wouldn't help Lowell, for instance, whose yoking with Elizabeth Bishop as one of 'the great duos of epistolary writing' (Angela Leighton) has resulted—to borrow a phrase from Thomas Travisano's *Midcentury Quartet* (1999)—in using one poet 'as a club to beat another'.

Finally, are letters works of literature in their own right? I share the view of Tom Paulin and Angela Leighton that 'a general poetics of the letter … is probably impossible'. There are too many variables: too many recipients with different relationships with the subject and too many purposes in the letters themselves. Are they at least autobiography? Yes, but again: beware. The answer to the question, 'Who is the *you* of your letters?' is generally 'It depends on who I'm writing to?'

ADAM KIRSCH AND MICHAEL HOFMANN: HOBBYHORSING

Adam Kirsch and Michael Hofmann are poet-critics, seasoned exponents of what John Gross called 'the art of talking on paper'. The former presents his cases more conventionally, while the latter proceeds with idiosyncratic gusto. Most recently Adam Kirsch has been given the broader remit in taking on literature *and* intellectual history in *Rocket and Lightship: Essays on Literature and Ideas* (Norton, 2015), whereas Hofmann offers an Anglo-European perspective on writers and artists in *Where Have You Been?: Selected Essays* (Farrar, Straus and Giroux, 2014). Both are passionate advocates of their tastes. It pays, therefore, in reading these two collections of review-essays to bear in mind the maxim *de gustibus non est disputandum, which Laurence* Sterne relevantly rendered as: '*there is no disputing against HOBBY-HORSES*'.

Aside from essays in the 'New York Review of Books,' the 'London Review of Books', 'The Times Literary Supplement', what first attracted me to these writers was their books. For Kirsch it was partly the subject matter of *The Wounded Surgeon* (Norton, 2005), his study of six, self-destructive American poets: Lowell, Bishop, Berryman, Jarrell, Schwartz and Plath. This served as a perhaps fated attempt at 'a brief biography' of the poetry, rather than a sensational look at their self-destructive lives (for that, one could turn to Jeffrey Meyers' *Manic Power*). There then followed the straight-talking, Arnoldian *The Modern Element* (Norton, 2008) where Kirsch waded in with, 'Over time, it has seemed less and less likely to me that criticism ought to offer disinterested assessments.' With Michael Hofmann I had been first drawn into the poetry, its gritty weaving of the personal and the public (in the shadow of Robert Lowell). *Behind the Lines: Pieces on Writing and Pictures* (Faber, 2001), his book of reviews, turned out to be a treat.

In *Why Trilling Matters* (Yale, 2011) Adam Kirsch lamented 'a literary culture suffering from a crisis of weightlessness, a feeling that literature has ceased to matter in the way it did for Trilling and his age'. *Rocket and Lightship* is another attempt to redress the situation, while also focusing on issues in cultural criticism. It is a morally serious if occasionally flawed work. My one *minor* quibble is with the unnecessary whiff of justification in the preface, which uses Matthew Arnold's dictum that 'poetry is at bottom a criticism of life' as a holdall for the essays, on the grounds that any kind of 'serious writing' will then benefit from lit. crit. Kirsch offers essays on media intellectuals and novelists. These, written for 'New Republic', 'The New Yorker', etc., may focus on a single text (such as Kazin's *Journals*), though often they offer commentary on the writer's ideas generally.

Centrally the essays concern Jewish writers—Benjamin, Kazin, Sontag, Ozick, Proust, Bellow, Arendt. 'As a writer, I'm interested in whether a coherent Jewish tradition exists across languages and countries,' Kirsch said in a 'P N Review' interview (209). In 'examining a writer's Jewishness' it is the intellectual rather than the religious aspect that interests him. So, for example, the starting point of an essay on Proust is in rabbinic literature. In another essay, Cynthia Ozick's Jewishness is said to be 'primarily a way to think about, and against literature'.

My one serious reservation comes with Kirsch's treatment of Hannah Arendt. (Like his wrong-headed, recent dismissal of Tony Judt in a review for 'Tablet') this calls into questions the reputation of a highly influential Jewish intellectual for a perceived 'refusal of solidarity' with Jewish circumstances. In 'Beware of Pity: Hannah Arendt' Kirsch recycles the controversy beginning with her treatment of the Eichmann trial (and her phrase the 'banality of evil', which identified a moral thoughtlessness). He finally sides with the critics who find her 'impersonal' and 'distant', this woman who worked for six years in Paris (1933–39) for Jewish refugee organizations.

He begins, however, with Darwin. 'Art over Biology' pursues the question of whether art itself is an evolutionary adaptation, like language, and the implications of that possibility. If it is, it must serve life in some way and, acknowledging this, Kirsch illustrates false directions in aesthetics and neuro-aesthetics. Even if there were to be 'a plausible Darwinian aesthetics' he concludes, 'it is hard to see how it would change the way we experience art, any more than knowing the mechanics of the eye makes a difference to the avidity of our sight'. 'Darwin at 150' deals with the tendency in anniversary texts to confound evolution with ethics, when centrally the 'animalization of humanity' and 'the sheer blindness of natural selection', should in themselves be enough to dispel any hierarchical notion of man and animals.

Kirsch notes the same tendency to endorse the notion of superiority, where Darwin wrote only of difference, in his review-essay on *The Origins of Political Order* (a Hegelian 'story of progressive enlightenment') by the end-of-history man, Francis Fukuyama. Kirsch identifies a paradox at the heart of Fukuyama's changed thinking about liberal democracy: that according to the author it is both ideal for all (the end point of social, cultural and political evolution) and yet, writes Fukuyama, 'Modern institutions cannot simply be transferred to other societies without reference to existing rules and the political force supporting them.'

More interesting to Kirsch is the self-styled 'hyperbolic' German philosophy of Peter Sloterdijk. Aside from its creativity, Kirsch reckons, 'One of the most appealing things about Sloterdijk's philosophy is that, like literature, it leaves itself vulnerable, instead of trying to anticipate and refute all possible objections.' He extends no such sympathetic engagement to Slavoj Žižek, the controversial Slovenian Marxist philosopher, who like Sloterdijk considers himself more interested in questions than answers. The difference is that with Žižek his critiques are 'arcane notions' (read 'confused') and their author 'a contemptuous foe of liberal democracy', while a darling of the American campus (and 'the thinker of choice for Europe's young intellectual vanguard', according to 'The Observer'). Kirsch notes that 'the treatment of Jews and Judaism in his work has long being unsettling—and in a different way from his treatment of, say, the United States, which he simply denounces'. Kirsch denounces Žižek in turn: 'Under the cover of comedy and hyperbole, in between allusions to movies and video games, he is engaged in the rehabilitation of many of the most evil ideas of the last century.'

Kirsch tackles two famous controversialists in Alfred Kazin and Susan Sontag. Reading the *Journals* of the former renders

Kirsch impatient with their note of 'self-hatred'. (Joseph Epstein recently described Kazin as 'a grievance collector of Homeric proportions'). Where Kazin's lacerate others too (like Bellow or Lionel Trilling, his *bête noire* and Kirsch's mentor) Sontag's journals are 'far too intent on her own inner experience... to care about her image'. Kirsch takes her from her early hedonism to later elitism. In a 2004 'Slate' obituary Christopher Hitchens showed himself indulgent of Sontag's stances: 'If she was sometimes a little permissive, launching a trial balloon only to deflate it later... this promiscuity was founded in curiosity and liveliness.' For his part, Kirsch is less forgiving, seeing reversals of position taking place throughout the writer's career, the point being: 'What matters about Sontag now—and this is an evolution typical of many or most critics—is not what she said, but why she said it; not the work, but the person who produced it, and for whom it served certain psychic purposes.' From the author of *Why Trilling Matters*, this is presumably a considered judgement on critics and their criticism.

Part way through the book Kirsch turns from intellectuals to novelists and they prove largely less flamboyant, though not David Foster Wallace, whose talent and commitment Kirsch sees as something of a throwback to bigger literary lives, like that of Saul Bellow. Kirsch is admiring of Bellow's work but amused at the hubris in the letters (shades of Kazan): 'Bellow's belief that what happened to him was of general, indeed cosmic, significance could seem selfish, as he well knew.' Proust too had great, if more selfless, ambitions. Like his contemporary, the poet Chaim Nachman Bialik, he attempted 'to make art a source of metaphysical value, in a way that religion used to be'. For Kirsch, 'What [Proust] is grappling with is the disparity between the artist's sense of commitment, which is absolute and infinite, and the finite, transitory nature of all human achievement.'

Prompted by the appearance of Wendy Moffat's *A Great Unrecorded History*, Kirsch offers his thoughts on E.M. Forster's sex life and its connection with his liberalism. He finds the biography lacking in revelation, overly fond at times and, in turning Forster into a champion of gay rights *avant la lettre*, distorting the truth whilst committing 'the error of making Forster's sexuality the sole determinant of his being'. This leads Kirsch to consider the novelist's negativity about the survival of liberalism and 'his sense that the novel was intimately connected with a social order that was doomed in Europe'. In the end Kirsch sees Forster's resignation not as frustration with portraying homosexuality *per se*, but in facing the limitations of all relationships.

Less revealing is 'The Last Men: Houellebecq, Sebald, McEwan' where Kirsch offers these authors as lightning rods to the zeitgeist in the way certain nineteenth century writers seem to have been (Flaubert, Dostoevsky). One might question his choices, though, and point to the fact that our saturation news coverage thrives on the contemporary mood. Certainly Kirsch has the measure of Giacomo Leopardi's nineteenth century malaise. For the Italian poet 'death does not just end life, it nullifies life, and the fact that we are going to die is the only fact that matters'. As Edmund Wilson noted somewhere, the poet's 'indictments against life' were invalidated by the fact he had never known its possibilities.

Another essay celebrates Zadie's Smith's comic vision and raises the question of her evolving postmodern techniques, while Kirsch's title essay is built of discrete observations on writing generally. Some are more obvious (e.g. 'Even philosophy, even history, never say anything true about the world, only about the writer's experience of being in the world.'). Others are less so ('authentic speech and writing are always productive of more speech and writing—indeed, that is the point of discourse, not to describe reality but to avoid silence.'). I found metaphorically rich, if a little fanciful, Kirsch's feeling that our discomfort with e-books is the way they cram 'souls' together in a data cloud—a fate similar to our own.

Rocket and Lightship makes stimulating reading, though Adam Kirsch has the critic's tendency to see in our times a dying fall. His recent review of John Berryman books in the TLS ends with, 'If we have no poets like John Berryman today, it is not because we are less ingenious than he is, but because our poetry seems to have so much less at stake.' I suppose it is healthy to find ourselves wanting—poets *and* critics—but praise where it is due. Jonathan

Derbyshire and David Herman prefaced their 'P N Review' interview with recognizing 'a thrilling generation of young critics, among them Ruth Franklin, Adam Gopnik and Adam Kirsch. Kirsch is arguably the most interesting of them all'. As his interlocutors argued, he is among a number of insightful critics of poetry, one whose moral seriousness is generally bracing.

It is useful to bear in mind Kirsch's comment that 'the critic's assertions are always, read truly, only propositions, impressions, requests for assent' when reading Michael Hofmann's *Where Have You Been?* a collection of thirty, punchy essays. Otherwise one might be swept along without the occasional, necessary demur. Where we mostly listen with interest to what Kirsch has to say, raising an objection here or there, one has to interrupt Hofmann in full flow. He is a noisy writer: nimble, passionate, eloquent, witty (In December he ended a review of Richard Flanagan's *The Narrow Road to the Deep North* with the barb: 'The book was described as having gone through many drafts, with Flanagan using those that didn't make it to "light the barbie". I can't help thinking this wasn't the right one to spare'). And he is self-assured. The one who writes 'Over time, I've become more sure of myself, and more taken with myself… I back my feel for words against just about anyone's' isn't kidding.

In the introduction to his first collection, *Behind the Lines*, Hofmann tells us that reviewing immediately appealed to him: 'It was first thoughts and second thoughts… flashes and inscriptions, swift, provisional, personal responses…'. It is the personal that is the attraction in his writing, 'the nervous authority of the reader' as he phrases it. Like all good writers Hofmann concedes, 'I have always written out of curiosity to find out what I thought of something.'

With *Where Have You Been?* the 'intellectual vagabond' and 'irresistible flaneur' of the blurb (How did he let that go?) offers high-spirited review-essays: 'Here, safely between covers, you will find my most regular and responsible writing, the hand on the shoulder, the earnest or incredulous voice in your ear, the animated gestures of deprecation or delight or indifference or bafflement.' He considers these essays both as 'homage' and, hopefully, literature in their own right.

The 'red thread' (think 'thread') of his life is here, he tells us. One of the filaments is clearly passion: '*Words in Air* is such a formidably and dramatically and lingeringly wonderful book, it is hard to know where to begin', he begins. 'That's the beginning; it hurts to stop quoting', he writes of an Adam Zagajewski poem. Having button-holed the reader, Hofmann loves the literary nod ('He does the police in different voices, and so on'; 'and when like Marvell to roll all his sourness into one ball').

Thinking aloud is another winning mannerism, offering the reader immediacy, as if he or she were listening in at the drafting stage ('I'm sure I overstate Thomas's femininity'; 'I haven't talked much about poetry'). Part way through writing of a translation of Zbigniew Herbert's collected poems Hofmann addresses us ominously: 'I sense, and perhaps you do too, that I've tried to put off the moment.'

The poet in him revels in verbal pyrotechnics. The Bishop/Lowell correspondence is 'a cocktail of infernal modesty and angelic pride. It's a further episode in Bishop's increasingly sweeping posthumous triumph over her more obvious, more ambitious, more square-toed friend. It's a rat-a-tat-tat Ping-Pong rally, an artillery exchange, a story told in fireworks, a trapeze show.' In the Frederick Seidel essay he is even more flamboyant: 'If *Poems* is a man doing a headstand, then it's man in a bowler hat, wearing a chalk-striped four piece-suit, with a handkerchief in his top pocket and a natty carnation in his buttonhole, giving you an eyeful of his heliotrope spats.' Such exuberance tends toward chains of descriptive approval. So Hofmann celebrates the 'unpredictability, storylessness, geographical unattachment' that characterises Zagajewski's poetry as much as his 'benign, animating, gently humorous imagination'.

Coupled with this vigour is Hofmann's readiness to introduce his readers to German idioms ('*Torschlusspanik*, fear of the gate closing; *Fernliebe*, heady and disinhibited) which is more conventionally educative. Equally so is his formidable use of allusion and parallel. What they give us is a drawing together of the community of European and American writers. They also raise the status of an undervalued one by drawing him into more exalted company. It can be overdone. In an essay on Robert Frost and Edward Thomas, for example, we also meet many other relationships (Pound and Eliot, Goethe and Schiller *und so weiter*, plus a nod towards Akhmatova and Brodsky) as well as references to Montaigne, Wodehouse, Orwell, Bellow, Chekhov, Brecht. There is often too much armour. James Schuyler comes with Lowell and Bishop, Kleist, Kafka, Horace and Brodsky.

Robert Lowell is to Michael Hofmann what Henry James was to Kirsch's Cynthia Ozick: a major influence and a lifelong battleground. A number of the early essays here have Lowell as subject or shadow (so much so that I started thinking of the book as *Where Have You Been, Robert Lowell?*) The beauty of the Bishop/Lowell letters—it seems to me—is in the symbiosis, not in their potential as ammunition for the currently all-conquering Bishopers. There are insightful remarks from Hofmann but they imperilled by the partisan nature of his theme ('Bishop's increasingly sweeping posthumous triumph'). To Hofmann and others Bishop is the reluctant poet, Lowell the brash self-advertising one. Don't be fooled. Despite her reticence Bishop was as eager as any poet is; Lowell was simply more obvious in his ambition. And what are we supposed to take make of Hofmann *playing* Lowell to aid his cause: 'Small wonder that Lowell (maybe) felt fraudulent' or Lowell 'praises her poems—it's a heretical thought, but it did cross my mind—without much sign of having read them'?

He calms down a little in his later essays. With Bishop he settles for sheer admiration, coupled with some insights ('Bishop liked to come across as wayward'). Yet he overdoes it. A book of hers is a 'funfair' and why do we need 'abjectly' in 'the ground note is often humorous ... but never abjectly depends on being so'. Lowell is still here, voiced as usual by Hofmann ('you can imagine Lowell muttering...'). At one point Hofmann makes the enlightened observation: 'The decades have worn against the writers of disaster... and the stronger the reaction against the so-called confessional poets, the more prominence accrued to Bishop's self-exemption'. Only when he actually writes *on* Robert Lowell alone and tries to remember initial impressions does the poet come back into focus for Hofmann. Then again he is the essential poet: 'he exemplarily converted life into literature... the range of his effects ... is unequalled.... he is unspeakably missed by his literature and his country ... in his absence, literary and civic life have both deteriorated'. (Perhaps it's better not to have dog in the fight when reading Hofmann.)

However, the jaw dropping assertion from *Where Have You Been?* comes elsewhere, in the first of two shrewd pieces on Ted Hughes where Hofmann writes, 'Hughes is at least arguably the greatest English poet since Shakespeare'. The evidence is not to be found in these pieces, though interestingly Hofmann finds that Hughes's early work, with exceptions, is 'not especially impressive', which is surely something of an overturning of received wisdom. He is right that *Birthday Letters* is 'pulled apart' by contradictory impulses. The book was seized upon with a joy which masked relief (as happens with late Bob Dylan). Hofmann has a good point, too, in remembering that pleasure with the book partly comes from the fact that it 'brought Hughes out from under the everlasting 1960s and his extended tenure of the laureateship'.

Hofmann's most attractive quality is his enthusiasm. His admiration for poets like Seamus Heaney and Les Murray is almost boundless. We have a sense of this in his thoughts on Heaney's haiku '1.1.87' and are left in no doubt with Les Murray, whose work carries the essayist to a far shore: 'Certainly, for new readers the imperative remains: start immediately, and start anywhere, and wonder, not where Murray has been—because for the last quarter century at least he has been waiting to be found, like an undiscovered or, rather, "undiscovered," continent—but where you have been, yourselves.'

Another attractive quality is Hofmann's snappy one-liners. Fred Seidel is 'a carnivore if not a cannibal in the blandly vegan compound of contemporary poetry'. Weldon Kees, whose disappearance was linked by some with Mexico (shades of Ambrose Bierce) 'is the nearly man of twentieth-century American poetry'. Hofmann is spot-on with the literary ambition of Berryman's *Dream Songs*: 'In this frantic vision, life is a race to posterity, and, once there, perhaps, a struggle for ascendancy.'

Part One ends with as rave about the Canadian poet Karen Solie. This essay first appeared in the 'London Review of Books' and is so excited that I bought the book nominally under review *The Living Option: Selected Poems*, as well as Solie's first collection (for poems that Hofmann lamented were missing from the selected). I have to say I wasn't disappointed.

Part Two of *Where Have You Been?* deals largely with European writers and artists. The Anglo-German Hofmann's attitude to translation is revealing. In a *The Guardian* review of a translation of Hölderlin, in November, 2004, he made the point that 'Many of the best poets give least in translation: Baudelaire, Puskin, Mandelstam, Heine, Lorca, Brecht. This is not only because they are more inward with their own language, but also because they have left most trace on it.' Here he tells us, 'I sometimes think there is no good news about translation, ever.'

What is most interesting is the effect of translation on this translator: 'I was happily bilingual till my midtwenties, when I began, by economic necessity, to translate. The matching of my two languages is an inner process, the setting of a broken bone, a graft, the healing of a wound.' Though he is respectful of the tradition and admiring of its best practitioners, one is still made aware of the cost to the poet-translator: 'This is all distraction on an industrial scale', though fortunately, 'the "still small voice" of poetry decibeled over'. Finally, when Hofmann writes that he wants his translating 'to make a difference', he wonders where his skill may become intrusive in the exercise, especially to those of us who expect the form to 'remain meek, clothy, predictable, a little old-fashioned'.

His essay on Arthur Schnitzler ends by comparing two translations, concluding 'only one of them writes English'. This reference to writing well returned to me when I reread his damning essay on Stefan Zweig. It may be the case that Zweig is 'the Pepsi of Austrian writing', wildly overrated today as in his own day. I read both the novel *Beware of Pity* and the autobiography *The World of Yesterday* and found neither stylistically 'putrid through and through'. Perhaps then it is the work of his translators (Phyllis and Trevor Blewitt and then Anthea Bell, whose translation of *The*

World of Yesterday was described by Zweig's recent biographer as a 'livelier and more persuasively colloquial version' than the 1942 original). It seems that these translators enhance their subject, or perhaps Hofmann is driven to extremes by the views of some of Zweig's contemporaries (especially his favourite, Joseph Roth), for according to Edwin McDowell in *The New York Times, Beware of Pity* was admired by readers as diverse as Freud, Einstein, Toscanini, Thomas Mann—and Herman Goering!

Hofmann pursues the enigmatic Robert Walser (1878–1956) largely with biographical sympathy and admiration, as he does Kurt Schwitters, whose collages made from second-hand fragments in order to 'rebuild' mirrored his sense of post-war collapse. To Hofmann 'Originality gave [his work] its moment. Personality held it together.' Personality drives the Austrian Thomas Bernhard, also. Hofmann sees his novels as 'sculptures of opinion rather than contraptions assembled from character interactions' and since the opinions are not differentiated they sound authorial. He warns against reading them as comedy.

There are many *obiter dicta* throughout *Where Have You Been?* One surprising one comes in a fond essay on W. S. Graham: 'I hold no special brief for the early poems of the '40s and '50s—they strike me as having been, for almost everyone then writing, two rank bad decades for poetry'. Eliot and Auden, Lowell and Bishop for starters? Of his two entirely negative essays in the collection the other is on Günter Grass's hypocrisy in not disclosing his teenage SS membership, given that he has served as a public voice in recent decades. *Peeling the Onion* is Grass's memoir that covers the period. What 'The New Yorker' referred to as 'a memoir of rare literary beauty' Hofmann concludes is 'whitewash'.

We may carp from time to time, but finally we admire Hofmann's performance for its effervescent insight. After all, he has 'spent years, sometimes even decades' waiting for some of the works he noisily devours before us. Writers and their hobbyhorses!

STEFAN COLLINI *COMMON WRITING*

Stefan Collini, *Common Writing: Essays on Literary Culture and Public Debate*, OUP, 2016

Stefan Collini is a historian of Victorian and modern British thought: good-humoured, stylish and witty, if always with a seriousness of purpose. *Common Writing* is his latest selection, a page-turning education in thirteen review-essays, half on literary culture, half on public debate: 'Mostly, they are about authors who, while making a mark in a particular literary genre or intellectual discipline, have also figured, however indirectly, in wider public discussion, or else about some of the media that have enabled such contributions.' The focus of these essays is on new biographies or new editions of the writers' work, and on what he has described elsewhere as 'the lineaments of sedimented identity'.

The book is again built largely of essays from the LRB and the TLS. It is a companion to *Common Reading* (2008), the title intended to signal an activity 'that is both shared and everyday'. Behind it we might hear Doctor Johnson rejoicing, in his *Lives of the English Poets*, on 'the common sense of readers uncorrupted with literary prejudices'.

Common Writing has a starry—if predominantly deceased—cast of poets, literary and cultural critics, professors, journalists and historians: public intellectuals. Some are not as celebrated today, it must be said. For instance, Collini discusses those in the 'English tradition of ethically driven progressive social commentary', like the Hammonds, Tawney, Hoggart and Titmuss. He also considers historians such as Eileen Power (impact overstated) and Herbert Butterfield (biographically enhanced) in contrast to Hugh Trevor-Roper (greatly gifted, insensitive, and lacking the magnum opus). Then there is the sentimental but serious J. B. Priestley, C. S. Lewis ('at times seeming to use surface depths to mask deeper shallows') and Maurice Bowra. This piece begins ominously: 'What is the best case that can be made for Maurice Bowra?' In contrast, Collini contextualises his appreciation of the work of the dated Day Lewis and the excellent Graham Greene in terms of their 'bloodstock details'.

Poets come off a little better. Collini welcomes A. David Moody's biography of Ezra Pound, as it 'eschews hindsight', essential in any serious treatment of early Pound's contribution to poetry. With Eliot, Collini is constrained by the fact that volume 1 of the Letters (1898–1922) had the Modernist sparks, while he is stuck reviewing volumes 2 and 3: domestic unhappiness, editorial correspondence ('the spirit does not leap at the prospect of so many thousands of pages of elaborate politeness').

Empson and Leavis provide more substance. There is a review of Haffenden's 'magnificent' two-volume biography of the former, as well as praise for Hilliard's 'excellent' book on 'Scrutiny'. We learn that Leavis had less impact on American campuses, whereas Empson's marvellously close readings suited the spirit of the New Criticism. However, Leavis's view of Literature as a vocation was paramount in influencing others: teachers, students (and the *Pelican Guide*). Collini is admiring of Lionel Trilling, yet circumspect: 'There is, for many of us, something vaguely oppressive about the thought of having to re-read Lionel Trilling now.' Even so, Trilling remains *the* cultural critic in the tradition of the Coleridge and Arnold. Collini reads very interestingly on Raymond Williams's contribution to British intellectual life, valuing Dai Smith's biography of the author of the seminal *Culture and Society*.

You might expect some fun when Collini approaches Kingsley Amis and David Lodge, after all he has admitted elsewhere to being drawn to Amis's and Larkin's, 'skeptical, human, funny idiom'. That idiom does indeed prove hard for him to resist, but inevitably the portrait of a man debilitating is rather sad to witness. Nevertheless Collini is willing to see the subtle potential of 'monochrome' in the writer's work. He is less sanguine about Joyce enthusiast David Lodge, whose later writing—essays and memoir—is felt to fall short.

An essay on 'Migrants' recounts the story of the indefatigable Nikolaus Pevsner, the German historian of English architecture and of Ernest Gellner, the stylish Czech social anthropologist. The Isaac Deutscher versus Isaiah Berlin conflict takes centre stage here, segueing into a consideration of Berlin's biography. The latter had, to a debatable degree, prevented Marxist historian Deutscher's appointment as Senior Lecturer at Sussex University, and then denied it. The affair was later seized on by Christopher Hitchens in a damning article in the LRB. Sensibly—in my view—Collini suggests there is little point in dismissing Berlin, the brilliant, gossipy establishment figure, as a weak and 'calculating Cold War ideologue'. Instead Collini makes out of the rhetorical exuberance of Berlin's letters a point that I believe applies to all correspondence: the necessity 'for a certain interpretative tact from the reader before [it] can be pressed into service as historical sources'.

A review of a biography of Roy Jenkins proves to be typically fair-handed, if the imagery is a little fanciful at times ('a man who, though never crowned as philosopher-king, became for a while the Crown Prince of social democracy'). Collini then moves from one who helped to sink the Labour Party to the Canadian professor (and Berlin biographer) Michael Ignatieff who was to 'wreck the fortunes of the Canadian Liberal Party'.

An essay on the media, reviews books on the TLS, the New Left Review and Radio 4, celebrating their survival skills. Another, on 'Social Analysis', deals with government reports: the ideological function of propaganda (which destroys the egregious metaphor of 'the level playing-field'); the dangers inherent in 'the relentless cultivation of individualism' by governments for the past thirty years; and the crucial dependence of statistical techniques upon language.

Collini is almost too engagingly even-handed at times. Qualifications like 'may', 'arguably' and 'such a view "risks"' are subtle but insubstantial, which is why he is uneasy with Christopher Hitchens, Tony Judt and Timothy Garton Ash, in what is for me his most-self-revealing essay, 'New Orwells?' All three are deemed too assured in their judgments (in reviews written before the deaths of the first two). Hitchens, of course, could take care of himself: 'His preferred genre is the polemic; his favoured tone mixes forensic argument with a kind of high-octane contempt.' Collini wonders how Hitchens will deal sensitively with his own hero, in *Orwell's Victory* (answer: they have a lot in common, some of it wrong-headed). He fears that Hitchens preferred role as contrarian might just be leading him into the wrong (i.e. Right) company—Amis *père* and others—and then by declension into a bore.

He is hard on Tony Judt in my estimation. Reviewing *Reappraisals* he finds Judt in many pieces 'gives a master-class in the role of the historian as public intellectual', but at other times 'he writes more in the vein of the prosecuting attorney'. Collini feels Judt's polemics are too certain, too passionate, too unambiguous. It is certainty again that troubles Collini with Timothy Garton Ash's scholarly journalism: 'Perhaps I would admire him still more if his journalism now gave a little more room, as his best essays do, to the hesitations and ambivalences that must be part of the attempt to understand on this heroic scale.'

And it is in these comments that I think we come closest to Stefan Collini's own ideal of cultural criticism (if we substitute that term for 'history' in his following observation):

> The best works of history rarely yield unambiguous support to any political cause or affiliation, and we look to the vocabulary, register, and cadence of good historical writing to communicate that chastened sense of complexity which otherwise can struggle to get itself heard in public debate.

The best literary/cultural criticism transcends the genre to address the moral life. The intellectuals Collini deals with, the ideas that motivated them and they in turn articulated to motivate others remain important, even in the shadows. I think of Geoffrey Hill's lines from 'Scenes with Harlequins':

> Even now one is amazed
> by transience: how it
> outlasts us all.

RICHARD HOLMES *THIS LONG PURSUIT*

Richard Holmes, *This Long Pursuit: Reflections of a Romantic Biographer*, Collins, 2016

In an observation that has stayed with me, Lionel Trilling wrote: 'Some of the charm of the past consists of the quiet—the great distracting buzz of implication has stopped and we are left only with what has been fully phrased and precisely stated. And part of the melancholy of the past comes from our knowledge that the huge, unrecorded hum of implication was once there and left no trace' ('Manners, Morals, and the Novel'). I mention this because the finest biographers—and I include Richard Holmes among them—are able to hint at least at noises off.

There is no coincidence in Holmes calling his passionately vivid biography, *Shelley: The Pursuit* (1974). In a real sense all Holme's biographical works are pursuits, physical as well as intellectual journeys, geographical as well as scholastic. Holmes has constantly returned to the image. As he wrote in *Footsteps: Adventures of a Romantic Biographer* (1985), '"Biography" meant a book about someone's life. Only, for me, it was to become a kind of pursuit, a tracking of the physical trail of someone's path through the past, a following of footsteps.' And again in *Sidetracks: Explorations of a Romantic Biographer* (2000): 'For me biography has always been a personal adventure of exploration and pursuit, a tracking.' The reason is that, as he eloquently explained of Shelley, the 'life seems more a haunting than a history'. In *This Long Pursuit* he reiterates the theme vigorously: 'I had come to believe that the serious biographer must *physically* pursue his subject through the past. Mere archives were not enough. He must go to all the places where the subject had ever lived or worked, or travelled or dreamed.'

He is nothing, then, if not a romantic biographer of the Romantics. In *Coleridge: Early Visions* (1989), for instance, he wrote in the preface: 'If he does not leap out of these pages—brilliant, animated, endlessly provoking—and invade your imagination (as he has done mine), then I have failed to do him justice.' And now, in *This Long Pursuit*, we learn he yearns to dance around the dinner table with Madame de Staël!

This latest book is substantially autobiographical, a reworking of lectures, articles and introductions, the third of the trilogy after *Footsteps* and *Sidetracks*. For Holmes the last leg is 'a sort of eulogy: a celebration of a form, an art, and a vocation that I have intensely loved over more than forty years, and which I still do not entirely understand'. A work of discovery and rediscovery, it is arranged in three sections: 'Confessions', 'Restorations' and 'Afterlives'.

Holmes has always been keen for us to glimpse the biographer's craft as he sees it. In *Footsteps* he recounted learning cardinal lessons as a young man in Paris, one being 'that the past is not simply "out there", an objective history to be researched or forgotten, at will; but that it lives most vividly in all of us, deep inside, and needs constantly to be given expression and interpretation'. In *This Long Pursuit* he reveals his own method of transcribing it: research detail to be written on one side of a notebook page and personal responses on the other—'The cumulative experience of the research journey, of being in my subject's company over several years, thus became part of the whole biographical enterprise'—hence the empathy, the passion, the material for these 'reflections' (and the nearly 200 working notebooks he has filled).

Holmes' first essay, 'Travelling', recounts with a touch of humour his geographical pursuit of Shelley, Stevenson and particularly Coleridge. 'Experimenting', the next, reminds us (with illustrations from the lives of the Herschels among others) that the age of the Romantic poets was equally a great age of scientific discovery and innovation. Holmes explored this in *The Age of Wonder* (2008), a book in which he tried 'to capture something of the inner life of science, its impact on the heart as well as on the mind'. In this essay he recounts being daunted by the prospect of introducing that book in a lecture to the Royal Society.

In 'Teaching' Holmes remembers how reflection on the academic potential of biography led him to design and teach an M.A. course at the University of East Anglia. Animating questions involved the seemingly transient nature of biographical knowledge, how perspectives change with period and access to new materials, how no one work is definitive. He considers, therefore, a new discipline: comparative biography. 'Forgetting' deals with 'nominative aphasia' and 'associationism' (including David Hartley's classic text of 1749) as well as current theories. There is also room for Proust and Porlock. Finally, 'Ballooning' finds Holmes 'in restless middle-age' taking up the noble sport but bringing back a highly curious account of Poe fictionalising Coleridge's experimental intrepidity.

As well as bringing science back into the Romantic equation, Holmes has also been alert to the contribution of women to the history of thought. He devotes part two of his new book, 'Restorations', to a handful of writers and scientists who deserve greater recognition: Margaret Cavendish ('Poet, polemicist, feminist, satirist, aristocrat, naturalist, stylist, eccentric and survivor' *and* the first woman to attend a meeting of the Royal Society); the Enlightenment writer, Zélide ('I find an hour or two of mathematics freshens my mind and lightens my heart.'); the brilliant and exhausting conversationalist and writer, Madame de Staël; the once-celebrated 'educational writer and champion of women's rights', Mary Wollstonecraft; and Mary Somerville, author of the best-selling *On the Connexion of the Physical Sciences* (1834) an early work of popular science.

Interesting as these narratives are, they are inevitably sketchy. With his more famous male Romantics, Holmes has the luxury of focusing on one theme, the life already being much travelled over. Here we must trust to the potential in his claim: 'biography as a form is destined continually to challenge conventions of silence and ignorance'.

In the final third of the book Holmes returns to his intimacy with these Romantic poets: Keats, Shelley, Coleridge, Blake and, in addition, Regency portrait painter Thomas Lawrence. As 'Afterlives' suggests he is concerned with reputations, with what Keats called the 'posthumous existence'. He is interested in the myths that have encrusted his subjects, with the biographies which have rescued them. He recounts working on his Shelley biography on a balcony overlooking the Spanish Steps in the apartment where Keats' died: 'It was the back room, the proper place for a biographer.'

Holmes goes on to discuss instances of Keats's survival in the popular imagination, including an apparent craze for literary tattooing (though he misses Galway Kinnell's wonderful 'Oatmeal', in which the two poets breakfast together). Always interested in the intensely personal biography, Holmes discusses Nicholas Roe on Keats (as he does Godwin's life of Wollstonecraft and Geoffrey Scott's Zélide).

Admitting to having earlier ducked the posthumous shenanigans around Shelley, he now seeks to make amends, to rescue his reputation from the popular myths of the 'incompetent sailor', 'the fated spirit', and the 'posthumous angel' of Mary Shelley's creation. With reference to the poet's watch, preserved in the Bodleian Library, he reflects on the difference between human time, historical time and biographical time. 'The dead may always be biographically immortal', he concludes.

Holmes then turns to 'revarnishing' the charming Thomas Lawrence, whose work 'transcended personal portraiture, and captured the spirit of the age' (though I would have preferred to see the seven minute 'likenesses' the precocious child made of the regulars at his father's coaching inn). In the final essay Holmes turns to William Blake.

He recounts in narrative detail how Blake was painstakingly, even heroically, rediscovered by the Victorian Alexander Gilchrist and his wife, Anne, and then how he has variously served succeeding generations, like the radical '60s. (I, too, once witnessed Allen Ginsberg chanting 'Little Lamb', while accompanying himself on squeeze box in Manchester, an image had to dislodge).

There is great similarity between Richard Holmes and the fated Gilchrist. As the latter's widow observed: 'He desired always to treat his subject exhaustively: … as a biographer to stand hand in hand with him, seeing the same horizon, listening, pondering, absorbing.'

ROBERT HASS & STEPHEN BURT

> Robert Hass, *A Little Book on Form: An Exploration into the Formal Imagination of Poetry*, Ecco, 2017
> Stephen Burt, *The Poem is You: 60 Contemporary American Poems and How to Read Them*, Harvard, 2016

There is a moment in *A Little Book on Form* where Robert Hass offers his students (and now readers) 'a small exercise. Take an afternoon and reread Wordsworth's "Tintern Abbey" and "Immortality Ode" and maybe one other Wordsworth ode or the first book of *The Prelude* and Coleridge's "Frost at Midnight" and his "Dejection: An Ode" and then read—written about twenty-two years later, the five Keats odes—"Psyche," "Melancholy," "Nightingale,", "Grecian Urn," and "To Autumn."' One's first reaction is that this is a demanding workout—but there is a point to it: 'I don't know if you will share my experience of them, but I found that when reading them in that order, the striking thing about the Keats poems was that they seemed so beautifully finished and a little old-fashioned.' This sort of statement is characteristic of Robert Hass's critical writings. It combines insight, admiration and commitment with an open personal touch.

In this highly stimulating, though hardly 'little', book the acclaimed poet and essayist goes beyond metrical rules and rhyme schemes, to consider the 'formal imagination in poetry'. He is searching for a language to explore its intuition and creativity. Hence the tentativeness of 'notes toward' in the following: 'It seemed possible to construct notes toward a notion of form that would more accurately reflect the openness and the instinctiveness of formal creation.'

Mercifully this is not nearly as abstruse as it sounds. In fact Hass offers quite a comprehensive course, developed to guide young poets at the University of Iowa Writers Workshop through two years of intense study. Beginning in 1995 Hass has added to these 'notes' which have swelled with the addition of so many examples of the poet's craft that *A Little Book on Form* offers an annotated anthology worth reading in its own right. In the interests of accessibility his approach has been to begin with consideration of the single line (the completed clause, the line, the one-sentence line, the one-line stanza, the experimental one line poem) and then to move to the two-line poems and stanza, to three and then four (from which 'almost all the likely formal propositions in both metrical and free verse poems can be derived'). He turns then to blank verse (one 'implicit model' for free verse), followed by poetic forms (sonnets, odes and elegies, etc.) to end with consideration of stress and how free verse works.

What is on offer is distance learning at the hands of a Berkeley professor, complete with frequent reading lists and occasional exercises. We meet a great deal of information along the way: the synoptic history of forms; examples from different cultures (including Asian, Chinese and Persian); explorations of craft. Hass's students took their course in three hour sessions, the second half—student-led—on form outside poetry. Seasoned readers will work out their own timetable, attracted by old favourites from Horace to Heaney, along with the pleasure of discovery. (I might note that English poetry effectively disappears from consideration in the twentieth century. There are an honoured few outsiders: Breton, Lorca, Heaney, Herbert, Miłosz, Neruda, Yeats. Otherwise it's Americans from Whitman and Dickinson to, say, Lyn Hejinian and the poet's wife, Brenda Hillman.)

The book is commendable for its pithy explanations and insights: 'The term romantic is a convenience for observing a shift in the notion of the poem from the idea that the work of the imagination was to make vivid and attractive the ideas that are available to us through reason or an empirical common sense to the idea that imagination was not illustrative, but creative, that the imagination embodied its own kind of knowledge, deeper, phenomenologically fuller, than the kinds of thing the other labors of knowing afford us.' Discussing the ode—the longest and perhaps the most interesting part of the book—Hass turns to the inward journey of thought in 'Frost at Midnight', to the poem's structure: 'I wanted to call attention to this rivery movement in the verse of this period because it tracks a different sense of mind [anticipating surrealism and stream-of-consciousness] ...It represents thought as something nearer to what we think of as imagination, a proceeding by intuitions having to do with likeness, with mirroring and echoing, with an oscillation between thought and sensation, discursive and mimetic modes.'

In an earlier essay, 'Listening and Making', Robert Hass remembered a friend taking exception to a comment he had made about 'metrical inversion' in a line by Robert Lowell. 'He said he liked the piece well enough, but that one phrase—that finical tic of the educated mind—had filled him with rage.' Hass added, 'I think I understand why.' Perhaps the good-humoured *A Little Book on Form* isn't for his friend, but it should be for many of us.

While Hass's chosen poems have largely been tested by time, Harvard professor Stephen Burt has the difficult task of illustrating contemporary excellence (1981–2015). *The Poem Is You* is a celebration, from sea to shining sea, of the current state of American poetry. (I venture the patriotic touch because Stephen Burt sees poetry's health and especially diversity as an image of America itself.) He illustrates its vivacity in sixty essays, each following the poem which is its subject, explicating, contextualising, biographizing and venturing into other fields in support: psychology, neuroscience, evolutionary theory, phenomenology and so forth. Diversity is certainly the key to the collection: 'the recondite and the demotic, the accessible and the challenging, mingle'. At the same time Burt repeatedly cautions that the chosen poems are only his take on the poetic variety to be found today. Thirty years from now, he suggests, the chosen poems might be 'in Spanish, or in Hmong, or in American Sign Language'. For less adventurous readers what is here may be confusing enough.

Although Burt does not make the point himself, he acknowledges that there are those critics like Marjorie Perloff who have long argued that 'models of poetry as conceptual exploration, resistant to speech, or perpetual experiment [have] replaced or displaced models of poetry as "lyric," or rendered it obsolete'. Certainly many of the poems in Burt's book are claiming or reclaiming what he likes to call 'space' from what had gone before (Zukofsky and Oppen, Lowell and Bishop). He defends Claudia Rankine's *Citizen: An American Lyric* (2014) as a bona fide recipient of poetry prizes as very sensible, 'if "poetry" means a text that brings together the many aspects of language in order to explore someone's, or anyone's, interior life, to challenge the transparency of common language, and to do something that mere exposition or narrative could never do'.

And so we have, in *The Poem is You*, an openness with forms—prose-sense deniers, a one-line poem, some computer speak, on-line alt-lit, a homophonic translation—but with common concerns and all, presumably, excellent. Burt's avant-garde choices are meant to open up questions of who is reading what and how we read it. Those gripping tightly to the lyric tradition may feel–using the old analogy of modern painting—that gallery walls alone confer status upon some of his chosen examples.

This is where Burt's admittedly excellent commentaries come to the rescue. He knows the poems; he knows the poet's background, techniques, and their public statements. He knows the poems that clustered around the one he chose for its representational nature. His method is to let us in on it all ('I chose this one because it shows how to read the others.'). Yet we may legitimately wonder at times if the ingenuity is in the poem or rather in Burt's exploration of it. Some of the chosen poems do not hold the reader's attention, or do not repay it. In these cases I felt—assuming I might be the mouldy fig– that an anthology served the poet poorly. Then again, shouldn't a poem be able to stand alone?

I seem to have fixated on the weaknesses of Burt's choices. Yet there are many excellent poems and poets too. There are highly informative essays on a number of poems by well-established poets like Miłosz, Ammons, Charles Wright and Komunyakaa, for instance. And there are memorable poems, like Merrill's 'Self-Portrait in TyvekTM Windbreaker', Glück's 'Lamium' and C. D. Wright's 'Key Episodes from an Earthly Life'. I have had interesting introductions, too—to Linda Gregerson, Kay Ryan, Joseph Massey and Albert Goldbarth among others.

The Poem is You (shame about the title) compels serious attention as news from the poetry front. For that alone it would certainly be worth reading—and we have the extra benefit of Burt's enthusiastic ruminations.

THE LAMENTATIONS OF ARTHUR KRYSTAL

> If you think that *Buffy the Vampire Slayer* deserves to be the subject of an academic dissertation in English or that the Tarzan books belong in the literary canon because they have been anointed by the Library of America, then you are living at the right time. Elitist literary culture is as defunct as Buffalo Bill, a semi-elitist reference that thirty or forty years ago would have been familiar to serious readers.
> – Krystal

As Jeremiahs go, Arthur Krystal is an affable, erudite one, who dispenses his opinions with humour but also with steel. As he explains in *Except When I Write*, he has learned from William Hazlitt: 'In his wonderful essay "The Fight," Hazlitt recalls overhearing one man say to another, "Confound it, man, don't be insipid" and thinking, "that's a good phrase."' Krystal thinks so, too. He does not try to match his master's 'subversive wallop' (nor scorch like Hitchens or garrotte like Epstein) but prefers a tone he once described as provocative but not offensive. Then there is the humour (('I can only speak for the person who brushes my teeth'), the disarming candour ('Like most writers, I seem to be smarter in print than in person') and the literary urbanity ('After all, a Wildean willfulness to be misunderstood underscores one's tastes, adding a certain élan to one's appreciations'). A typical Krystal essay or review balances insight, sense and humour, trawling back through the past of an issue, liberally illustrating it with quotations from interested parties. (For this we forgive him some old targets and the occasional 'judicious repetition' of opinions and references.)

There are now four slim, infinitely quotable books of essays: *Agitations: Essays on Life and Literature* (2002): *The Half-Life of an American Essayist* (2007); *Except When I Write: Reflections of a Recovering Critic* (2011); and slimmest of all, *This Thing We Call Literature* (2016). Krystal (born 1948) is a regular contributor to 'The New Yorker' and 'Harper's Magazine' among others, where he writes and reviews on any number of subjects, from God to night time. He is also an editor on the work of Jacques Barzun, his teacher, and a screenwriter to boot.

For me, he is at his most interesting as a literary essayist and there he focuses on essentials: 'In short, no art without craft; no craft without individual sensibility; and no art-object without the artist's negotiation between tradition and innovation.' A student of the canonical tradition, his lamentations on the state of literature, like Hazlitt's, begin in personal observation ('the romance of books is swiftly disappearing') and proceed from the premise that 'art has always been the product of talent, skill, inspiration, and labor; and so, to a degree, has been the appreciation of art'. Consequently art is the responsibility both of its creators and its audience. It is Krystal's view that both sides have been failing badly, so badly in fact that the know-nothings, the politically suspect and the mercenary have taken over.

Agitations introduced us to Krystal's perspective on what he has recently called 'this age of diminished expectations', where taste has been reduced to a matter of personal preferences. He caused a stir with the essay 'Closing the Books: A Once-Devoted Reader Arrives at the End of the Story', first published in 'Harper's' in 1996 and included here. Essentially Krystal argues there that he can no longer find pleasure, meaning or merit in literature. He concedes that it is difficult to recapture the excitement of discovery one first has as a young reader and also that our experiences in life dull the impact of like experiences in literature. However, he sees other stifling forces involved. The media has been 'devaluing the idea of privacy' and thereby impoverishing the writer's imagination. Further, the literary climate has been smothered by the academy, 'that confederation of professors and curricula which over the last three decades has reversed the respective status of criticism and belles lettres'.

In 'The Rise and Fall of Theory' we hear that those 'superior' professors saw in 'novels and poems ... semiotic tracts that reflect all sorts of nasty, royalist, elitist, patriarchal, sexist, and imperialist sympathies'. In cutting the text down to size they served to politicise and further alienate audiences. Yet Krystal reminds us that 'art is not foremost in the business of rectifying injustice or inequality; it is not about the suffering masses. It is about those who are born with a need and a gift to create, and about people whose nature and intelligence compel them to seek and understand such creation.' To Krystal being literary is comparable to being musical, not militant.

Universities are the custodians of literature. In 'What Do You Know?'—on the decline of embarrassment at ignorance—he writes, 'Students are urged to get hip to what "knowledge" and "culture" really signify: the power struggle between classes, races, and sexes.' In 'Death, It's What Ails You', he worries that the remoteness of dead writers seems to be accelerating alarmingly. Not only is Dryden dropped, he argues by way of example, but Milton too, in favour of Stephen King (a popular example with Krystal of someone having greatness thrust upon them). And yet poets also deserve a kicking.

'Going, Going, Gone' turns specifically to the decline of poetry, its modernist practitioners creating a chasm between the 'text' and conventional readers: 'The irony here is that in ridding itself of formal characteristics and adopting free verse to portray the world more realistically, in language approximating the vocabulary and rhythms of ordinary discourse, poetry succeeded in losing what little audience it had left.'

Krystal has been disappointed in print about poetry since at least 1996, feeling that poets are over-hyped, with critics 'assigning greatness where there is only intelligence and competence'. Back then he named names: Helen Vendler, John Ashbery, Rita Dove. Not so in his new book, *This Thing We Call Literature*. 'LISTEN to the Sound It Makes' takes-on the deafness of contemporary poets. He laments the dearth of memorability in modern poetry, which he ascribes to a lack of interest in its musical nature, in the rhythm, the metre. With acknowledged exceptions (Wilbur, Walcott, Heaney at times) he feels the day the music died was somewhere around 1977, its requiem Larkin's 'Aubade'.

Paradoxically—and this he acknowledges—Krystal's preference has always been for reading a poem and not for hearing it read aloud.

So the music has been internalised: 'the tempo, the emphasis, the feelings are synthesized in us'. The poet's voice is constantly forging the reader's. He does not damn poets for incompetence. In fact he finds 'intelligence, shrewdness, irony, and humor' in many practitioners (some named), but not an interest in music. Krystal's problem with the 'atonal' nature of contemporary poetry is compounded by his sense that continuity has been severed with the past and its poetic wealth. Essentially, as Trilling explained in *Matthew Arnold*, 'Natural magic and moral profundity—these are the two attributes of great poetry.' Krystal can no longer find them.

There is no one way to answer that, unless it is to give lists of the 'musical' poems Krystal omitted to mention. When the essay appeared in 'The Chronicle of Higher Education' quite a few of the responders did give lists. One argued hip hop and rap were the current poetic musical locus; another pointed to the fact that the poets Krystal liked were dead and anthologised and therefore more often seen; another questioned the automatic connection of music with metric regularity. Others might have blamed the universities for turning poetry into metaphysics, or into emails among friends. They might have wondered if perhaps Krystal's own nostalgia has something to do with his beef. At any event, the comments showed there is breath in the argument yet.

It is not Hazlitt, but the spirit of Lionel Trilling which permeates *This Thing We Call Literature*. Like the 'Closing the Books' essay, it is 'essentially a lament and not a condemnation of the general literary culture' although there *is* condemnation of those who trumpet the new as the great, or elevate the second rate. Creative works are being talked up wildly because of the absence of the real thing, or because it is in the interests of the talkers (critics, professors, publishers, gallery owners) or, as Rebecca Watts argued, on the part of cultural commentators who 'are playing a part in the establishment's muddle-headed conspiracy to "democratise" poetry' (See PNR 239 'The Cult of the Noble Amateur'. At numerous times, when reading Krystal, the mind turns to her reasoned argument).

Two essays in the collection deal with genre fiction, those novels 'delivering less rarefied pleasures'. One concerns 'Time' magazine's book critic, Lev Grossman's contention that genres are hybridizing and hierarchies collapsing, an argument Krystal engages with. (He also interestingly contrasts the opening of Christie's *Murder on the Orient Express* with Ford's *Parade's End* to illustrate how Christie's language wants us to settle in to the narrative, while 'Ford demands that we pay attention'.) Krystal also makes the point that anyway enjoyment is not a matter of choosing between the high and low, since quality always comes down to craft: '[Elmore] Leonard has his skills *and* his place in literature without exactly being part of literature as Trilling understood it.'

Ultimately, though, this high-low business does matter greatly. In 'A Sad Road to Everything', Krystal suggests the tension which exists between the individual and society is at the heart of what literature is about and that literature 'charts our changing relationship to the issues that intrigue us'. It is vital, therefore, that literary writers 'interrogate reality' to explore the human condition. To break down the barriers to what constitutes serious literature, then, to give everything equivalence as publishers do when sales drive critical reception, is more than worrying. Literature is, to Krystal, what Matthew Arnold called 'a criticism of life'. And if all this smacks of elitism, so what? 'Literature is an art and not meant to be convenient… This doesn't automatically exclude the less sophisticated, but it might, and so be it.'

The other elephant in the room is, of course, 'the canon'. The essay 'What is Literature?' begins with a narrative of the canon's history: 'a way of establishing a national literature that would build on the Ancients and vie with other nations'. Incorporated into university syllabuses in the 1920s, it held sway until the 1970s and 80s when the so-called 'culture wars' undermined its legitimacy, because of its supposed exclusivity, paternalism, oppressiveness, reverence, and hierarchical, patronising nature—in other words its justification of 'the prevailing social order'. Acknowledging the canon was at least 'exclusionary by nature', 'a result of the middle class's desire to see its own values reflected in art', Krystal comes to its defence 'as a convenient fiction, shaped in part by the material conditions under which writing is produced and consumed, while simultaneously recognizing the validity of hierarchical thinking and aesthetic criteria'. We live, inevitably, in a world of Top 20s.

Krystal brings us up to the moment with 'The Shrinking World of Ideas' where he argues, in effect, that science has built a flyover where once stood Trilling's 'dark and bloody crossroads where literature and politics meet'. The Second World War and the Cold War had raised crucial moral issues, which literature, history and philosophy were there to address. Trilling became a proponent, therefore, of the idea that literature was a reason for living. (Now he is merely 'literature's superego', 'a suffocating ghost' according to Adam Kirsch, in *Why Trilling Matters* (2011).) Even fifty years ago, according to Krystal, 'we opened books not just to learn about the content of a writer's mind but to hear the right words in the right order telling us things we sensed to be true'.

Eventually critical theory derailed the 'humanistic charter' of the arts and now scientific disciplines have triumphed, especially neuroscience because 'our preferences, behaviors, tropes, and thoughts—the very stuff of consciousness—are by-products of the brain's activity'. Where we once saw—with critics like Barzun and Trilling—'no fissure between moral and aesthetic intelligence,' we now see synapses.

Occasionally an Arthur Krystal essay focuses on a single eminent critic. In his new book, his longest essay is a consideration of Erich Auerbach with his seminal work of comparative literature, *Mimesis*, 'the apex of European humanist criticism'. Krystal's presents a well-rounded portrait of a man who seemed to share Dante's sense of tragic destiny, who literally and temperamentally came to be defined by exile and thought, a critic with occasional failings, but a master of the philological approach to literature.

Krystal's interest in Auerbach suggests there is life in high culture yet. If it is defunct then, as Lesley Chamberlain wrote in defence of George Steiner in a recent 'TLS' letter, 'If there are generations out there who have never registered high culture's early twentieth-century objection to democracy's downsides, and the commodification of everything, then they are missing a vital chapter in the history of ideas.'

And yet there is still so much to be argued over in the pages of Arthur Krystal's collections. After all, reading is a serious business—or it should be.

JAMES WRIGHT: A BIOGRAPHY

Jonathan Blunk, *James Wright: A Life in Poetry*, Farrar, Straus and Giroux, 2017

James Wright found in poetry a disciplined means of self-preservation against the mental torment, the alcohol-fuelled mayhem his life sought. A fine poet, a charismatic teacher grounded in the metrical tradition and New Criticism, he followed a different path to the so-called Confessional, the Beat and the New York poets of the period, prompted by his assimilation of Latin verse and the poetry of Germany and South America. *In The Branch Will Not Break* (1963) and *Shall We Gather at the River* (1968), probably his best known collections, he moved toward freer forms which could accommodate the vernacular and eventually prose.

Wright, the man, lived at a pitch of intensity which sends the reader reeling. His selected letters, *A Wild Perfection*, reveal a passionate, restlessly experimental figure. He can be 'hysterical and profane', humiliated and deeply apologetic, compassionate and brutally frank. He knew his gift, if at times faint-heartedly, but grew to be his own most merciless critic. Of his first collection, *The Green Wall* (1957), he wrote it 'stank'; his second, *Saint Judas* (1959), was '*still* second rate'. He was to describe *Two Citizens* (1973), in an appreciative letter to Dave Smith, the poet who had reviewed it with 'intelligent good will', as a 'botched effort', a 'bad book'. The letters give a visceral sense both of Wright's demanding expectations of his work and what it cost him in his search for technique.

A bipolar condition fuelled his mental states, wreaking havoc with the life and the poetry at times. In May 1958 he wrote to his teacher, John Crowe Ransom: 'If I could curb my personal hysterias, then perhaps by the same token I could purge my verses of their violence.' In the following year he told James Dickey, 'I have been getting the shuddering horrors, indescribably so, and frequently going to pieces, sometimes in really mad and violent ways... Worst of it is that it hits me as pure egoism.' Two years later he confessed to Anne Sexton, 'in my real self, I am way off in the darkness, and sometimes the light, dazzled beyond vanity, at war with sloth'. Industry caused the pressures it kept at bay. In the mid-1970s he still wrote of attacks in which he felt 'a loneliness of the soul, in which I feel an appalling sense of abandonment and loss'. Such turbulence alternated with periods of calm, with amazing productivity, with generosity and genuine feeling for family, friends and students.

Wright grew up unhappily in the town of Martin's Ferry, Ohio, on the West Virginia border ('that unspeakable rat-hole'), where his father worked for the Hazel-Atlas Glass factory. It gave Wright a subject: the desperation of lives, the dark waters of the Ohio River and of the self. As Robert Hass explained, his famous preoccupation with, 'the suffering of other people, particularly the lost and the derelict, is actually a part of his own emotional life. It is what he writes from, not what he writes about.'

After a year's absence from school caused by a nervous breakdown, Wright began 'to rise from the dead'. Recognising that the G.I. Bill would fund his studies, he enlisted in the post-war army at graduation, which took him to Japan. In 1948 he enrolled at Kenyon College in Gambier, Ohio, where he learnt German, began translating poets and contributed to Ransom's 'Kenyon Review'. Graduating with honours, he married and received a Fulbright Scholarship to study German literature in Vienna. There he discovered Trakl's poetry. The following year Wright enrolled in graduate school at the University of Washington in Seattle, with the intention of preparing for settled employment teaching literature.

Those years 1954–56 were crucial in his development. While being taught by Theodore Roethke and Stanley Kunitz, he met Richard Hugo, Carolyn Kizer and David Wagoner. He also began a lifelong correspondence with Donald Hall. W. H. Auden chose his first collection, *The Green Wall*, for the Yale Series of Young Poets during the time he worked for his PhD (on Dickens). In 1957 Wright began teaching at the University of Minnesota. He struck up friendships with James Dickey and Robert Bly, with whom he visited and worked on translations.

In 1959 Wright's depression and heavy drinking contributed to his separation from his family. It was also the year in which his second collection, *Saint Judas*, appeared, when he immersed himself in Spanish and Latin American poetry. He continued to co-publish translations of Trakl and Vallejo, extended friendships (Louis Simpson, John Logan) but was denied tenure at Minnesota:

> At that time I was so god damned miserable that the only thing I could do was translate Theodor Storm from German, have a bad love affair, get sick, go to hospital, get visited by John Berryman (who went and taught my class while I was sick), get habitually drunk, teach very well when I could bring myself to make a class, and, naturally, get fired.

Wright then taught at Macalester College in Saint Paul. *The Branch Will Not Break* was published to acclaim, especially for its directness and 'deep image' poetry (surreal and arguably sentimental). In 1966 he began teaching at Hunter College, at which time he met his second wife and the couple began their love affair with Europe. He published *Shall We Gather at the River* as well as translating poems by Neruda, before being awarded the Pulitzer Prize for his *Collected Poems* (1971). *Two Citizens* appeared two years later. There were periods of exhilarating European travel, of depression brought on by stress, but the awards, appointments and poetry continued to come: *Moments of the Italian Summer* (1976); *To a Blossoming Pear Tree* (1977); then posthumously *This Journey* (1982). Wright attended a White House tribute to American poets in 1980, the year in which he died of cancer at 53. Five years before his death he had acknowledged: 'I have inflicted a good deal of pain on others and on myself during my lifetime. But God know I have suffered inwardly quite enough hell to pay for it.'

It is Jonathan Blunk's job to deal with all that. His authorized biography follows slowly on the heels of *Above the River: The Complete Poems of James Wright* (1990) and the 2005 selected letters (to which he made a significant contribution). It is a sympathetic yet judicious biography, a necessary corrective to the self-laceration in Wright's letters. It also conveys the immense vitality of the man for whom poetry, as Donald Hall wrote, was life. The particular danger with a rollercoaster life like Wright's is for his biographer to be distracted by the drunken antics, thereby losing touch with the work. Blunk avoids that. He gives insight into the unpublished journals as well. Also, encouraging his reader to look to the collections for the poems, he still manages to explore a good number of them.

That Blunk knows his subject is made clear at the outset, where he focuses on the critical summer of 1958 when, with one collection behind him and a second effectively completed, Wright seriously debated quitting poetry. We are then shown the prolific adolescent composer of sonnets, being apprised frequently of the hundreds of poem drafts Wright produced even before publishing. He had, as his biographer explains, a 'musical intellect'. A 'typewriter is for me simply a piano on which to improvise melodies and fragments', he wrote. He could not stop. Wright also possessed a phenomenal memory which allowed him to recite comprehensively in public which, along with a sonorous voice, contributed to his popularity.

Blunk is abetted throughout the biography by the deployment of shrewd insights and assessments from Wright's friends, with blisteringly revealing comments from the man himself. For example, to his semi-fictional muse, Jenny, he wrote in 1959 of his total dedication: 'It is the struggle between my inner self (poetry, for which I apologized in order to *live*) and the horrible gray world of deterministic hopelessness where I was born and which I only partly escaped.' In the last decade of his life, joying in Southern Europe, he confessed, 'I'm getting sort of tired of the darkness. There is something to be said for the light, also, after all.' In his work he had moved beyond compassion to what one critic called 'benevolence and grace'.

Wright once said he wanted 'to be a grown man'. His sense of un-entitlement confounded this for years. Blunk's fine biography illustrates that the trajectory of his life, like that of his work, moved towards a maturing, more uncluttered identification with the light. Reading this biography—with *Above the River* and *A Wild Perfection* to hand—is an inspiring experience.

ANTHONY RUDOLF *EUROPEAN HOURS*

Anthony Rudolf, *European Hours: Collected Poems*, Carcanet, 2017

Rudolf's *European Hours* (Carcanet, 2017) is an intriguing, not always accessible, but finally very rewarding book. The reader increasingly aligns with his wry perspectives through work from four periods (1964–2013), plus 'Two Long Poems' and a sample of 'Proses'. It begins with a prologue 'invocation' *To ancestral Europe: your Iberia, my Austria-Hungary. (To London…).* Presumably this prayer is to Rudolf's own history, familial and aesthetic, and to that of his companion, the artist Paula Rego, as well as to her as teacher and inspiration.

The early poems speak of absence and elsewhere, of living 'on the edge, on edge'. Many are concise, their diction clear, but their reference unrevealed; some are 'fragments'. They seem coded, wilfully strange. 'Stone' and 'pebble' are recurrent metaphors. In 'Necessary Fiction', for instance, thought and emotion are unmoored from 'the mind's bedrock'. These may have the old biblical association with truth or they may be images of withdrawal, a melancholy in keeping with the influence of Stevens ('One must have a mind of winter') or by Octavio Paz:

> I borrow from you
> *stone*, move onto
> *sun*, and recall
> your poem which "comes
>
> full circle / forever
> arriving".
>   – '6.30 P.M. on the Dot'

The exercise of translation is, of course, also a mediation of another's experience and I had a sense in Anthony Rudolf's earlier poems of a consciously weakened 'I'. 'Kensington Palace Gardens', for example, 'announces / perfection of a mood I thought / dead for ever' but we come no closer to that mood, or to the self that it returns to. Primarily he is the conduit. 'A Presence' both celebrates the 'the quest / of one I translate' and records that 'of my presence / I know nothing'. The security of belonging, of identity escapes the poet.

He is instead the observer, always recording and repeatedly returning to the arts, to reading and, particularly, seeing ('We recreate time / in writing, as painters / recreate space'). Rudolf has a highly sophisticated sense of art and order. As he writes, addressing the reliefs of Michael Michaeledes:

> I want to walk
> around them.
>
> In a space like the space
> they create inside my head
> where I walk
> around my thoughts
> cleansed of ancient signs
> and dead would nots

Drawn into Natalie Dower's paintings with their light-filled angles and 'mind, set / against /disorder':

> I empty my
> head to a vacuum
> that I may leave
> room

Many artists are addressed and celebrated—Balthus, Chagall, Morandi, Hopper among them—almost always in terms of their influence on Rudolf. Some are personal friends like the recipient of 'East Sixth Street, 1966'. In 'Bonnard: The Last Picture', however, he enters into the consciousness of a painter considering his last canvas (*L'Amandier en fleurs* with its fortuitous symbolism). Clearly Rudolf's friendship with Rego has influenced them both (He figures in her paintings, including the cover portrait of *European Hours*). The world itself is seen with a painterly eye, as in 'Reveille' or 'Amsterdam'.

Poets also emerge frequently, unsurprisingly given that Rudolf is a veteran translator. Hölderin, Rimbaud, Celan, Cavafy, Bonnefoy reflect his lifelong commitment to European poetry. Part of the appeal of translation for Rudolf is his engagement with Europe and his Jewish heritage and this is reflected in a number of poems, such as 'Song Recital in a City Church', which considers the passion of music amid the ironies of history.

'Reading Stevens in Hospital' gives us an insight into Rudolf's approach to understanding the work of his masters:

> I read each phrase, each line, re-read
> the one before, the next, one more
> each time, the way I always do

and the brief 'Process Verbal', illustrates his enthusiastic sensitivity to diction, in this case to Lorine Niedecker's disarming poetry.

There is frequent humour in *European Hours*, including a witty rejoinder to Auden's 'Musée des Beaux Arts' in 'Breughel to Auden'. Meditating on an Auerbach picture with a friend, in 'The True Inflections...', Rudolf plays off the artist's densely worked style: 'Behind her, through the window, realistic / buses cross the bridge.' Then there are many examples of his fondness for puns, clearly a habit of mind. Of Morandi's tonal reproductions he writes, 'it has taken me / twenty years to get the picture'. Elegies also deploy them. 'Final Proof—'for Jon Glover and i.m. Jon Silkin'— dispels the funereal with various puns, beginning with the title:

> In the East End
> stonemason's showroom
> I read, re-read
> (final proof,
>
> the poet is dead)
> the large letters
> outlined on
> 'John' Silkin's tomb-

> stone, the writer's
> own words included:
> 'the word surrounded
> so by light'.

The punning continues after the blessing until, 'I bury myself / in his late poems'.

If death is a preoccupation (see 'Fran Sinclair', 'Three Poems of the Grave', and 'Last Poem of Karl Kraus (1936)') then so is love, most memorably in 'Noonday', 'Pillar Box', 'Well Walk NW3' and 'Branca's Vineyard':

> I drink the wine a painter of the sacred
> and doctor of the heart pressed into being,
> then, for a moment, lingering alone,
> wineglass in hand, pen upon this paper,
> inhale an ancient oneness which I'd thought
> lost for all time, except when I make love
> with the woman who has just spoken to me
> and broken the spell, as spells are always broken.

The 'Proses' section at the end of the book offers short, insightful prose pieces. There are ruminations on poetry's mission and a judgment on Rudolf's process. 'A Coherent Deformation: Arturo Di Stefano' serves as a credo for poetry: 'art and life give each other meaning and this is the dialectic of the imagination, which keeps us human'. In a piece on Vilhelm Hammershøi, Rudolf asks and answers the question: 'What or why does it matter that he painted these pictures? It matters because he paid attention.' It also matters because the artist has no choice: one painting, like one poem, like 'one phase of life', leads ineluctably to the next until the end. The 'Notebook' jottings also record Rudolf's angst: 'Little by little, I came to understand that I had spent more time in defeat and creative darkness than I needed to, than is already built into the process.' By the end of the book we warmly endorse the poet's wish, 'With luck, I am unlearning the comfortable role of an eternally melancholy juggler in a painting by Watteau.'

THE LIVES OF ROBERT LOWELL

> I can't tell you how I dread the future with biographies
> and *Lizzie*, to say nothing of Cal, who will never be even
> touched with the truth of his own being and nature.
> – Elizabeth Hardwick to Elizabeth Bishop
> (18th October, 1973)

In *Reading Chekhov: A Critical Journey* (2001) Janet Malcolm wrote of 'the inescapable triviality of biography', since the artist's doings are 'the mere husk of the kernel of our essential life'. There may be all sorts of things wrong with this, though it also feels true in some way. Nonetheless biography can be a revealing, fascinating and potent force. It can illuminate the work of an artist, affect our perspective on it and, most worryingly, overwhelm what is supposedly its raison d'être.

All three outcomes have been the fate—to date—of the biographies and reminiscences of the American poet, Robert Lowell (1917–77), once the premier poet in the English speaking world. First came the brilliant but severe *Robert Lowell: A Biography* (1982), by Ian Hamilton, which effectively tarred its subject. Then came Paul Mariani's admiring *Lost Puritan: A Life of Robert Lowell* (1994), honest and informative, but insufficient to redress the balance. There followed *Collected Poems* (2003), *The Letters of Robert Lowell* (2005) and *Words in Air: The Complete Correspondence Between Elizabeth Bishop and Robert Lowell* (2008) all of which have done something for the reputation, along with a host of other studies and essays over the years, notably by Helen Vendler, Richard Tillinghast, Alan Williamson, Steven Gould Axelrod and William Doreski. There have been romantic memoirs by Kathleen Spivack, one forthcoming by Sandra Hochman and a scandalous outing by Jeffrey Meyers. In short, there is a continuing Lowell industry, though of late more focused on the life than the poetry.

Now we have the much anticipated *Robert Lowell: Setting the River on Fire*, by Kay Redfield Jamison, the reviews of which—by Lowell intimates—are startling ('I'm happy that I've lived long enough to read it.' Frank Bidart; 'In this astonishingly multidimensional portrait of Robert Lowell, Jamison makes him live and breathe'. Jonathan Raban). Jamison, an eminent psychiatrist, makes it clear that hers is not a biography but 'a psychological account of the life and mind of Robert Lowell; it is as well a narrative of the illness that so affected him, manic-depressive illness.'

The photographs on the covers of the three major studies signal their degrees of sympathy. The Hamilton book bore a slightly manic illustration and, in paperback, a photo of an unkempt Lowell, shock of greying hair, eyes averted. The Mariani offered a 'Life' portrait from 1947: the young Lowell as a Hollywood dreamboat. Jamison's biography has a photo by Gisèle Freund of an alert Lowell, wearing jacket and tie on a Parisian terrace in 1963. Hers is the portrait of an intellectual.

Robert Traill Spence Lowell IV—Cal to his friends—had a privileged Bostonian upbringing, marred by a difficult home life and a struggle with self-control at school. Unhappy at Harvard, he was taken in by the Fugitive poets of Tennessee, Allen Tate and John Crowe Ransom, following the latter to Kenyon College, Ohio, where he made lifelong friendships, including that with Randall Jarrell. He began writing difficult and authoritative poems fuelled by religious imagery and intolerance for the fallen world of New England and Europe. The publication of the Pulitzer Prize winning *Lord Weary's Castle* in 1946 made his reputation.

Lowell was much honoured in his life, book after book winning awards. He developed wide literary friendships, constantly revised his poems and his style, and was offered prestigious teaching appointments. He also developed a public persona: telling off presidents, opposing the offensive militarism of WW11 (for which he was imprisoned as a conscientious objector) and marching against the Vietnam War. At that time he dabbled briefly in politics as an 'aid' to Eugene McCarthy in 1968 and flirted with the Kennedy clan.

Lowell was frequently hospitalised from 1949 onwards with bipolar disorder—the latest victim of an auspicious New England family line—which expressed itself in bouts of intense work, religious zealotry, infidelity, lavish expenditure and destructive behaviour, spiralling into breakdown and guilty depression. Apparently, in the early stages of a manic attack, Lowell was 'seductive, flush with words and ideas and confidence', hardly even recognisably ill. Soon, as he described it to Elizabeth Bishop: 'These things come on with a gruesome, vulgar, blasting surge of "enthusiasm," one becomes a kind of man-aping balloon in a parade—then you subside and eat bitter coffee-grounds of dullness, guilt etc.'

A dramatic, though temporary, conversion to Catholicism accompanied his marriage to the first of three writer wives, Jean Stafford, a marriage productive but destructive. Later his zeal would find expression not in religion but in love affairs. Elizabeth Hardwick, his second wife, was in good part responsible for Lowell surviving the attacks of mania. In contrast he found his third marriage, to Caroline Blackwood in England, initially rejuvenating but eventually intolerable. Lowell finally returned to life with Hardwick, dying in a taxi cab outside their home.

All this is the material for the two biographies and this new study of the life and mind. What is interesting is: what is considered; what is omitted; where the interpretative accent lies; and, ultimately, how close we come to Malcolm's 'husk' and 'kernel'?

Ian Hamilton's authorised biography of Lowell recounts key episodes well and gives lots of mayhem on the way, but is not even understanding enough of the 'mere husk' of the life. It is a portrait of the poet as bad boy. In Jamison's words, 'The Lowell that Hamilton chose to portray is loutish, mad, humorless, a snob, and an overrated poet.' Unsurprisingly, some reviews seized on the image; it made excellent copy. The reader senses from the off that Hamilton does not particularly like his subject. Armed with Lowell's own negative recollections—from prose pieces such as '91 Revere Street' and the letters ('I was so abristle and untamed')–Hamilton warms to his task of presenting an 'ominous nativity'. Lowell's father is 'less than forceful', his mother appalling: 'she would spend whole afternoon waiting for the doorbell to ring so that her servant could announce that she was not at home'.

Enter Lowell, 'utterly enthralled' by the authoritarian ways of a mother he despised. Subjected to the barbarism of private school, he 'is remembered as dark, menacing, belligerent... always ready to take his own unpopularity for granted'. His interest in toy soldiers and military history is seen as grounds for his 'bloodthirstiness'. When Lowell turns to intellectual pursuits Hamilton describes only an 'awesome deliberateness in Lowell's metamorphosis from lout to man of sensibility'. At Harvard he is 'the young malcontent'. The poet's own amusing description of his arrival at the Tates' house in Tennessee is dismissed for the 'sneakily whimsical but condescending tone' that 'was to become familiar to Lowell's Southern friends throughout his later life'. Faced with the paradox of presenting a brutal conscientious objector, Hamilton decides: 'Most of his childhood heroes had been military heroes, and he had shown himself to have a rare appetite for both tyranny and violence, but he could see little that was splendid in the way modern wars were fought.'

When it comes to the bad behaviour, Hamilton refuses to join the dots. It is as if everything before Lowell's first manic attack is simply brutish behaviour or rebellion. And yet Hamilton knows the plot; he knows what's coming. Even Lowell's fierce, blinkered mother recognises in Lowell's behaviour a 'mental seizure'. Again, after her death, Hamilton writes 'a new voice is to be heard in the letters'. There are, for instance, 'callously brisk accounts of his new financial gains'. Yet this is clearly taken from an acutely manic letter to Lowell's friend Blair Clark, which his biographer fails to make clear.

Hamilton has no access to Lowell's hospital records and anyway limited sympathy for the mania. He gives, for example, Lowell's lengthy description of a psychotic episode, following it with the observation that it is 'chillingly consistent with the tone he used to recall childhood misdeeds. There is an amused, tolerant, near embarrassment as Lowell recalls the "mischief" he has done—in both schoolroom and asylum.' To Hamilton it seems self-indulgence. Jamison, who has access to the records, has the context: 'Tellingly, Lowell does not write about the subject he broached most often with his doctor: his unshakeable fear that he would go mad again.'

Hamilton also fails to pursue the other Lowell. As Hamilton's friend Al Alvarez wrote in his *Observer* review of the biography, it is 'as if the eminently sane man who wrote the poems ceased to exist in his last years. I find this misleading.' According to writer Peter Taylor, Hamilton missed the fact that 'He was a wonderful friend; he could make you feel good about anything.... He had the most marvelous sense of humor; he was the gentlest person and the most loyal of friends.' Hamilton also fails to explore this tribute of Hardwick's, written at a time when she was most hurt by Lowell's betrayal: 'I have always felt that the joy of his "normal" periods, the lovely time we had, all I've learned from him, the immeasurable things I've derived from our marriage made up for the bad periods. I consider it all a gain of the most precious kind.'

Where Hamilton scores—aside from his thorough coverage of the public persona—is with the poetry, when he likes it. He cogently explains the evolution of style that produced Lowell's masterpiece, *Life Studies*, in 1959: 'He had become expert at contriving [prose] sentences that could be elevated and yet speakable, and had found a literary voice that could encompass something of his social self ... The obvious next step for Lowell was to perceive that some, if not all, of these considerable gains could be carried over into poetry.... The "excitement" of poetry could vitalize and be restrained by the sturdy, detailed worldliness of prose.'

When he does not like Lowell's poetry, as John Carey acknowledged in his review, Hamilton 'quotes damaging criticisms' and 'adds some of his own'. Not infrequently he is flip. After *Lord Weary's Castle* the poet 'now deals not in destruction but in decline, and he no longer pretends that God is on his side'. So 'For the Union Dead' is 'his first step towards extending the possibilities of his self-centredness: towards treating his own torments as metaphors of public, even global, ills'.

Reviewing the second major biography of Lowell, *Lost Puritan*, his friend Grey Gowrie wrote in the 'The Daily Telegraph' (February 11th, 1995) that Paul Mariani 'has a less forensic mind than Hamilton and on occasion writes slackly.' However he described the portrait that emerged of the poet as being truer than Hamilton's. Unlike his predecessor's biography Paul Mariani's is sympathetic enough—'tactful', as Richard Wilbur judged, 'poignant' according to David Ignatow—to see his subject at times through his friends' eyes and therefore brings us close to the 'husk' of Lowell's life.

It is certainly a more approving biography. Mariani noted in his preface: 'my admiration for Lowell and his work only increased as I entered more deeply into his life.' After a dubious beginning in which he imaginatively ranges through Lowell's mind in early July 1954, Mariani settles into a detailed narrative, perhaps lacking Hamilton's stylistic flair, but more interested in the man and less dramatic about the drama.

Mariani treats Lowell's early family life with a little more restraint, dwelling on the influence of the maternal grandfather ('the man who had so shaped him and his mother') as well and Lowell's father and mother ('Charlotte Hideous' Jean Stafford's called her). The welcome addition to the life, however, is the detail on Lowell's first marriage, to Stafford. We share more than her colourful personality and the poisonous, witty comments of her letters, as Mariani brings into focus Stafford's influence on early Lowell. He also invests a little more time in describing the young poet's formative time with the Tates, Ransom and Kenyon. He introduces others with walk-on parts, which develop the narrative, such as publisher James Laughlin (of 'New Directions') and later Philip Levine, who counters the general admiration by offering a negative assessment of Lowell, as a self-involved teacher at Iowa.

Mariani is no apologist for Lowell's behaviour. He notes on more than one occasion how Lowell distanced himself from his own occasionally violent domestic acts. Also, while he resists the pressure to be dramatic about Lowell's harrying of his wives, he does not hide his subject's dominating manner or infidelities. Yet he is sympathetic in dealing with the pressures Lowell is under.

Mariani is often interesting on the poetry, on 'Skunk Hour' for instance, 'Lowell's "Dover Beach"'. In 1953 'He spent all his spare time writing now, telling Tate that it broke "one's heart each time fighting one's verbiage and awkwardness to the real flesh."' He presents the urgency and frustration Lowell experienced at attempting to evolve as a poet. He had to unlearn, as it were, the lessons of Eliot and Tate, the pressure on tradition, the belief in constantly reinvigorating the old metrical forms, to embrace the lived life in his poetry as he begins to see William Carlos Williams has done. Lowell is aided in this recognition by his readings with the Beat poets and a new feeling for at least freer verse. Yet even at his most successful in experimenting with more relaxed rhythms, he acknowledges that he misses 'the carpentry of definite meter'. Then when he turns to sonnets he finds, in Mariani's words, 'a way of mixing the instant with the deeper horizons of history, what he called the "flash of haiku to lighten the distant"'. In his last book, *Day by Day*, published weeks before his death the poet had turned again, this time solely to free verse.

Mariani is also effective at presenting Lowell's meditations on his art, by mining the letters and late poems. Lowell comes to think of the 'seedy grandiloquence of *Notebook*'. Reading through his *Selected Poems*, he sees his old preoccupations treated in too similar a way ('half-amused to think he could ever have thought of himself "as a tireless surpriser"'). He wonders what he is doing in England, why a true artist would want to leave his familiar landscape 'and while his method was "formidable enough to turn out new poems," it was not so easy—or even possible—to turn out new subjects'. Finally though, Lowell confessed to Frank Bidart, poet and executor, 'that he didn't know what the value of his work would finally be', but he felt he had 'somehow "changed the game"'.

Kay Redfield Jamison's *Robert Lowell: Setting the River On Fire* is ambitious: 'I am interested in who Robert Lowell was, how he came to be the man and poet he was, and why his poetry matters; in what we can learn from his work about the ambition of art, the necessity for art… the strands that link madness to action and imagination…… I am particularly interested in why character…matters so deeply in understanding both art and mental illness.' In a way the book is a gift to psychiatry, for Lowell is the ultimate public case study, a subject so highly documented by himself and his friends in poems, essays, letters, remembered conversations, memoirs. 'Hardwick and Lowell left a written legacy of madness, imagination, and determination that is unmatched.' Jamison's starting point, then, is the documentation, 'the lighted way into it'.

Immediately the reader has the illusory feeling that the subject's intimates had held back until now, waiting for a writer like this. For instance, in two early pages Jamison gives testimony to Lowell's unique, stimulating brilliance from Alan Brownjohn, Helen Vendler and Esther Brooks (a former ballerina, who gave an acute portrait in the essay 'Cal Remembered'). In Hamilton's biography we find the three also there, but late in the book and commenting on Lowell's behaviour. Similarly, if we turn to the indices of the three biographies we find entries in the Jamison for 'friendships' and 'generosity and kindness'. Hamilton has no such headings. Mariani has 'friendships'. Not damning of course but perhaps a small indicator of the slant of the books.

Jamison begins by restoring Lowell to his ancestors, beginning with Harriet Brackett Spence Lowell, the poet's great-great-grandmother who died insane, and to the New England literary tradition to which he was heir. Generally there is a relative dearth of action, a focus on character more than incident. Much of the detail of conventional biography is missing, as are certain episodes: details of his student years in the South; a blow-by-blow of the first marriage; the courtship of Elizabeth Hardwick. There is little of Lowell's political activities, of his relationship with other poets, and little on his lovers or students—no Plath, for instance. This should not work to the book's advantage but it does, raising a mirror to the mental life actually more than to the personality.

The mania is central, as is explaining what Lowell's bipolar disorder actually means and meant to him. Particularly relevant is this description of symptoms, from the diagnostic criteria for mania and depression (2013): 'Excessive involvement in activities that have a high potential for painful consequences (e.g. engaging in unrestrained buying sprees, sexual indiscretions, or foolish business investments).' Lowell's reputation has been hurt by his infidelities, his repeated attempts to leave Hardwick for younger women ('All life's grandeur / is something with a girl in summer').

Yet his wife, though repeatedly heartbroken by them, saw Lowell's betrayals during illness as an attempt to begin a new, healthier life, a 'kind of flight' in her words. The identification with men of violence—another blow to Lowell's reputation—becomes, as Jamison explains, something Lowell shared with 'many patients with manic delusions'. To read a Lowell biography without this understanding is to dismiss his behaviour as typical Lowell high-handedness.

What Jamison achieves is to make the life a whole, to make it meaningful, to see its essential courage. 'Lowell came back from madness time and again, reentered the fray, and kept intact his friendships. He kept his wit and his capacity for love.' The manic episodes are no longer only tragic breaks in the living and writing routine but the accelerating rhythm that also produced the work: 'Mania took his poetry where it would not have gone'. In the dry periods 'it disturbed the embers and breathed back the life into his poetry'. To Jonathan Raban Lowell once reported 'I write in mania and revise in depression.' If he could only control the mania, he would have accepted it, cost and all. It could not produce great poetry but it could get the motor running. Whether in fact the early poetry suffered from the manic flights and the later poetry suffered from the lithium remains contestable.

Jamison filters Lowell's unpleasant behaviour—the broken confidences, the betrayals, the violence—through his mania. In so doing she gets closer to the genius and courage and this, presumably, is what his intimates so admire about the book: 'Few can prevail against mental illness as severe as Lowell's; still less can they reenter the mix of life, as he did time after time.' She invokes comparison with explorers (Scott) and poet-warriors (Sassoon). Her conclusion is that 'Robert Lowell knew civic valor. Sixteen times and more he had been down on his knees in madness, he said. Sixteen times and more he had gotten up. He had gone back to his work, entered back into life. He had faced down uncertainty and madness.'

What is the dark side of the man, his illness aside? Jamison does not allow, as Hamilton did, for 'an element of simple mischief, of sly, childishly perverse outrageousness' in his breakdowns. The furthest she will go is to make comment on 'the relentless mind' and 'vaulting ambition' (I am reminded of a comment by Lincoln's law partner: 'His ambition was a little engine that knew no rest'). It is as if Lowell's mania is enough for the reader to deal with and the wonderful qualities of the man must be ranged against it. This is Jamison's way. Although she cautions her readers at the outset that no-one can more than partly understand the mind of another, she comes enviably close to illuminating moments of what Janet Malcolm referred at the outset to her subject's 'essential life'.

In the January 6th edition of the TLS this year, the 'NB' column had this to say of Lowell in its anniversaries: 'In the 1960s and 70s, Lowell was No 1... Nowadays he scarcely figures in the Top Twenty. His early formal verse is too highly wrought for modern taste, and his late work too diffuse.' In my view there are no American poems of the last fifty years that stand with 'The Quaker Graveyard in Nantucket', 'Waking Early Sunday Morning' or 'For the Union Dead' as public poems, or 'Man and Wife', 'The Old Flame', or 'Home After Three Months Away' as painful, personal testimonies. One can argue that all day, but not about the bankability of a dramatic life:

> I have sat and listened to too many
> words of the collaborating muse,
> and plotted perhaps too freely with my life,
> not avoiding injury to others,
> not avoiding injury to myself—
> to ask compassion
>   – 'Dolphin'

Robert Lowell has received more 'compassion' than he might have felt he earned. It is time to do justice to his poetry again. For us, at least, the 'essential self' is there.

ACKNOWLEDGEMENTS

I would like to thank my publisher, John Lucas, and also my wife, Chris, for her help with the book (as well as for her patience in appearing a second time on a cover of mine). I would also like to thank the editors of the four magazines in which most of these pieces first appeared (or are about to): Michael Schmidt (*P N Review*), Patricia McCarthy (*Agenda*), Steven O'Brien (*The London Magazine*) and Elaine and Jon Glover (*Stand Magazine*).

PART ONE

With the Topnotch Tates at 'Benfolly', *P N Review* 227, 2016

Archibald MacLeish's Faded Star, *Agenda* online 'Testaments' issue 2017

Malcolm Cowley Among the Poets, *P N Review*

On Allen Tate in Paris, *P N Review* 238, 2017

Robert Penn Warren at Oxford, *P N Review*

Seeing Robert Lowell Plain, *The London Magazine* Aug/Sept 2017

All's misalliance: Lowell in England, *Agenda* vol 51 Nos 1–2 June 2017

Maxine Kumin at Fifty, *Agenda* online 'Retrospectives' issue 2012

The Hard Losses of Louise Glück, *Agenda* online 'The Power of Poetry' issue 2017

PART TWO

Czesław Miłosz in Exile, *Agenda* vol 52 Nos 3–4 summer 2019

Time away: Louis MacNeice in America, *P N Review* 245, 2018

Charles Tomlinson and America, *The London Magazine* April/May 2019

PART THREE

Alexander Herzen in London, *The London Magazine* Dec. 2016
The Shelf Life of Robert Browning, *P N Review* 208, 2012
Ford Madox Ford, *The London Magazine* Oct. 2016
Remembering Wilson & Trilling, *P N Review* 247, 2019
William Empson & America, *The London Magazine* April/May 2018
Regarding William Styron, *The London Magazine* Oct./Nov. 2018
Al Alvarez at Risk, *Agenda* Vol 50 , Nos 1–2 Sept. 2016

REVIEWS

Jim Burns & Jonathan Ellis, *Stand* vol 15 (4) 2017
Kirsch and Hofmann: Hobbyhorsing, *P N Review* 225, 2015
On Stefan Collini's Common Writing, *P N Review* 235, 2017
Richard Holmes This Long Pursuit, *P N Review* 234, 2017
Robert Hass & Stephen Burt, *P N Review* 237, 2017
The Lamentations of Arthur Krystal, *P N Review* 244, 2018
Jonathan Blunk, James Wright, *P N Review* 241, 2018
Anthony Rudolf's European Hours, *Stand* vol 16 (4) 2018
The Lives of Lowell: three biographies, *P N Review* 237, 2017